Adolescent Crisis
Family Counseling
Approaches

Eva Leveton, M.S., received her Master's degree from San Francisco State College. She was trained in family therapy at the Mental Research Institute in Palo Alto. Currently she practices family therapy as an Associate at the Family Therapy Center of San Francisco, where she is a founding member. A former psychologist for the Child Study Unit of the University of California at San Francisco School of Medicine, she has served as a consultant in family therapy at the Wright Institute in Berkeley, the California School of Professional Psychology, Langley-Porter Neuropsychiatric Institute, and Marin County Mental Health Services. Ms. Leveton is a well-known teacher of family therapy, and is the author of the widely translated *Psychodrama for the Timid Clinician* (Springer Publishing Company, 1977).

Adolescent Crisis
Family Counseling Approaches

Eva Leveton

Springer Publishing Company
New York

Springer Publishing Company, Inc.
200 Park Avenue South
New York, New York 10003

84 85 86 87 88 / 10 9 8 7 6 5 4 3 2 1

Library of Congress Cataloging in Publication Data

Leveton, Eva.
    Adolescent crisis.
    Bibliography: p. Includes index.
    1. Adolescent psychotherapy.   2. Family psychotherapy.   I. Title.
RJ503.L48   1984   616.89'156   84-10502
ISBN 0-8261-4500-0

Printed in the United States of America

Advice to society could be: for the sake of adolescents, and of their immaturity, do not allow them to step up and attain a false maturity by handing over to them responsibility that is not yet theirs, even though they may fight for it.

[D. W. Winnicott, *Playing and Reality*. New York: Basic Books, 1971, p. 146.]

Contents

Preface

This book rests on 20 years of clinical experience with teenagers and their families, counselors, teachers, probation officers, therapists, and doctors, in various settings. During that time, the number of agencies working with adolescents multiplied. More and more skilled workers were in demand. Training lagged behind the growing social need. As the history of my work with one particular agency, Youth Advocates of San Francisco, parallels the changing scene, it serves to introduce the reader to this book.

Family counseling became a part of the Youth Advocates program when Huckleberry House for Runaways, the parent agency for the present system, was sheltering the "flower children" of the 1960s. Youth Advocates is a San Francisco Bay Area youth agency that provides temporary housing for teenagers, family counseling, employment and legal counseling, a mobile counseling unit, and foster home placement services. As a consultant in family therapy, I worked with the staff of Huckleberry House and, later, Youth Advocates, in a variety of ways. I taught basic concepts of systems theory and family therapy to the staff; I helped settle problems that arose between staff members and their clients; and, perhaps most important, I acted as "family therapist" to the staff itself, in an effort to use the same principles we were learning to apply to clients and their families when unhappiness and miscommunication affected staff relationships.

Although my terminology was not always acceptable to the staff members (who sometimes believed they behaved in a more objective, professional manner), I often made the analogy between the Youth Advocates staff and a regular family. The structure was similar both in terms of authority, commitment, independence, and feelings of love, anger, and frustration—keeping in mind, of course, that in a real family these issues take on a far greater degree of intensity. Youth Advocates was run by three directors who clearly functioned as parents. The directors determined policy, created new places of work, retained final authority in hiring and firing, took public responsibility for failures of the system, and, reluctantly, found themselves in charge of getting most of the funding for the agency. The staff of the various facilities represented the older children engaged in various degrees of struggle for independence or dependence with the directors. The clients often seemed like small children, demanding much from the rest in the way of energy, care, and planning. I saw myself as an aunt. Although I wasn't particularly visible in the structure and my name wasn't on the door, everyone thought of me as someone who, like the director's older sister, usually got on well with the kids because she had no special interest of her own to defend. I visited quite a lot, as much as two or three hours a week, pleased when both parents and kids trusted me enough to ask me to give advice or arbitrate conflicts.

During the course of my work I found that many of the issues concerning both family counseling and staff relationships had occurred over and over again. There had been a good deal of staff changeover. As the agency had grown, many new staff members arrived. So often, when working with a combination of old and new members, I had wished that we could somehow convey what we already knew to the newcomers. I had wished for a handbook to use as a reference to help them get acquainted with some of the issues we faced. *Just what is meant by family counseling? Why shouldn't a counselor get angry with an overly restrictive parent? How could one work with a cotherapist far more experienced than oneself? How could one deal with a kid who brought drugs into the house?*

Many counselors and volunteers working with adolescents and their families at Youth Advocates lacked training. Though many had a background in education or social services, they knew little about family development and dynamics. Their training in this area occurred "on the job" and was augmented by supervision with trained professionals, many of whom volunteered their services.

Two problems proved difficult to overcome. First, the counselor often lacked formal training in child and family development, since individuals with advanced degrees in these areas seldom took jobs with the pay scale offered at Youth Advocates. Second, even those counselors who had university degrees had received little that would serve as preparation for short-term counseling with adolescents, because the category had not been in existence long enough to reach the university. Each generation produces volumes on the crises wrought by its adolescents, yet, until recently, solutions almost always involved individual or group therapy of long duration. As family therapy developed, books written to help the students began to include short-term work. These, however, usually assumed that the student was already well versed in individual development and dynamics.

My work at Youth Advocates was directed at helping the counselor find a way through the maze of family counseling by providing a practical approach to counseling families with adolescents and by exploring personal history as well as basic theory and dynamics where relevant.

That was the impetus of this book, as my experience at Youth Advocates was repeated at several other youth agencies both here in the Bay Area and in other parts of the country. When I began writing it, I simply made notes of material with particular value to staff members of the various agencies where I was working. As I organized the material, I found that it fell into several sections. The first section is intended as an orientation to my personal style and as an overview of basic family systems theory and family rules.

The second section deals with general problems facing the family counselor working with adolescents. Crisis counseling is discussed, general techniques described, and personal challenges examined.

The third section deals with clinical material from family counseling sessions with adolescents. Cases are presented in some detail in order to demonstrate both a typical selection of problems and to discuss the counselor's choice of techniques in each particular context. Cases were selected on the basis of the author's experience as a counselor and consultant in various youth agencies. It must be clearly stated that there was no attempt at the selection of a scientifically representative sample. Omissions are inevitable, due entirely to my directing my efforts at selecting those situations that seemed both to represent the most frequently raised problems in consultation and to provide the reader with relevant reading in the field.

Suggested Readings:

Beggs, Larry. *Huckleberry House.* New York: Ballantine Press, 1968.

A Word About Pronouns _____

From time to time, the reader of this book may find him- or herself startled that there's been a sex change. He/she had been reading right along about a counselor named Fred, aptly modified by male pronouns. Now, suddenly, she/he is reading about Susie, and the gender has changed. If the reader is bewildered, it's a sign of the times. An exclusive use of the male pronoun doesn't seem right anymore. Nor does an exclusive use of the female pronoun seem to be justified. What is one to do? The solutions appearing earlier in this paragraph have been tried. They do not appeal to me, as I feel affected by something akin to stammering when reading paragraphs dotted with he/she's or him- or herself's or she/he's. Therefore, in this book, always prepare for a change of sex. Some counselors are male; others are female. Sometimes "one" refers to "her"—other times to "him."

Acknowledgments _____

I would like to thank my husband, Alan Leveton, M.D., for his steadfast support and fearless criticism; George Lane, for his helpful comments; Martha White, Ph.D., for the eclecticism chapter; and Fred Ford, M.D., whose teaching in my early years in this field helped formulate many of the basic assumptions on which this book rests.

A grant from the Tides Foundation, administered by the San Francisco Studies Center, partially funded the writing of this book. Some of the ideas and case material first appeared in a simpler version in the teaching film "Children in Trouble; Family in Crisis." I am grateful to the Department for the Administration of Criminal Justice at the University of California, Davis, for permitting us to use the material, and to Alan Leveton for working as my co-therapist with many of the families whose stories appear in the film and in this book.

Adolescent Crisis

Family Counseling Approaches

I

An Eclectic Approach to Family Systems

1

In Praise of Eclecticism

[*Students addressing Eva Leveton:*]

"What kind of therapist are you, anyway?"

"You're not a Freudian, are you?"

"Is this going to be this 'touchy-feely' California stuff?"

"I see what you're saying, you just follow your feelings, that's all."

"You know, I realize that I don't know any more about why you work the way you do, after hearing you talk, than I did before."

"Is there a place where I could find a kind of a model for what you're doing?"

"Does it ever get less confusing?"

It is hard to learn from an eclectic. The student who learns by following a specific psychological theory and approach has the opportunity to develop some clarity about her own choices. She frequently has the gratifying experience of observing a client demonstrate something she has learned and the even more pleasant experience of successfully using techniques suggested by the model she is studying. But, while following a particular approach lends clarity to the clinical experience, it presents some difficulties as well. The sense of clarity may be falsely reassuring. The student who views behavior in terms that allow her to fit everything into place often finds herself, despite every attempt to correct her errors, confronted by behaviors that simply don't fit into the scheme or techniques that don't accomplish their goal. One of the troubles besetting our field is that adherents of a particular point of view seldom acquaint the student with its limitations. (A notable exception is Peggy Papp, who presents her work in the context of some of its problems. See end-of-chapter references.) On the other hand, every student of a particular discipline is aware that there are theories and approaches different from her own. Should she choose? How? She often becomes even more confused as she comes into contact with others who have made their choices.

Confronted by a demanding, whining woman, whose history suggests that she was inadequately mothered by a woman not unlike herself, the student finds that each discipline offers a different way of working. The Freudian learns to analyze her patient's behavior, history, and dreams, in order to determine the nature of her defensive structure and the stage at which her psychological development was arrested. She hardly needs the confirmatory evidence presented by her patient's dreams of mountains of sweets barely out of reach, to know that the analysis will need to deal with material repressed since early infancy, that it will last for years, and that it will test all her powers to resist her patient's manipulations.

Given the same patient, the behavioral therapist might determine that the woman's smoking habit is her most pernicious problem and proceed to work out a short-term, intense treatment program with behavioral rewards and punishments, at the end of which the patient would be considered cured.

One family therapist, confronted by the same patient, would insist on seeing her with her entire family in order to help her find more successful ways of making her wishes known, by looking at the family patterns that have allowed and even promoted her distancing behavior. Another family therapist might encourage her to complain at regular intervals at home, with her husband and children, with her own parents, and at her job, to achieve a cure through paradox.

I could go on finding different hypotheses and different approaches, but that is not my intention. I only want to suggest that each different discipline looks at different aspects of the same case, and it is not always easy for the student to choose among them.

One way to examine these differences is to view them as addressing themselves to various levels of the personality. The Freudian addresses herself to the deep-lying aspects of the personality, often buried since a patient's early childhood, in order to effect major change. The behavioral therapist addresses herself to the removal of a bothersome symptom or complaint that will have the effect of making her patient's life more pleasurable by its absence. The family therapist addresses herself to the interpersonal functioning of her patient and his immediate family, in an attempt to correct dysfunctional patterns of behavior that lead to symptom formation. Other disciplines address still other levels at which the person functions: The group therapist, for example, may address herself mainly to the individual in his social context, while the body therapist works mainly to help alleviate stress as it is accumulated physically.

Some students have a preference for dealing with one of these levels and are able to identify themselves with one or another primary discipline. Others find that they want to be more flexible than their particular discipline allows. A student of a particular discipline has few choices when she runs into difficulty. If she is creative and steadfast, she can seek to improve the discipline until it encompasses the difficulty she encountered. A body therapist, for example, may find that her patients want to talk with her about the associations that arise in them when she is working on their body awareness. She may find that, rather than adopt one of the other "talking" therapies, she can develop a particular way of talking with her patients that specifically fits her discipline. If her method is accepted by her peers, she will have enhanced her discipline. Another student, with a more pedantic frame of mind, will choose to narrow her point of view when encountering difficulty. A body therapist, for example, might handle the problem of a patient who needed to talk about his experience by automatically referring such an individual to a "talking" therapist. A third student may want to switch to a new discipline that holds more promise. A fourth may attempt to synthesize different disciplines so that she can switch levels as the work demands it.

I have chosen the latter path. It means learning as much as possible and using it whenever possible. Its limitations are obvious. Trying to live in a constantly experimental position is difficult in times where one of the most frequently uttered needs of patients (people, students, parents) is "I want an answer." The eclectic therapist must be ready to contend with comments that assert that her work is unscientific, lacking in cohesion, and impossible to organize. She must accept uncertainty as a condition of life, and the results of her work as the most— and possibly the only—evidence of her success or failure. Still, a large number of social workers, counselors, psychologists, psychiatrists, nurses, teachers, priests, and ministers, and legions of clinical workers are eclectics, who do their work as well as they can, reading and attending a class here and there, gleaning as much information as possible to help them with their complex task. This book is an attempt to take the reader along as an eclectic therapist makes her rounds.

A clinical work such as this one usually appears under the aegis of an "ism"; adolescence, in particular, has been written about by practitioners richly versed in Freudianism, Sullivanism, and gestaltism, to name but a few. If not a disciple of a particular theorist, the writer is often motivated by her enthusiasm for a new approach. Family therapy, for example, has been enriched by structural, paradoxical, strategic, and, most recently, epistemological approaches. This book is less easily identified. It attempts to describe choices made by an unrepentant eclectic, choices made on the basis of all the information available at the time. If that is too general a statement, let me attempt to sketch a few details.

What makes an eclectic? I have always thought it was an inner predisposition acted on by someone who, on the one hand, found it impossible to become a follower of any one leader and, on the other, was not sufficiently original to develop a system of her own. She is a synthesizer rather than an originator, a person who builds up a fund of information large enough to produce a relevant hypothesis or approach for each particular case.

In my own case, the predisposition to eclecticism undoubtedly relates both to a rebelliousness that makes consistent following difficult for me and to an inherent conviction about the complexity and variety of human behavior that makes me skeptical of any one theory or approach. My professional training began at Stanford University where I quickly became resistant to the behavioristic approach. Stimulus–response theory held little fascination for me. The truth of numbers did not impress me. If eight out of 35 monkeys failed to reach for a box to step on to get a banana, I was less interested in what that suggested about the population of monkeys than in what each particular monkey might have had in mind. Perhaps some were hungrier, others hated bananas, and still others hated the same old experiments. Perhaps some of the successes had special relationships to the experimenters or represented a population of firstborn or otherwise privileged monkeys. I could never persuade myself to believe in a sufficient conformity of context or experience to draw conclusions about relatively simple situations. The more complex aspects of human relationships seemed even less accessible to the experimental approach. The kind of truth I was after needed to appear in its own context.

Luckily, I also had classes which taught by example. Case histories illustrated the Freudian material, lending it the texture and richness that I had been missing. In reading Sullivan, I found the first clinician that took himself and his own actions into account in describing what went on during therapy. In and after graduate school, I found clinicians willing to let me observe their work with patients, sharing their thinking as well as their feelings. Two of the most important contributions to my clinical development arrived with the 1960s: the teaching of systems theory and family therapy at the Mental Research Institute in Palo Alto, and the development of experiential techniques through the encounter movement. Classes from family therapists such as Alan Leveton, Fred Ford, Virginia Satir, and Ben Handelman helped me integrate my personal history, my educational background, and systems theory and also taught me some ways of talking with the families I saw. Fritz Perls worked with me in a group setting, letting me experience the effects of his theory and approach. Moreno's work helped me to develop my own approach to the use of psychodrama. The climate in which so many experiential methods flourished—body movement, drawing, body awareness, family sculptures—enriched my own work with more and more choices. At the same time, I was part of the Family Therapy Center in San Francisco, an association of peers who assisted my development through constant and stimulating interchange.

There are, of course, some general precepts that describe my way of working. Presenting them here will help shed some light, I hope, on the reasons behind the choices made in the clinical work in the following chapters. First, let's discuss briefly one of the problems that attends eclecticism, which is what to call the person or persons with whom one works. Patient? Client? Family? Family members? Groups of people important to each other? One works with individuals for whom one of the preceding is exactly the right term, and one finds new terms for others, but it is impossible to find the right category for discussing them all together. I am of the generation for whom the word "patient" comes to mind most easily. Perhaps an identification with my father, who was a medical doctor, led me to think about myself and my patients; perhaps my long years at the University of California Medical Center account for my preference. At any rate, it's my favorite term, and I hope the reader will put up with it in the following pages, knowing that it refers to individuals, families, and groups with whom I stand in a therapeutic relationship.

Now let's move on to a discussion of the categories I want my students to explore:

1. The patient's context.
2. Child development, madness, and common sense.

3. The use of self.
4. Therapy in depth.
5. The role of the therapist.
6. "When you're in trouble, get help."

The remainder of this chapter will be devoted to these six precepts.

The Patient's Context

Each individual comes from a family, lives with important others, works or goes to school, supports himself or depends on others, and leads his life in his culture with philosophical or spiritual beliefs that help guide him, with dreams and fantasies that give him hope. [The individual functions on many different levels.] My first objective is to acquaint myself with him on as many levels as possible; to do that, I want to find out all I can about the various contexts in which he has lived and currently leads his life.

Individual therapy often presents a particular roadblock to this pursuit, since words are all too often the only medium through which information is exchanged. Dependent on words alone, or at least on words and gestures, individual therapy has much in common with romantic love. The patient comes to the therapist with his illusions and the therapist contributes her own projections. For a period of time, both people attempt to please each other, carefully sifting out unwanted behavior which, in the presence of a third party, might emerge quite spontaneously. The context is dyadic, one on one; no third or fourth person with whom to engage or get feedback is present. However, individual therapy can be enriched by experiential techniques, such as role-playing, in which others important to the patient's past and/or present life emerge in a vivid and colorful way. Photographs and letters also help to augment verbal information. (These active techniques are described more fully in Chapter 6.)

An alternative comes from the fields of human systems theory and family therapy. Since systems theory provides many of the hypotheses with which I work, I attempt to include important others whenever I can. When my patient lives or works with others who play meaningful roles in his life, I will ask them to join us in our work. I have seen many varieties of "important others," from the immediate family to the extended family; from visiting parents of adult patients to children of divorced families with both sets of parents; from relative outsiders such as teachers, social workers, or probation officers to friends, roommates, fellow workers, or employers. In short, for me, the individual emerges more clearly the more I see him relate to others who matter to him.

It is important for the reader to realize that, in all these inclusions, my goal is to work more successfully with the patient or family who originally came to see me. In order to attain that goal, I want to remain as flexible in my choices as possible; therefore, while I frequently include important others and may ask a patient to include his family at least once, I do not follow any rule that says that they need to be included all the time. My further choices will depend on the particular needs of my patient. If he is in a phase of his development where he needs help with his interpersonal life, we may continue to work with others. If he is in need of narrowing his social context in order to work on problems that demand more privacy, we will work alone. Parents, for example, are seen with their children some of the time, but not when they want to attend to the business that affects their relationship as a couple. A member of a couple may, in turn, ask for time alone with the therapist, to discuss inner problems not requiring the presence of the other person. That, too, is workable, as long as the therapist takes responsibility for evaluating the therapeutic use of any shift that occurs, rather than letting it emerge in a haphazard fashion.

A difference in the cultural backgrounds of patient and therapist provides another opportunity for the therapist who seeks to understand the patient's context. Although cultural differences are often perceived as a hindrance to therapy, they can prove enriching to the therapist who is willing to be a "tourist" in the sense of asking the patient to help educate her about his culture. Cultural information can be a bridge to greater understanding. A white therapist seeing a black family, for example, will need to learn the meaning of words and gestures used in the black idiom. A home visit can help acquaint her with her patient's circumstances. The black patient who senses that his therapist's desire to inform herself about his life is genuine usually will be happy to help educate her. Assuming sameness where large cultural differences exist, on the other hand, can lead to the usual tensions produced by false assumptions, this time between therapist and patient.

Students often interpret my enthusiasm for learning about a patient's context as a request to learn as much as possible about a prospective patient or family *before* beginning therapy. That is not my intent. Therapy, for me, means working in the present as much as possible. Individuals are encouraged to talk about what concerns them in the present tense, to deal with emotions they experience during the therapeutic hour, to talk to the others in the room about present concerns. As they proceed, the past will become relevant, and so will other parts of their context, such as their jobs, other relatives, and so on. At such times I include new people in the therapy, or set about an active investigation of the particular part of the patient's life that has become relevant.

Child Development, Madness, and Common Sense

A clinician must learn to diagnose symptoms. Like a tracker following traces of footprints and disturbances in the sandy ground, conjecturing about the size and activity of the animals he wants to find, the clinician must learn to look at individuals caught in a difficult situation and work backward, uncovering the tracks that led them there. A tracker draws conclusions from every sign at his disposal—the degree of moisture in the ground, the way the wind is blowing, a feather here, a clawmark there. A bent twig may signal that the animal has taken an entirely new turn. The clinician, too, must form hypotheses continually about the past, present, and future movements of her patients.

The patient's upbringing lies in his past. A clinician needs to know as much about normal growth and development in this patient's culture as the tracker needs to know about the habits of the animals he tracks. The richest part of my own education was the study of child development. Every adult carries with him the child he once was. Frequently an individual who is frozen in a particular, rigid, adult stance is transformed by the expressive vitality brought on by a memory of childhood. A gesture, a facial expression, a sudden start can unveil an enthusiastic seven-year-old child where a depressed, middle-aged person was sitting. Other people adopt an adult style on the basis of habits learned at a time when their psychological development slowed. The bossy little eight-year-old girl who tells everyone what is right and wrong, the sad-faced, fat little boy waiting for someone to buy him an ice cream cone, the 12-year-old kid who always was first in a fist fight—all these come to therapy in their grown-up guises. The clinician who can recognize them will have an invaluable key to therapy.

I learned about child development in a number of ways. During the 10 years I spent at the Pediatric Child Study Unit of the University of California giving psychological tests to children and interviewing their parents, I became acquainted with a large range of intellectual, academic, emotional, and psychosomatic functioning. Observing my own children's growth and working with normal children from nursery-school age through high-school levels helped me acquire a feeling for normal development. I tried to read about child development not only from the clinical, pathological point of view, but also from the normal, creative, educational angle. Seeing families in family therapy provided me with the opportunity to observe a variety of contexts for growth and development in different classes and social contexts. Many authors helped me—Erik Erikson, Piaget, Frostig, and Spock, to name but a few—and my reading was brought to life by taking advantage of every opportunity to observe. "Always working," some of my friends would say when I talked about what I had seen, but for me it wasn't work. It was, and remains, an endlessly fascinating pursuit.

The therapist is stimulated constantly to review her own life. The problems brought to her will echo her own; the family roles of her patients will recall her own family. Her ability to make use of what she has learned from personal experience is of vital importance if she is to help others, especially with childhood. Her vivid recall, her own interest in and acceptance of her child-self, her own sense of play, all will enable her to touch the child in others. My own early fear of heights, my childhood preoccupation with play-acting and talking with horses, and my vivid recall of the fairytales my grandfather told me have provided many a bridge to a patient's past. Laughter, wonder, puzzlement, fantasy, and play are seldom anticipated by individuals entering therapy. These qualities can provide unanticipated and productive ways of joining with the patient and helping him grow.

In counseling others, the mixture of observing others in normal and stressful situations, of reading the views of others' notions of possible cause and effect, and of discussing these situations and observations must be augmented by a body of knowledge sometimes referred to as common sense. I am referring to the solutions passed down from generation to generation in every culture. Child-rearing practices, philosophic wisdom, methods of healing and giving pain relief, and ways of calming psychologically disturbed individuals are known and handed down by each generation of each family. Our own, largely urban culture has become so intellectually snobbish and committed to seeking the help of experts that common sense has been forgotten as a source of wisdom in human situations. Milton Erickson's stories about his children and the farm community where he grew up, and Carl Whitaker's tales of his own life and times have done much to help therapists become more tolerant of what once was considered material "irrelevant" to the clinical situation. Patients often feel isolated, as though coming to therapy marks them as peculiar. They fear their problems are so difficult that only a long-term and complicated technical solution will help. That is not always true. There are times when common sense will do much to solve a problem. The clinician who tells tales of other families in similar situations, who makes suggestions for approaches a patient may try, who is willing to transform herself into the "village philosopher" when required, is often welcomed by a patient starved for such talk.

Common language has become just as important to me in talking with my patients as common sense. We are always talking about concrete life situations in our work, yet I have always been puzzled by the professional's need to shift to a special vocabulary, whether it be technical in nature (terms like "repression," "regression," "ego-ideal," or "love object") or the current mental-health jargon (i.e., "peak experience," "sensory awareness," "encounter," or "communication skill"). Each individual uses words charged with emotion as he describes events that led him to seek help. I have done my best whenever possible to respond to the patient with equally concrete, human language.

If the study of childhood and normal development enables us to form some notions about where our patients have been, the study of madness tells us something about where they may or may not be going. White middle-American culture leaves little room for madness. While other cultures provide niches in the form of shamanism, witchcraft, or eccentricity, our culture provides few places for those considered mad who refuse to be medicated or hospitalized. Madness is usually discussed only in negative terms. Despite the best efforts of such proselytizers of madness as R. D. Laing and Carl Whitaker, the helping professions remain, by and large, representatives of the popular point of view in their phobic, negative treatment of psychosis. They associate insanity with something terrifying, loss of control, an ever-escalating burning intensity, a point of no return, or total withdrawal. In other words, they describe only the most extreme stages of insanity and none of the creative, freeing, intense irrationality also found in such a state. A view of psychosis as it relates to inspiration, creativity, and dreams is neglected for a point of view of psychosis as an illness that must be deadened with drugs or locked up on a ward.

The clinician is usually confronted by a rigid pattern in an individual or family, a pattern that has become useless and repetitive, stifling growth and change. Greater rigidity usually spells greater hopelessness. Suppression of the dream, of the crazy creativity that might break through the pattern, will lead the intensity to submerge until it gathers enough force to become destructive and confirm the original fears. The clinician who wants to experience the full range of life in her sessions must become acquainted with madness, so that she can track its suppression and help release it in healthy doses of fantasy, anger, and creativity, lest it turn to rage or withdrawal from normal life. Because psychosis has such a bad reputation, signs of unconventionality or loss of control in the expression of anger or the expression of unusual ideas are often feared by patient and clinician alike. It is important for the clinician to get over such a fear, if possible, so that she can stimulate her patient to release energy without becoming afraid. To do this, the eclectic clinician can do no better than spend some time on any ward for psychotic patients. Having some personal experience with those considered so very different from the rest of us will provide her with clues about what is wrong and will make the descriptions she finds in books by Sullivan, Laing, Whitaker, and Searles more understandable.

Learning about psychosis will help the clinician understand some extremes of human behavior that she might not otherwise observe. First, the psychotic ward is full of people who have contained stress until they could contain it no longer. It is not an easy place to be, but it will educate the clinician about the processes that produce the kind of people who are feared by so many. The intrusiveness of parents, the lack of privacy, the build-up of rage where there is no release for anger, the solipsistic speech where plain talk must be avoided for fear of causing pain—all the aspects that make the psychotic experience in its extreme state so painful and destructive—must be known by the clinician who wishes to help her patients avoid them.

It also is likely that the clinician who becomes acquainted with psychotic individuals will encounter her own irrational self, her own anger and fear, part of the time. If she stays long enough to talk with her patients and gets to know them individually, she may learn ways of taking care of herself in such moments, such as speaking plainly about what is occurring and getting help, if necessary. Even more important, however, her contacts with her patients will introduce her to an emotional candor and a vivid use of metaphor seldom encountered except in young children.

An acquaintance with madness is, in my view, as necessary as an acquaintance with childhood and common sense if the clinician is to successfully track human experience.

The Use of Self

The interplay between the personality of the therapist and that of the patient is one of the constants of therapy. So often the student imagines that she is or should be an all-powerful but neutral healer. When she grapples with the problems of her work with others, she may neglect the relevant aspects of her own experience in or outside the therapy situation, in favor of analyzing her patients. This would be a mistake.

I have discussed my own need to know the relevant context, both in my struggles to learn psychological theories and in doing my work with patients. Knowing the background of any given situation is important for my own reality testing, and it is crucial for my patients as well. I would feel that I was depriving my patients of valuable information if reports of my own experience were not part of the therapy. (The "what," "when," and "how" aspects of sharing the therapist's experience are discussed in detail in Chapter 8.)

Therapy in Depth

Earlier in this chapter we discussed the different levels of psychological functioning. Some therapists use a continuum ranging from "superficial" to "deep" to view the various levels of therapeutic endeavor. A superficial problem is one lying close to the surface, dealt with by a kind of therapy that does not delve deeper. For example, a person who wishes to meet more people may seek help from a therapist willing to rehearse him in some techniques for meeting strangers and to provide him with information as to where he can meet the kind of people he is seeking. If that is the extent of the work, a superficial goal will have been accomplished. Meeting more people may have all kinds of profound consequences in the patient's life, but these are not explicitly addressed in the treatment. On the other hand, he may encounter a therapist who encourages him to look at the deeper-lying reasons for his shyness by drawing on memories of his early school experiences or his identification with a shy mother or father. Working through these earlier experiences may free the patient to the extent that he no longer needs coaching or advice in actually meeting a stranger.

I try to teach students to become flexible in their view of themselves and their patients, so that they can address the deeper levels of the personality as well as the more superficial ones. Psychological work always occurs at several levels. Deep work occurs to some degree even if the therapist does not make it explicit. A person who simply attends a nonsmokers clinic, for example, will feel the reverberations of the work in his past and present relationships, no matter whether the technique intends it.

Each of the levels of psychological work has a physiological component—for example, a greater or lesser amount of tension or relaxation in particular parts of the body, or a change of breath, or a change of color in the face or hands—because, of course, we react physically as well as psychologically and we store our memories along with our physical reactions.

The therapist must learn to shift her attention from the psychological to physical and back again, in addition to moving back and forth between the past and the present, fact and fantasy, and social and individual levels. At any given time, my goal is to help my patient work at all the levels accessible to therapy, if that suits his needs. The dance of therapy is never quite predictable, because each step depends on the readiness of both the therapist and patient. Considering these various levels enables the student to search out the areas of relevant work the patient is ready to accomplish.

The therapist can also deepen therapy by addressing himself to the patient's search for meaning. We live in a society where the pursuit of pleasure and material comfort is emphasized, while little attention is paid to the inner search for meaning and integrity. The isolated patient often complains of a sense of emptiness. He may be the kind of person whose response to the pressure of making a living has resulted in a series of meaningless training and job situations. The young lawyer, for example, exhausted by his competitive schooling and examinations, often finds himself confined to doing seemingly mechanical research during his first few years in practice. The sense of satisfaction he has hoped to gain in the defense of justice has disappeared from view, and he wonders how he could have fought so hard to get such a pedestrian job. Others, successful and more satisfied at work, have lost touch with the imagination. Unable to remember their dreams or include fantasy and play in their lives, they complain of their dry, workaday experience, of their inability to take pleasure in the material gains they have achieved.

Here the therapist has the chance to help her patient enrich himself by perhaps reacquainting him with the person he once was, the one who had hopes and dreams, who knew what was important and meaningful to him. On the other hand, confronted by a person who had little awareness of such matters in his childhood, the therapist may have to help him discover a more meaningful existence.

Not all levels of therapy can be addressed in each case. Therapy is most rewarding when the therapist can be flexible enough to move from one level to the other, challenging his patient to integrate the superficial with the more profound levels of his difficulty, the physiological with the psychological, symptom relief with the search for meaning. The work with material from early childhood, with fantasies, dreams, and renunciations, with pent-up grief and family secrets, is enriching for both therapist and patient. These deeper levels of therapy provide the constantly shifting field that sustains my interest in my work.

The Role of the Therapist

A therapist can take on many roles—friend, parent, teacher, peer—and the relationship that typifies her work at any given time will depend on her personal style, her view of her work, her flexibility, and her reaction to her patients. Some therapists, frequently those who are adherents of one specific discipline, take on primarily one role and fit their work around it. The social worker in the black ghetto is well known for her ability to behave in a way that fits her environment: a friendly but tough peer, someone who knows the ropes but will not act in the condescending manner of a professional. Some psychoanalysts, on the other hand, are known for their emotionally cool, professional manner. Nothing seems to shake their equilibrium. The patient experiences the analyst as an expert, a professor, or as an authority figure.

Patients project many roles on their therapists. As the work of therapy changes, the patient often has different views of and requirements from his therapist. Initially, he may wish the therapist to remain at a distance, professional and reassuring. Later in the relationship, the therapist may find that her patient regards her as a friend, or that he relates to her as though she were a member of the family. Families, in particular, put pressure on the therapist to play one or another of the roles that fit their particular system, such as aggressive child, weak father, or protective mother. At each point, the therapist has an opportunity to move into a new or different relationship with her patient, or to frustrate her patients' needs and make the results of that frustration the topic of therapy.

An eclectic can take on various roles with her patient as the demands of her work with him change. Just as the parent is strongly authoritative at some points of his child's development and gradually becomes more and more of an advising friend, so the therapist also changes her stance in relation to the patient. I am not talking about role-playing; rather, I am talking about the stretches in personality that challenge every parent and therapist. In fact, the therapist must be able to shift without role-playing, if the patient is to develop trust. Every organic process has variety and sameness. Cycles of growth occur in therapeutic relationships just as they do in a garden. If the patient is to learn to trust his therapist, he must learn to know her as a human being with integrity, which in this case implies a predictable sameness in her behavior. If, for example, he can trust the intention of his therapist, trust her knowledge about what she is doing, trust her ability to ask the patient for help when she is confused, and trust her accessibility as a human being, then both he and his therapist can grow and change together.

Without losing her integrity, a therapist may behave in different ways. She may be talkative in one session and silent in the next. She may be emotionally distant or emotionally close. She may chat with her patient or she may limit the therapeutic hour to the discussion of important material. All such behaviors, and many others, may occur in one hour or in various hours, and all are potentially positive in their effect as long as the therapist remains recognizably herself to her patient. The therapist and the patient form a new system. In family therapy, it is hoped, the therapist becomes a new part of an ongoing system, an agent of change. It is of vital importance for her to be a model of open, trustworthy communication.

The concept of open communication often contains a dilemma regarding the right of privacy. Openness can vanish in the face of coercive pressure from other individuals who may be perceived as intrusive by someone wishing to keep something private. Openness, here, is intended to mean that there is no content that will be barred per se from the discussion. Potentially, any subject can be discussed with any person at any time. The qualifiers are the relevancy of the communication and any individual's right to privacy at any given time.

The therapist also must be willing to be open, not only about her own feelings and possible relevant experiences, but also about her intentions. Thus she must attempt to conceptualize as she works, so that when she is appropriately challenged she will not need to mystify her patient; instead, she will be able to be explicit about her work when she wants to be. She may choose to talk at any given time, just like any other member of the therapeutic context. Her readiness to talk about what she is doing, when appropriate, can help her patients test reality and can serve as a model for open communication.

"When You're in Trouble, Get Help."

The therapeutic context is fraught with possible distortions. When I picture the complex interweavings of my own background and of my patients and their families, the wants and needs that exist in each of us at every moment, our hopes and fantasies, and our fears of catastrophe, and when I add the conundrums of any communication, it often seems to me a minor miracle that we do come to understand each other and work successfully to achieve a goal that pleases all of us. Of course, that is not always possible. There are times when, even after the therapist has done her best to clarify the situation and has enlisted the help of those with whom she is working, the work comes to a standstill. An impasse has been reached, and those involved in it directly cannot see a way out. Unresolved, such an occurrence leads either to endlessly repetitive and frustrating treatment or to the termination of therapy.

There is tremendous power developed by any human system, by which I mean the entity that develops when people are in an important relationship with each other. Anyone who understands this power is not surprised that such impasses occur. Presumably it was the "stuckness" of the patient that led him to therapy in the first place. In the following pages, we will see many of the repetitive patterns patients bring to the counselor: the parent who fails again and again to discipline his child; the adult who cannot stop his own self-destructive behavior; these are familiar figures. It makes sense that the therapist would be exposed to the same unsuccessful pattern the patient repeats in other important life situations. If the patient cannot discipline his child, he too may show signs of lack of discipline and begin missing appointments. If he is self-destructive, he may drink or take drugs before he comes to see his therapist. Yet the beginning therapist often fails to expect such behavior. Partly because she sees herself as a helpful person, different from those individuals responsible for her patient's symptoms, partly because the patient has responded by behaving more positively both in therapy and in his life during the beginning phases of treatment, the young therapist often forgets that all important relationships are fraught with ambivalence and that the patient's negative feelings also must find expression in therapy.

At best, an impasse serves to educate the therapist about her patient's experience. Her patient comes in complaining that he can't seem to find any satisfying friendships or work situations. When the patient starts talking about the failure of the treatment and his desire to switch to someone else, the therapist often reacts with a mixture of feelings. She may feel somewhat disappointed initially, but, on examination, she may come to understand the connection between her patient's symptoms and his complaint. As she gets over the feeling of personal rejection, she may develop some confidence in addressing an issue of vital importance to her patient, and so the work continues.

This does not always happen, however. There are times when the therapist is "hooked" by a complaint. Usually this takes place when the patient represents an important person in the therapist's own background, from whom negative feelings are not easily tolerated. The patient may mention the therapist's lapses of attention with the same kind of contemptuous biting tone the therapist's mother used, and the therapist may find herself feeling vulnerable and defensive and may say some things she may come to regret.

Needless to say, impasses that require help are not limited to patient's complaints. A therapist can become blinded to a patient's difficulty because of a dynamic of which she herself is unaware. She then may find herself angry at or frustrated with the patient who keeps returning to the subject. A deep-lying conflict in the therapist also can be stimulated by a similar conflict appearing in a family she is seeing. Again, her clue to seek help will come from her genuine puzzlement about her own reaction or that of her patients.

At such times, it is important to get help. Someone outside the system often can see what is going on. It may be sufficient to talk the situation over with a colleague or consultant. It may be necessary to tape-record the deadlocked therapeutic session, so that the consultant can get a flavor of the process, or it may be helpful to ask a colleague or consultant to join the session to help clarify communication. This is a procedure seldom adopted in our field, except during our training, because the fear of being seen as helpless or inadequate reigns supreme. However, it is also one of the best ways for a therapist to get help in seeing one or more patients. With the consultant in charge, the therapist can relax sufficiently to explore her own feelings until she can reach a point where she can communicate without counterattacking her patient. Frequently, successful communication can be reestablished in one meeting. The information that is learned in such an interview will prove invaluable the next time such an impasse occurs.

Carl Whitaker is a therapist who believes so completely in the value of another therapist working with him that he prefers working as a member of a therapeutic team, even in individual therapy. In many classes in advanced family therapy, the student learns to incorporate the comments of a supervisor who is either present in the same room or just outside it, viewing the work through a one-way mirror and able to communicate with his student either by telephone or by entering the room.

The student may wonder how such a strategy could fit the analogy of the therapist as parent, used previously. Parents don't ask others to comment on how they are doing with their children. It's true that such a procedure is probably as rare among parents as it is among therapists. Yet family therapy asks parents to do precisely that: to employ consultation while they are parenting their children. This compares well to former times, when the extended family was still in existence and there was nothing unusual about another family member observing an impasse between parents and children and commenting. Grandparents, uncles, aunts, siblings, and cousins often commented on a process gone awry from a vantage point both close to the immediate situation and at the same time less directly involved than the combatants. Visiting among members of a large extended family often meant asking for the advice of another, less-biased family member about a difficult situation. Asking for help is a type of modeling often completely neglected by therapists and parents in the context of a culture that demands mastery.

Suggested Readings

Alport, Gordon. The fruits of eclecticism. In Gordon W. Alport, *Selected Essays*. Boston: Beacon Press, 1968.

Boszormeny-Nagy, I., and Framo, J. *Intensive Family Therapy*. New York: Harper & Row, 1965.

Brill, L. (Ed.). *The Basic Writings of Sigmund Freud*. New York: Modern Library, 1938, 1966.

Brown, Tom, Jr. *The Tracker*. New York: Berkley Books, 1979.

Chapman, A. H. *Harry Stack Sullivan, The Man and His Work*. New York: Putnam's, 1976.

Erikson, Erik. *Childhood and Society*. New York: W. W. Norton, 1963.

Ford, F. R., and Herrick, J. Family rules/family life styles. *American Journal of Orthopsychiatry,44*, 62–69, 1974.

Gesell, A. *The First Five Years of Life*. New York: Harper & Row, 1940.

Green, Hannah. *I Never Promised You a Rose Garden*. New York: Holt, Rinehart and Winston, 1964.

Haley, J. *Uncommon Therapy, The Psychiatric Techniques of Milton Erickson*. New York: Norton Press, 1973.

Hall, C. S. *A Primer of Freudian Psychology*. New York: New American Library, 1954.

Jackson, Don (Ed.). *Therapy, Communication, and Change*. Vols. I and II. Palo Alto: Science and Behavior Books, 1968.

Jones, Ernest. *The Life and Work of Sigmund Freud*. New York: Basic Books, 1953.

Jung, C. G. *Man and His Symbols*. Garden City, NY: Doubleday, 1964.

Keeney, B. P., and Sprenkle, B. H. Ecosystemic epistemology; critical implications for the aesthetics and pragmatics of family therapy. *Family Process*, 21, 1–19, 1982.

Leveton, A., and Leveton, E. Children in trouble, family in crisis. A series of 5 training films demonstrating a family counseling alternative. University of California at Davis, Administration of Criminal Justice, 1975.

Minuchin, Salvadore. *Families and Family Therapy*. Cambridge, MA.: Harvard University Press, 1974.

Moreno, J. L. and Moreno, Z. *Psychodrama*. Vols. 1 and 3. Boston: Beacon Press, 1969.

Napier, August, with Carl Whitaker. *The Family Crucible*. New York: Harper & Row, 1976.

Neill, John R., and Kniskern, David, P. (Eds.). *From Psyche to System, the Evolving Therapy of Carl Whitaker*. New York: Guilford Press, 1982.

Papp, Peggy (Ed.). *Full Length Case Studies*. New York: Gardner Press, 1978.

Perls, Fritz. *The Gestalt Approach, An Eye-Witness to Therapy*. Palo Alto: Science and Behavior Books, 1965.

Perls, Fritz. *Ego, Hunger, and Aggression*. San Francisco: Orbit Graphic Arts, 1966.

Rosen, S. *My Voice Will Go with You, The Teaching Tales of Milton H. Erickson*. New York: W. W. Norton, 1982.

Satir, Virginia. *Conjoint Family Therapy*. Palo Alto: Science and Behavior Books, 1964.

Searles, Harold F. *Collected Papers on Schizophrenia and Related Subjects*. New York: International Universities Press, 1965.

Skinner, B. F. *About Behaviorism*. New York: Vintage Books, a division of Random House, 1976.

Spock, Benjamin. *Baby and Childcare*. New York: E. P. Dutton, 1976.

Whitaker, Carl, and Keith, D. Symbolic–experiential family therapy. In A. Gurman and D. Kniskern (Eds.), *Handbook of Family Therapy*. New York: Bruner-Mazel, 1981.

Winnicott, D. W. *Playing & Reality*. New York: Basic Books, 1971.

Winnicott, D. W. *Therapeutic Consultations in Child Psychiatry*. New York: Basic Books, 1971.

2

The Family as a System

A system is an assemblage of objects unified by some form
of regular interaction or interdependence.
[*Webster's New World Dictionary*, World Publishing Co.,
1964.]

Family Counseling and Systems Theory

Psychological counseling was based for a long time on the notion that
psychological problems were problems of the individual. Since healing
in our society was the province of the medical profession, psychological healing was conducted along much the same lines as physical
healing. While it has long been recognized that psychological forces
manifested in a person's job or family situation contribute to his
physical symptoms, it has been assumed that the individual alone
should be treated for them. If the problem was physical, he was given
medicine; if the symptom was psychological, he was given therapy
which sometimes included medicine. The context of the patient's
problem often was considered but was thought of only as part of the
cause, seldom as part of the cure. By bringing the entire family into
treatment, family therapy challenged some of the basic assumptions of
treating psychological symptoms, which were now seen as residing in
the entire family rather than the individual alone. The symptomatic
individual was labeled the *Identified Patient*, meaning that he was the

person identified by others as having symptoms, while the family counselor saw the whole family as dysfunctional. Family therapy as it was developed on the West Coast evolved as a consequence of and in adjunct to systems theory and communications theory. To understand the family as a system, we need to have an overview of some of the basic tenets of systems theory.

In any living system, such as the human body, simple notions of linear cause and effect prove inadequate to explain or describe the dynamic events that make up the life process. A clinical laboratory, for example, can determine the numerical values for carbon dioxide and oxygen in a sample of blood. What determines these values, however? The answer, if it attempts to account for the working of the applicable system of body functions, is necessarily complex.

To begin with, the amounts of oxygen and carbon dioxide needed to maintain a "healthy" condition are variable. For each gas there is a range of concentrations consistent with average, expected functioning. Events that occur in the daily life of the individual affect this range. Exercise, for example, may reduce the oxygen temporarily and increase the carbon dioxide. When that happens, all of the system's parts go to work to help restore the normal balance. Heart rate increases, facilitating the removal of excess carbon dioxide from the muscles and supplying them with oxygen. Breathing deepens and becomes rapid, facilitating the intake of oxygen and the expiration of carbon dioxide.

To make things even more complex and interdependent, the capacity of the blood to carry oxygen and carbon dioxide is influenced by other parts of the body, such as the brain, liver, bone marrow, and kidneys. The kidneys can excrete excess carbon dioxide in the longer term, in the form of bicarbonate, while the bone marrow can manufacture more red cells, which in turn can carry more oxygen, with the brain mediating the whole process.

We have roughly outlined some of the complexities of one body function to show that, when something is altered in any part of this living system, other parts of the involved chain start to interact in an attempt to compensate for the change. As long as they are able to do so, the normal range of concentration of carbon dioxide and oxygen can be maintained. When compensation no longer works, however, dysfunction results. Instead of normal breathing and lack of pain, there may be fatigue, muscle pain, even fainting. This process illustrates the interdependence of parts of any system.

Family systems also have their interdependent chains of reactions. A family is a living system whose members interact regularly and with various degrees of dependence on one another. Any event affecting one member spreads its ripples of influence over the others. "When one member of a family hurts, all hurt" is a maxim that was drawn from early communication theory and can be seen as basic to seeing the entire family in treatment. When one family member gets in trouble, physically, psychologically, socially, or academically, systems theory suggests that all members of the family are affected and some will alter their behavior visibly in order to compensate, to keep the family in balance. When a parent becomes depressed, for example, the whole family must find different ways of relating to him and making up for the losses in family activity caused by his depression. One of the children may react by becoming more parental, while another may take on the job of challenging and provoking the father into better health. A shift in family roles ripples throughout its members. In another family, an absent mother is replaced by her daughter's motherly behavior. In still another, a recently grown-up child forces his mother to find other outlets or compensations for her mothering activities. Sometimes these shifts or compensations are made in the service of growth, such as when a mother finds a satisfying career to take the place of parenting her now-grown children without giving offense to her husband, who is also ready to have her shift to greater absence from the home. At other times, these shifts and compensations take the form of desperate efforts to keep things the same when the world demands change and growth. In such cases, these accommodations are called symptoms, as in the following case, where school phobia can be seen as an attempt to compensate for the void in a parent's life.

Paula: "When Mom's lonely, I stay home."

Paula is 11 years old. Her life in her family, school, and social circle seemed normal and happy until her parents were called to school because of her increasing absences. As the family talked, it became apparent that Paula's absences from school coincided with a change in her father's job that required him to be away from home several days out of each week. Paula had always been a special friend and companion to her mother. Now, as she saw her mother's loneliness and sadness, Paula had decided to stay home with her during the day, inventing excuses about minor illnesses, with which her mother, in her time of need, went along.

Paula is the identified patient, the symptom carrier in the family. The therapist who deals only with individuals and their symptoms may look into Paula's family background and her present school adjustment for clues to her problem and then use these in order to help Paula understand what is wrong and change it. The family therapist, however, sees Paula's school phobia as a signal that something is wrong in the whole family system, which has failed to handle successfully the more frequent separations of the parents.

Homeostasis

Every family develops a range of expectable behavior. Some families move several times a year; others have stayed in one town for generations. Some families include outsiders easily; others remain mostly among themselves. We each have a notion of a balance in our own family, of boundaries and limits, the breaking of which would constitute a shock or a crisis to the family's existence. This concept of dynamic balance we call *homeostasis*. In Paula's family, for example, the family homeostasis had depended to a large degree on her father's presence in the home every morning and evening. When that homeostasis was upset, the family regrouped and, in the process, Paula developed the symptoms of school phobia.

The processes by which families attempt to maintain homeostasis are called *homeostatic mechanisms*, predictable patterns of interaction that help the family maintain a feeling of stability and sameness in the face of the stresses of normal living. When Mom gets sick, the oldest sister is overheard dealing with her brothers in the same way that Mom usually does. In a family where there has always been a family clown, this job is passed from one child to another as circumstances change. Family systems are described as functional when their process serves to promote the healthy growth of family members; they are dysfunctional to the extent that they retard the growth of family members and create symptoms in one or more of them.

In some families, homeostasis depends on dysfunctional processes. A family may require one "bad" member, for example, where Dad perhaps is the "saint" and Mom the "sinner." In the small town where they live, everyone pities him because of her embarrassing escapades. He finally divorces her and marries another "saint." Suddenly his oldest son starts to get in trouble. There is a new "sinner" in the family.

Billy: The Sad Clown in a Grieving Family

Billy and his family were seen for an initial interview at a probation department. In the week before the interview, Billy had been arrested for shoplifting and then had run away from home for two days. Three months prior to the interview, Billy's mother had died suddenly of a stroke. The family consisted of the father, who worked as a construction worker; Michelle, aged 16; and three brothers, Billy, 15, Ronny, 14, and Danny, 12. All three boys had been enrolled in special classes for educationally handicapped children and had gotten in frequent trouble at school for their immature behavior. The father was a heavy-set, middle-aged man with a deep voice and some apparent self-consciousness about his choice of words in the unfamiliar setting of counseling. Michelle was an attractive teenager who sat next to her father throughout the interview and kept a watchful eye on her brothers, all of whom were small for their respective ages and inclined to wiggly, immature ways.

As we talked with the family, it became obvious that the recently deceased mother had been the parent-in-charge in the family. She had been at home while the father worked full time and attended lodge meetings two evenings a week. The family had always been close; few outsiders were included in their activities. The primary compensator in this bereaved family appeared to be Michelle. She had taken on the major responsibility for disciplining her brothers. She looked somber and grave for her age, seemingly forcing her voice at times into the pseudomature phrases she chose. Her family seemed to accept the change as natural. Billy told a story of how another child in the neighborhood mistook his sister for his mother when she answered the door. Ronny and Danny used the interview to ask Michelle to stay home with them even more, rather than visit her girlfriends. The father looked at his daughter–spouse with obvious pride. As long as Michelle could handle the strain of her inappropriate role, a semblance of the family homeostasis had been recovered.

All was not well in the family, however, and since neither Michelle nor her father were able to perform adequately in their parental roles, the boys appeared to have taken it upon themselves to attempt to restore the homeostasis in their own childish ways, thereby being labeled symptomatic.

The problem in the family had to do with expressing grief. The family had always had a style that vacillated between Dad's authoritative, extremely rational approach and the mother's playful, sometimes wry joking. Strong feelings weren't often expressed except in a clowning way. When the family's grief precluded the usual clowning and joking, they appeared stuck without a way to express their necessary tears, rage, and tenderness. Father, who had always seemed so strong and totally in charge, looked obviously depressed and at a loss as to how to handle the family. In response, the boys increased the energy of their clowning. They jumped on the sofa as though it were a trampoline, poured food from one plate onto another, used the cups for juggling, and so on. In school, they cut up by entertaining the other children with their antics whenever the teacher's back was turned. Billy's stealing had been an effort to show off in front of his friends, but it also was another attempt to restore the family homeostasis. The clowning was intended both as a way of restoring the playfulness that had disappeared with Mother's death and as a way of provoking Dad to once again become the strong, authoritative father they were missing.

These examples demonstrate homeostatic mechanisms at work in the family's attempts to heal its own wounds, to restore a disrupted balance. Self-help of this nature often has a price in the form of symptoms occurring in one or more family members. Paula's school phobia and Billy's and Ronny's behavior problems are casualties in the family's attempt to heal themselves. But homeostatic mechanisms do not always produce symptoms. In fact, homeostasis often is maintained through the subtle ways by which a degree of comfort and predictability is legislated in all families. The mother who cautions her child against too great a risk lest he worry his father; the father who tells his daughter to try out for a play because he knows it will fulfill one of her mother's fondest dreams; the child who comes down with a cold just as her parents start to quarrel—such behaviors as these function to help the family when its homeostasis is threatened. A crisis, which by its very nature presents a threat of major proportions to family life, throws the family's ways of attempting to restore balance into bold relief and often produces symptoms.

When homeostatic mechanisms are working properly, they produce a predictable, comfortable sameness in family life. The comfort here refers to the knowable, understandable quality of life, not necessarily its ease. Families vary greatly in the behaviors they can accept as normal and with which they can be reasonably comfortable. There are marriages, for example, that are regulated by a certain amount of absence of one member, while others depend on as much togetherness as possible. In some families, the father is seen as the authority who legislates by yelling and screaming at the children, and so a kind of discomfort appears when he is quiet. For most families, homeostasis is achieved when life is going along without shocks or imbalances and within the family's expected level of pain and discomfort.

The same homeostatic mechanisms that produce feelings of normality in any family mitigate against change when the family is in treatment. The beginning family counselor often is puzzled by the family's reluctance to take up options that clearly would work better for them in times of stress. It seems to him that the family wants to stay miserable because he fails to comprehend the family loyalty to its old ways.

The family, however, developed its ways of coping without a family therapist. They come to counseling with the notion that they already know how to behave with each other. "You don't upset, Mother. Period. No outsider is going to change that. Nobody talks about Dad's drinking. Period. If you do, there's no telling what will happen. You don't even think about what would happen if you did. And here's this lady asking if he has anything hurting or if we know when he's hurt! Better do something to change the subject. This is getting scary. Anyway, what's Dad got to do with Junior? He's the one who stole the car. We should be talking about him!" The family in trouble tries all of its old familiar ways to get out of trouble. When they are unsuccessful, they often are seen by counselors who find that the very mechanisms that once promoted comfort now must be challenged to promote change. When the counselor suggests a change, he challenges family loyalties and encounters the family's resistance.

Family therapy usually starts during a time of crisis, when family homeostasis has been disrupted; thus, therapy provides a further disruption of the family balance, in the presence of the counselor. Because the counselor will suggest new ways of relating, the family will resist, believing that the old ways are the safe ways. The more skilled the family counselor and greater his understanding of each particular family system and the homeostatic mechanisms that have served to keep it in balance, the less he will oppose that resistance by demanding an immediate change from the perplexed family.

Content and Process

One of the problems facing the beginning family counselor is how to sort the deluge of information the family presents into a comprehensible whole. The general belief is that the more one knows about a given problem, the better one understands it. Following that belief, families usually begin by attempting to make sure that the counselor learns all about what happened during the events that brought them to therapy. They want to relate exactly what was said, by whom, when, and so forth. Moreover, each family member has a unique point of view and an explanation for what went wrong.

Jane: The Silent Patient

The crisis involves Jane's wanting to drop out of school, so her parents come prepared with her school history. Mother persuasively recounts the changes that took place in Jane after three new boys were bussed into her class from another neighborhood and cites quotes from the mothers of several of Jane's friends to back up her point. Father and Mother join in expressing their dissatisfaction with Jane's teacher, whom the father regards as an effeminate man and mother describes as having his own problems, which caused him to treat Jane unfairly. Mother talks about her efforts to reassure Jane. Father describes his program of helping Jane with her schoolwork. Jane sits quietly through these explanations, close to her mother.

In this situation, the family counselor is thrown immediately into conflict. The family wants him to digest the information, yet, right there in his office, while he is trying to follow the complex unfolding of events, something seems to be going wrong. The parents keep talking, and Jane, who is the center of the problem that brought the family, seems to be left out. He feels incompetent to understand the situation fully and helpless in view of what's going on.

Communications theory suggests that the differentiation of content and process is vital to the understanding of families. For the therapist, the details of the family history and records of their daily existence—all answering the question, "What?"—are labeled the *content* of the family's communication. The *process* is the information that describes the family's functioning in terms of "how" things work in the family.

Beginning family therapists tend to feel overwhelmed by content. Each family, with its unique history and present circumstances, is the undisputed expert on its own content. The beginning counselor is discouraged, since, if he can manage to follow them at all, he knows he will never be able to master the complexities of the family experience in terms of factual events. The family has him beaten at the start. The family counselor needs ways of categorizing what he sees and hears other than memorizing dates and places. Using the concept of process, the counselor can sort the verbal and nonverbal information he receives into a comprehensible view of the family. Since process is the concept that helps the counselor to understand how the family functions, the counselor seeing Jane and her parents, for example, can make sense of what is going on by noticing that her parents' communications seem to concentrate on two goals. Verbally, they strive to blame outside circumstances for what is wrong while keeping Jane from talking, and nonverbally they suggest a coalition between Jane and her mother. If he can change the family's agenda from recounting content to working on the family process, he can comment in a way that produces more vital, personal information and also includes Jane in the discussion. While family content is infinitely detailed, process is limited. There are only so many ways a family can interrelate. In order to achieve homeostasis, the family must produce repeated ways of handling their common tasks.

How does a given family function? The answers to this question should inform the family counselor about major areas of concern. Here are some questions that can be used as guidelines in looking at the family process:

1. How does the family handle feelings?
    a. Are feelings expressed openly?
    b. Can members express pain to one another?
    c. Is there a taboo about the expression of anger? of tenderness?
    d. Is anyone in the family depressed?
    e. Is the family openly affectionate?
    f. How is sexuality handled?
2. Who's in charge?
    a. Are the parents in charge?
    b. Is the father in charge more than the mother? vice versa?
    c. Are there conflicts about the use of authority?
    d. Is it a pseudodemocratic family where everyone is supposed to be equal but the children really rule?
    e. Is one of the children in charge of a parent who is symptomatic?
    f. Is anyone in charge?

3. Who is counted out?
   a. Has Junior always been a failure?
   b. Does Mom look at herself as a "nothing" except for her children?
   c. Is anyone in the family consistently labeled stupid, crazy, sick, or bad?
   d. Does Dad feel he didn't make it?
4. What is the parents' marriage like?
   a. Are they close or distant?
   b. Are they friends?
   c. Are they enemies?
   d. Do they have any contact? What kind?
   e. Do the children carry messages between them?
   f. Do the children side with either one in an argument?
   g. Are they satisfied with each other? disappointed?
5. Are there coalitions in this family?
   a. Do they remain stable? change?
   b. Do Dad and Sister make a team against Mom and Brother?
   c. Do some siblings regularly gang up and exclude another?
   d. Is there one member of the family who usually plays helpless and forms a coalition with another member against whoever is on the offensive?
6. How does this family handle closeness and distance?
   a. Are they a family that touches easily? a lot? only on ritual occasions?
   b. Is there room for privacy in this family, or is physical and/or mental space easily invaded?
   c. Can family members tolerate intimacy? to what degree?
   d. Does the family regulate distance by fighting? departing? living parallel nontouching lives? fussing? blaming? refusing to separate?
7. What is the style of communication of the various family members?
   a. Are they soft-spoken, careful to avoid hurting feelings?
   b. Are they loud, boisterous, melodramatic?
   c. Are they matter-of-fact, unemotional in tone?
   d. Do they send clear messages?
   e. Do they listen to each other?
   f. Do they interrupt each other?

     g. Do they conduct parallel conversations?
     h. Is it easy or hard to understand their meaning?
     i. Do they seem to say one thing and mean another?
8. How does the family handle differences?
     a. Can Dad and Mom disagree? How do they go about it?
     b. Is it possible for a younger child to disagree without being punished, ridiculed, or pooh-poohed?
     c. Is this a family that discusses issues, openly airing differences?
     d. Are differences hidden in this family for fear of hurting someone's feelings?
     e. Do differences cause arguments that end in fights and in someone getting hurt physically and/or psychologically?
     f. Do the parents sermonize about or discuss issues of discipline with the older children?
     g. Could you imagine a child in this family feeling free to grow up to be quite a different person from both of his parents?

These are only some of the questions that can be asked about a family's process. As the counselor fills in the picture of a family's process, using the preceding guidelines, he will come up with more questions of his own to help complete his view.

After answering some of these process questions, the counselor will be able to develop a more complete picture of what it's like to live in the family he is counseling. In Jane's family, for example, he may find more evidence that Jane provides little room for emotional expression. The family engages in a multitude of activities; conversations are usually factual and routine. While lip-service is paid to Dad as the head of the family, Jane's mother disqualifies him in front of the children: "He exists only for his business; he has no feelings for people at all." Jane's mother, as coordinator of the family program, is clearly the real head of the family. As the mother talks, her nagging dissatisfaction with the emptiness of her very busy life becomes clear, although she never labels it as such, referring instead to her tiredness and growing nervousness. Seeing Jane rebelling against school has resulted in the mother's subtly encouraging her daughter to drop out. On the one hand, she joins the father in sermons on the need to attend school; on the other hand, she shows an avid, excited curiosity about Jane's exploits when she cuts school. Jane has always felt close to her mother; her dropping out appears to be in part an effort to please her mother and help her live vicariously.

Looking at the family process also helps the counselor formulate goals and strategies for working with Jane's family. A primary goal is to disentangle Jane and her mother from their respective "rescuer" and "victim" roles so that each can devote her energy to her own life and development. The counselor's strategies include learning more about the marital life of the couple, teaching the whole family to communicate their feelings directly, and teaching the parents to give clear, consistent disciplinary messages. Based on the information from the initial interview, he realizes that he needs to know more about the father's functioning in the family—that, in fact, he may have joined the family in its disqualification of the father in the first session. In his plan for the second session he can review his goals and strategies in order to take charge of the treatment and avoid being caught unaware in the family system.

Every family will come to the first interview with the primary goal of acquainting the counselor with their lives through the delivery of reams of content; in every initial interview, the counselor must use the information he hears and sees in order to make some formulations about the family's process. If the counselor confuses content and process, he may draw conclusions based on content alone, which can be quite misleading. Since no two families react in the same way exactly, even the most startling content, such as the death of Billy's mother, cannot be assumed to have a single, useful meaning. No amount of information about the experience and timing of her death would lead us to understand the function of Ronny's and Billy's behavior problems or inform us about Michelle's function as mother substitute. Another family, with different homeostatic mechanisms, might have handled the same situation quite differently. The information vital to the counselor does not lie in a description of the event of the mother's death; rather, it lies in the answers to questions about how the family dealt with it.

Suggested Readings

Ackerman, N. *Treating the Troubled Family*. New York: Basic Books, 1966.

Anderson, Carol. *Resistances: A Practical Guide to Family Therapy*. New York: Guilford Press, 1983.

Boszormeny-Nagi, I., and Framo, J. *Intensive Family Therapy*. New York: Harper & Row, 1965.

Bowen, Murray. *Family Therapy in Clinical Practice.* New York: Jason Aronson, 1978.

Framo, J. L. *Explorations in Marriage and Family Therapy.* New York: Springer, 1983.

Guerin, P. J. (Ed.). *Family Therapy: Theory and Practice.* New York: Gardner Press, 1978.

Haley, J. *Changing Families.* New York: Grune and Stratton, 1971.

Hoffman, L. *Foundations of Family Therapy.* New York: Basic Books, 1981.

Jackson, Don (Ed.). *Therapy, Communication, and Change.* Vols. 1 and 2. Palo Alto: Science and Behavior Books, 1968.

Leveton, A., and Leveton, E. Children in trouble, family in crisis. A series of 5 training films demonstrating a family counseling alternative. University of California at Davis, Administration of Criminal Justice, 1975.

Minuchin, Salvador. *Families and Family Therapy.* Cambridge, MA.: Harvard University Press.

Napier, August, with Whitaker, Carl. *The Family Crucible.* New York: Harper & Row, 1978.

Papp, Peggy (Ed.). *Family Therapy, Full Length Case Studies.* New York: Gardner Press, 1978.

Satir, Virginia. *Conjoint Family Therapy.* Palo Alto: Science and Behavior Books, 1964.

3

Family Rules

All systems, living and mechanical, are governed by rules. The rules of the system provide the key to the question of how a given pattern in a system repeats itself. The rules by which a family operates, then, provide an explicit description of its process.

The difference between a homeostatic mechanism and a family rule is that the latter is more specific. A homeostatic mechanism in Billy's family is to clown when things get serious or painful. A family rule in Billy's family about clowning seems to be that when Dad is in pain one of the three boys (but not Michelle) clowns.

The term "family rule" normally suggests rules that govern discipline. "Don't interrupt your father." "Children over eight take turns washing dishes." "No one touches Dad's stereo set." The rules that govern family systems are much more elusive than rules of discipline. Although these rules govern family interaction, they usually are carried out unconsciously.

The rules for each family system are formed by the marital couple when they meet. For example, John, meeting Mary, sees her as an attractive, happy-go-lucky, outgoing person who looks like she'll be able to help him with his shyness. Mary, on the other hand, sees John as a handsome, attractive man with a brilliant mind and an ability to organize his life with a clarity that she envies. John and Mary are aware of these thoughts. They admire each other greatly and they tell each other often how fortunate they are to have met a person who is not only attractive but also so helpful. They are not aware that concurrently each is developing a set of rules about how to relate to the other.

(These rules are not entirely new, of course, in the sense that both John and Mary learned to communicate in their original family systems and chose partners that were able to follow some of the rules they already knew.) The first rules already are made: John is to take charge of the direction of their lives and major decisions; Mary is to be in charge of the relationships the couple encounters. A very likely subrule in this system is that John will behave in a dominating, direct manner, while Mary will be more submissive and self-disqualifying, for, although both are taking charge of a vital part of their life together, John's is validated as the more important role in his social context.

In a short time, John learns that Mary's confidence waxes and wanes. At social gatherings, she is full of self-assurance. Alone with John, she becomes unsure easily, especially when challenged intellectually. The couple soon ceases to play games like Scrabble or Chess for their diversion and John learns to avoid direct challenges. When a lemon chiffon pie which he found "a little too sticky" becomes a source of hurt and blame for an entire day, John also learns to avoid criticism, in order to avoid a tearful, infantile Mary who doesn't resemble the confident, lively woman he is courting. John is beginning to adopt the rule, "Don't upset Mary through direct challenge or criticism." Later this rule may be expanded to "Communicate dissatisfaction indirectly." As the family grows, the children will learn not to challenge their mother, communicating their negative feelings indirectly or through their father.

Meanwhile, Mary is learning that, although John really seemed to be delighted by her talkativeness in the beginning, he cannot be counted on to listen all the time. She has come to recognize a certain absent look and sudden start when she asks him a question, followed by reassurances that he has, indeed, been listening. She feels John doesn't really pay attention to her when she talks and discovers she has to make a special effort to get his ear when she has something important to say. Her conversations thus come to have two openings. The first, used most frequently and intended to help her save face if John is not listening, is, "I'm not sure if you're interested, but . . ." or, "Of course I don't know much about these things, but my opinion is . . ." or any other version of a prediction that she will not be listened to. Her second method, reserved for important occasions, is to start a conversation in tears—tears that flow in recognition of how difficult it is for her to be heard, in anticipation of another failure. She soon finds out that when she cries, John will pay attention to her. In fact, he will do anything to stop her crying. In short, the rule for Mary with John is,

"Mary belittles herself." Later in their lives, these family rules are likely to develop the form, "Children don't have to listen to Mother."

Mary's self-disqualification may have another function as well: It serves to keep John firmly ensconced in the one-up position and protects him from potential challenge. Mary has noticed that, not unlike herself, John reacts negatively to direct confrontation and challenge. Although he seems so sure of himself handling his many intellectual and practical responsibilities when clearly in charge, he seems to become less sure of himself when challenged. John, who had no difficulty with words, who in fact liked to teach and explain, had become loud and rude when a friend argued politics with him. He had been upset for days about his loss of control. When an openly competitive situation arose at his work, John also seemed to "lose his cool," spending many sleepless nights worrying. Mary had never been intellectually ambitious. She practiced self-depreciation partly in an effort to let her husband remain unchallenged.

Of course, it would be farcical to assume that, on meeting one another or shortly thereafter, Mary and John had a conversation that went like this:

JOHN: Hi, I'm John and I like to be looked up to. I will work hard and take charge of our life and do my best to deserve it. I often get so caught up in my work that I neglect my social life; I hope you'll help me by becoming my bridge to other people. Though I talk very clearly, I have never learned to listen very well, but you can catch my attention by crying, because I'll do anything to help both of us avoid emotional pain.

MARY: Thanks for telling me, John. I don't like emotional pain either, so I think we'll get along well. I will be glad to help you get along socially because I'm good at that, if you will just tell me what to do with the rest of my life. I feel happy when I'm with others. But alone, I really get muddle-headed and confused. Since I've always been timid and unsure around my father, I think I could learn to be that way with you also if it will make you feel better.

Although such a conversation did not occur when John and Mary got together, the unwritten contract was made as though it had, and John, Mary, and their children will use it to pattern their ways of relating to

each other. Family counseling is used to bring these rules into awareness and thus allow family members to question what they are doing
and begin to have more choices.

Tammy: "Feel free to tell me what I want to hear."

Tammy is a 16-year-old girl who was seen at probation because
she had run away from home for the third time in the past five
months. She came to the interview, sullen and silent, to face the
rest of her family: her mother, a strong, stubborn-looking woman;
her 17-year-old sister; her 18-year-old brother; and her father, a
man older than expected, white-haired, with a mild, submissive
bearing. Throughout the interview the struggle between Tammy
and her mother was apparent; verbally and nonverbally, the two
squared off, each committed, above all, not to give in to the other.

The interview with Tammy and her family was long and complex.
There were two family rules in this family system that resulted in a
double bind for Tammy. The first rule was, "Mom is the absolute
leader," which was upheld by the family members as they echoed
Mother's point of view and gave no argument or even a show of
differences in the family. Moreover, all family members looked
toward Mother for clues as to how they were to respond. The
second rule was, "Don't show sadness." In Tammy's family, it
was not difficult to be angry—as long as the mother was not the
target—and a kind of lip-service to loving feelings was easily paid.
When a situation called for sadness, however, the family either
turned the feeling into another, such as anger, or distracted themselves with a logical argument.

Tammy's double-bind was illustrated in her attempts to talk about
her running away from home. Although the mother encouraged
Tammy to talk by reiterating, "You can come to me with any of
your feelings," Tammy felt stuck. She related that she had come to
her mother with her feelings of sadness about a friend's move to
another city, only to be told to shut up. When she had talked to her
mother about the boyfriend with whom she now wanted to run
away, she had been punished severely. As Tammy talked, she
began to cry, and the mother became visibly impatient, telling her
that certain subjects were taboo. Tammy's bind was that, if she did
not talk about her sadness, she was defying her mother's invita-

tion (really more like a command), "You can come to me with any of your feeings," and thus accusing her of being hypocritical and threatening her control in the family. If she talked frankly, she was punished for breaking a family rule and, again, in the position of blaming her mother.

Roy: Just a Chip off the Old Block

Roy was interviewed in the family counseling unit of the probation department because he had been arrested for possession of marijuana. He had a record of several previous arrests for stealing a car and possession of illegal drugs. He was the 16-year-old son in a family with three other grown children, David, 20, Julie, 18, and Mary, 19. Just prior to the family interview, Roy's mother and father had separated. All members of the family, including the father, were present in the interview.

In most of Roy's family, there were clear rules about breaking the rules. Mother, older brother Dave, and sisters Julie and Mary all followed explicit rules, such as, "Don't get in trouble with authority," "Avoid family fights," "Conform to society's rules." For Dad and Roy, however, the rule seemed to be, "Get in trouble and provide some excitement for the rest of us." We saw the antecedents for this rule in Mom's memories of what attracted her to Dad: "He was crazy . . . he'd do anything, he and his friends . . . I'd always been the quiet type myself, too quiet maybe. I still am." The whole family described Dad's escapades and frequent angry outbursts with a mixture of fear and admiration. Later, when we talked with Mother about Roy, we saw the same mixture. Roy had always gotten into trouble and thereby amused his mother and also worried her. We saw her give him double messages in which there was subtle encouragement to act out. In a discussion about a misunderstanding in which Roy dug up "Dad's bush" rather than a "dead bush," Mom remembered her amusement more than her consternation. She recounted how she drove all over town in order to help Roy replace the bush, again helping him to see that she would support his escapades. Julie seemed to reach a full understanding of this family process when she said, "We see Roy like he's a television program. We're amused by what he does." Later, both girls commented on Mom's tendency to cover up

errors that Roy made, rather than letting him take the consequences and learn from them.

Thus we see Roy caught in a family scene that subtly encourages
his antisocial behavior while paying lip-service to forbidding it.
Many of the youngsters seen for behavior problems come from
families with rules similar to Roy's. Punishing the youth and then
sending him back to a family where in effect he is rewarded for his
behavior will do little good. Treating Roy without treating his
family will have little chance of success. Family counseling can
attempt to attack one of the root causes of the problem by making
the family rules explicit and working with the entire family system
in order to accomplish change.

The foregoing discussion has concentrated on dysfunctional family systems and their rules. The family counselor will see many dysfunctional families, but family rules occur in all family systems, and the
rules change as families grow. John and Mary, for example, are headed
for trouble only in so far as their rules become rigidly applied. If the
rules work to help fill some of the gaps in each other's personalities, a
slow change may occur as John and Mary grow older. Discovering
more meaningful goals in her life may help Mary learn to be more
assertive. If John's family and social life teach him the interpersonal
skills he has been missing, he may become more interested in what
others have to contribute to his plans. The rules that once insured quite
separate functions then may be changed to include the other person as
the rules for mutual protection become less vital to the system.

Family rules are those rules that determine repetitive and predictable interaction among family members. The rigidity or flexibility of
those rules is governed by rules about rules, or "meta-" (Greek for "in
relation to") rules. Family rules are challenged as the family grows. If
family members are to adapt in the many crises that will besiege them
and also accomplish the various expected stages of growth without
developing symptoms, the rules that govern their behavior must be
flexible. A metarule that says "our rules cannot be changed" is sure to
result in symptoms. The metarule that promotes growth is, "Rules are
expected to change as the family grows." In each family there are
specific rules about changing the rules.

Most rules are potentially functional. The rule, "Mom is the leader," for example, can work just as well as "Dad is the leader" or "Both
parents lead." These rules remain functional as long as they have a
metarule that says, "Family members are permitted to talk about how

the leader is doing," thus giving permission to comment. If, however, the self-esteem of the parent(s)-in-charge is so shaky that any comment or change in role, however temporary, would engender feelings of worthlessness and not being needed by the family, the rule will be rigidly enforced and result in family dysfunction. Only families with metarules that allow modification of behavior and flexibility have potential for accommodating to the stresses of everyday life without developing symptoms.

Suggested Readings

Ford, F. R. Rules/the invisible family. *Family Process, 22*:2, 135–145, June 1983.

Ford, F. R., and Herrick, J. Family rules/family life styles. *American Journal of Orthopsychiatry, 44*, 62–69, 1974.

Ford, F. R., and Herrick, J. A typology of families: Five family systems. *Australian Journal of Family Therapy, 3*, 71–81, 1982.

Leveton, A., and Leveton, E. Family rules. In A. Leveton and E. Leveton, Children in trouble, family in crisis. A series of 5 training films demonstrating a family counseling alternative. University of California at Davis, Administration of Criminal Justice, 1975.

Luthman, S., and Kirschenbaum, M. *The Dynamic Family*. Palo Alto: Science and Behavior Books, 1974.

Satir, Virginia. *Conjoint Family Therapy*. Palo Alto: Science and Behavior Books, 1964.

II

Process, Techniques, and Challenges

4

Crisis Intervention in Youth Counseling Settings

San Francisco's Huckleberry House for Runaways developed in response to the waves of runaway teenagers that washed over the Bay Area in the "flower-child" era, the 1960s, a time when alternative youth services evolved in many parts of the country because existing agencies were unable to cope with the growing number of teenagers in trouble. A teenager would run away from home and find himself unable to cope in the new city. In San Francisco, he then would contact Huckleberry House, either because he'd already heard of it back home or because someone in the community suggested it. There he would find counselors, a place to stay temporarily in the company of others in the same plight, and adequate food, all given on the one condition that he would agree to involve his family in one or more interviews to help resolve the family crisis brought on by his running away. Thus "crisis intervention" and youth services became linked.

Since then, youth services have grown into more comprehensive systems, providing help with drug-related problems, housing, foster home placement, employment, and school problems, for example. It no longer is necessary for a young person to develop a crisis or run away from home to contact a family counselor. Huckleberry House has grown to become Youth Advocates, where a teenager may drop into one of several facilities to visit a friend, look around, or perhaps develop an interest in one of the programs initiated by the Mobile Unit, a van that visits the high schools and conducts informal "rap sessions," dream groups, and drop-in counseling. The youth is seldom "in crisis." He is simply in need of someone to help him talk about his problems. Similar changes have occurred in probation departments, where family counseling has become a frequently used alternative to punishment or incarceration for minor offenses; in high schools, which have involved families in their counseling and guidance programs; and in many neighborhood groups in large cities, where facilities have been added for teenagers and their families to attend regular counseling sessions.

The counseling available to the youth and his family usually will be called "crisis intervention," whether there is an actual crisis or not, because many of the original youth services were funded for "crisis intervention" or short-term treatment. Long-term treatment is a luxury seldom available unless the counselor is working in the traditional child guidance setting, and even there it has become increasingly rare. We will focus on two kinds of short-term therapy: crisis counseling and short-term treatment of noncrisis situations.

Family crisis counseling means seeing a family in a state of shock. Something has shaken the family's usual balance, reverberating in the community with such force that outside authorities have suggested counseling. The family finds itself facing a double dilemma, the crisis itself and the need to include an outsider, the counselor, in the family problem.

The family's sense of shock requires the counselor to proceed with care and sensitivity. Like the nurse in the emergency room, he must develop an understanding of what is wrong and prevent further damage from occurring. At the same time, the counselor has the job of forming a relationship for which very little groundwork has been laid. Unlike the nurse in the emergency room, the counselor cannot present himself in a manner that is quietly helpful and barely noticed by the family. While the nurse often remains in the background of a medical emergency, the family counselor occupies center stage during crisis counseling.

Families in crisis seldom choose to attend family counseling sessions on their own. For them, family counseling frequently represents the least bad of several horrifying alternatives. Imagine, for example, that Nora has told her parents that there is only one place she'll speak with them—in a family session; otherwise she'll leave town without telling them where she's going. Fred's probation officer has made it clear that the only way he can keep from booking Fred in Juvenile Hall is through the family's attendance of family meetings. Such families have seldom heard of family counseling before their child got in trouble. Now that they have heard of it, they regard it with a mixture of curiosity, fear, cynicism, and contempt. They experience, and usually demonstrate, a strong resistance.

Families express their discomfort with the counseling situation in a number of ways, all of which resist the counselor's attempt to get acquainted. Some families refuse to say much of anything in the beginning, leaving the counselor confused as to whether he's offended them in any way, or they're just depressed. Other families challenge the authority of the counselor in a variety of ways, demanding that he show his academic qualifications before they will talk with him, asking him for suggestions, medication, a diagnosis, or placement for their child in an institution or foster home, in an attempt to control the interview from the beginning. Some families talk endlessly about the subject that brought them. Still others persist in recounting one detail after another in relentless pursuit of finding a cause for their problems. All these families have one thing in common: They are coping with the problem of airing personal, private problems in a setting that is new to them. They are embarrassed and ill at ease. Their ways of communicating represent anxious attempts to retain control of the new situation. If they let the stranger take over, who knows what might happen? Even those who know how to speak openly and freely about their family difficulties are reluctant to do so on first meeting someone new.

Confronted by the family's resistance, the unprepared counselor often finds himself upset and disappointed. He feels that the family fails to appreciate his efforts to be helpful and supportive. He forgets that the family, in the middle of the crisis that brought them, hardly notices him, except as an intruder. Unlike the emergency room nurse who knows that her patients' cries of pain are usually unrelated to her efforts, the counselor often lacks an understanding of the way that families express pain, and believes he is to blame for what is going wrong, inadvertently letting the family defeat him in the first few minutes.

The crisis counselor must learn to understand that the family's resistance to counseling is an expression of their fear and pain. The child who has produced the crisis with a symptom such as running away, taking drugs, or stealing feels guilty and defensive for obvious reasons. Parents often experience overwhelming shame because their child's symptom marks a large part of their life's work as a failure. The family may have had little or no previous contact with the language of counseling, so they may become more and more estranged and suspicious as the counselor earnestly exhorts them to "establish clear communication" or "express your feelings honestly." The very notion of talking problems over with a stranger may be distasteful to the family with strong traditions of privacy. Moreover, many parents who enter a youth service agency for the first time feel that they've entered enemy territory. The informal atmosphere, the posters on the wall, and the age and dress of the counselors seem to some parents to be an extension of their teenage child's most alienating qualities. If the place looks like a teenage hangout, what chance is there that they will be listened to?

The counselor who finds himself struggling with the family's initial resistance usually can function more successfully if he remembers, first, that the apparent antipathy expressed by the family is a reflection of their fear and, second, that this family needs help. The shock of a crisis not only makes a family feel vulnerable and defensive but also unbalances this family's usual functioning enough to produce an opening in their ranks, an opening that allows the family counselor a chance to be helpful.

Usually, every member of the family is upset. Something has happened that never happened before. A child ran away or got arrested, or O.D.'d and had to go to the emergency room. In the days following such an event, each family member starts to ponder the family process. Even the most taciturn, action-oriented father now has some thoughts about what produced the disaster at hand. Some of the others, who had thought about these issues before but neglected to talk about them for one reason or another, are now eager to talk. No matter what they are saying, it can be assumed safely that almost every individual is experiencing a degree of helplessness and looking to the counselor for understanding and support. Each member of the family wonders, "How did this crisis come about?" "What do I have to do with it?" The family counselor can use the family's intense need for support and understanding to help counteract their initial resistance. Let the following case serve as an example. I have broken it down into three "strategies," all of which evolved during the course of the counselor's initial interview with this family.

Carmen: "We love you. Why did you run away?"

The counselor's first strategy is to overcome the initial resistance. Her tasks are (1) warming up the family, (2) helping the family to express feelings without making things worse, and (3) helping the family to talk about important things.

COUNSELOR: Hi. I'm Edith Burney, and I work here as a counselor. I'm glad to meet you all. Could we go around with names once? It's fine with me if you call me Edith, by the way.

MOTHER: I'm Carmen's mom. My name's Betty.

FATHER: And I'm her father, Bob. Glad to meet you . . . I guess. . . . [*Attempting to laugh in the face of obvious anxiety and tension.*]

COUNSELOR: This is always the hard part, these first few minutes. I can see you're sighing, Mom.

MOTHER: Well, this is just, well, it's just . . . I don't know. . . . Why doesn't someone else say something, I'll be all right. [*Swallowing her tears.*] I really don't know. . . .

FATHER: We just don't know exactly why we're here, if you know what I mean. This isn't exactly our cup of tea, I mean.

COUNSELOR: I do know. Let me tell you what I'd like you to do.

FATHER: Well, maybe you could start by answering a few of our questions. We don't really know what this is going to be about, if you know what I'm talking about. For instance, what are you, a psychiatrist or psychologist, or what? What's the difference, anyway?

MOTHER: Yes, I was wondering, is this related to psychiatry? You're not a psychiatrist, are you?

COUNSELOR: No, I'm just a counselor here. [*At this point, the counselor notices that the family looks as uncomfortable as ever and that she, too, is beginning to feel tense and apologetic. How will she get started? What about Carmen, the girl who ran away? She decides to take charge in a way that is designed to circumvent the family's anxious questioning and address their own feelings about the situation.*] I'll tell you what I'm thinking. I'm thinking that I could try to answer your questions, to try to make you feel more comfortable—which I really want to do—or we could just start, and you could kind of develop a picture of what this is all about as we go along. If you have any questions afterwards, I'll be glad to answer them. [*Checks to see if there are any nonverbal signs of agreement. She is relieved to note that both parents are nodding their heads.*]

The counselor decides that she has given the family sufficient support to begin.] Here's how I'd like to start. I want to hear something from each of you about what's important for you right now. Something about how you are feeling about what's happened and what you want. [*She looks at each member of the family, encouraging the person who looks least resistant to speak first.*]

MOTHER: Well, I don't know what to say, I'm so upset.

COUNSELOR: That's important. Say more about how you're feeling.

MOTHER: Well, isn't it obvious? When Carmen ran away it was just terrible for all of us [*begins to cry*], and . . .

COUNSELOR: [*Speaking directly to mother in an effort to support her enough so that she can begin to be explicit about her own feelings, rather than just blaming Carmen.*] It's all right to cry. Could you tell Carmen directly what you're feeling right now?

MOTHER: I just keep asking myself, Why? Why? Why? Why couldn't we ever talk about it? You didn't even give us a chance!

COUNSELOR: [*Wanting to stop the potential blaming and defense between mother and daughter, she encourages the mother to talk further about her own feelings by starting a sentence for her to finish.*] And I feel . . . ?

MOTHER: I feel . . . I feel all mixed up, I guess. I don't know what I feel, I don't think it's such a big thing to expect that your daughter would talk something out with her mother. . . .

COUNSELOR: I feel hurt? Disappointed?

MOTHER: I do! I do feel hurt. . . . [*Crying more openly.*] We're not that bad, I keep thinking, but we must be. . . .

COUNSELOR: Now you're guessing why Carmen left. Why don't you ask her if she sees you as bad.

MOTHER: Well? [*As the mother looks questioningly at her daughter, there is a silence.*]

COUNSELOR: Looks like you feel on the spot, Carmen. [*Carmen nods imperceptibly.*] I can see that. . . . Well, maybe you could start by telling your mom you feel on the spot.

CARMEN: I feel on the spot, Mom. [*Gives a self-conscious smile.*]

COUNSELOR: Is your mom right? Is it hard for you to talk about this kind of stuff with your folks?

CARMEN: Yes.

COUNSELOR: Could you tell your mom something about what makes it hard?

CARMEN: Well, I know if I say something you'll just get upset. [*The mother's eyes are brimming with tears. Father breaks in.*]

FATHER: Well, wouldn't you be upset if your own daughter ran away from home? What do you say when the phone rings, when a neighbor asks, "Where's Carmen?"

CARMEN: That's all you care about, what the neighbors are going to say, isn't it? You don't even care about me!

COUNSELOR: Stop a minute, Carmen. [*She has the feeling that Carmen is saying something very important, something that would get lost if the family were allowed to continue the fight they have started.*] Carmen, is that the way you feel? Like they don't care about you?

CARMEN: [*Starts to cry also.*] Yes.

COUNSELOR: Because . . . ?

CARMEN: Because . . . because you just don't care, that's all. It's always Dad's business and Mom's school and everything I ever do is just wrong, that's all.

MOTHER: But Carmen!

COUNSELOR: Did you know Carmen felt that way?

MOTHER: No, I never, I even thought . . .

FATHER: We both thought it was time to leave her alone, you know . . .

MOTHER: Yes . . .

COUNSELOR: Sounds like there have been some misunderstandings here. Let's find out how this came about.

The initial resistance is abating. The counselor's friendly, firm tone seems to reassure the parents that they will be heard. Her questions lead the family away from the shaming and blaming that they dread and stress the importance of stating feelings and checking out assumptions. Every member of the family has spoken up. The counselor's leadership apparently has been accepted by the parents, who already are learning a new way to look at what is wrong. Now she can settle down to the work of understanding the family process.

Some teachers of crisis counseling feel that, when a family is in crisis, the counselor's primary goal should be to help the family find a practical solution to their most pressing problems. Probing psychological background and relationships appears to be a luxury that should be addressed after the practical aspects of the crisis have been solved. In my opinion, however, understanding family process remains crucial because it means understanding how any solution will be used by the family.

There is no plan that cannot be sabotaged by a dysfunctional family process. A diabetic child may fail to be given his medicine by a mother and father who deny that he is in shock. A teenager who seemed adamant about being placed outside his home runs away from the placement on the first night and is found hanging around his old neighborhood. Understanding how the family solves problems—who is active, who is passive, who is weak, who is strong, who is protected by whom, and so on—will help the counselor to develop a plan that will fit the context and will be less vulnerable to the family's usual ways of sabotaging.

Exploring the communication in Carmen's family led the counselor to believe that this was a family in which there was a good deal of mutual isolation and loneliness between parents and child, interrupted only sporadically by their heated arguments and graphically illustrated by the symptom of running away. Carmen and her parents were not close, and each covered the distance between them with explanations that added to the pain that produced it. The parents felt that they couldn't seem to help Carmen any more, that she'd grown away from them and was looking to others for her deeper needs. Carmen felt her parents just wanted to get rid of her, that they weren't interested in her in the first place and were happy to take advantage of her greater independence to pursue their own goals more fully. She was especially hurt by her mother's going back to school but had never discussed it with her. The father had felt left out from the time that Carmen's adolescence began, when he had felt that his wife had become overly protective of Carmen and had encouraged her to turn away from the activities that the family had enjoyed together. Up to now, each member of the family had converted pain into distraction. Instead of doing something about their feelings of loneliness and isolation, a new pursuit was begun, until, finally, Carmen had run away from home. The family needed to learn a new rule: "Don't just do something! Stand there!"

Now the counselor was ready to begin her second strategy: deciding what part of the crisis could be resolved in a few interviews. The counselor was developing her hypothesis about why Carmen had run away. She thought that it had to do with the family's difficulty in coping with Carmen's adolescence. The parents apparently had meant to encourage Carmen's independence, but their actions had produced loneliness and isolation instead. In order to develop a plan for the next few sessions, the counselor needed to know more about the family process, especially the relationship between Carmen's parents. Since the counselor observed a lack of closeness and warmth between Carmen and her parents, her guess was that this feeling also existed between the parents themselves. She set out to explore this possibility.

COUNSELOR: Well, Carmen, it seems like both you and your folks have felt kind of left out by each other. Like the other person didn't care. [*Turning to the parents, and looking from one to the other.*] What about the two of you? How does that go between the two of you? Do you ever feel he leaves you out?

MOM: Well, not so much anymore. I mean . . .

COUNSELOR: But before?

MOM: Well, I don't know. I mean, maybe it was just being young and being a mother. It was just that—well, you know, I used to try to tell you this [*to her husband*], I just felt like he was out in the world and I was just at home, you know.

COUNSELOR: [*To Father.*] What was that like for you? Do you remember those days when Carmen was little?

FATHER: Well, not that well, I guess. But I do recall that those were hard times. Aren't they for most people? We were pretty young when we got married.

COUNSELOR: How young?

FATHER: We were both 18. [*Smiles self-consciously.*]

COUNSELOR: And do you remember those days?

FATHER: Well, sort of. I just knew that if she just got busy going to school again, she'd be all right. But there wasn't time for that then.

MOTHER: It was hard. [*Looking at her daughter.*] Honey, I wasn't much older than you are now. I just didn't know what

	I was doing or where I was going. I loved you a whole lot, though. But Dad was so busy!
COUNSELOR:	And now you're busy too!
CARMEN:	You'd better believe it!
COUNSELOR:	What do you mean?
CARMEN:	Well, that's the way it is in our house. Got a problem? Get busy! I've tried to tell them there are other things in life but. . . . Forget it.
COUNSELOR:	*[To parents.]* Did you know that Carmen had been worrying about the two of you?
MOTHER:	No.
FATHER:	Yes, in a way. She has something there, I guess, but it's hard to change.
MOTHER:	And we are the kind of people that do best when everyone is working! *[Adopting a more cheerful tone.]*
COUNSELOR:	But all the sadness gets lost . . . and some of the closeness, too, I think. Seems to me we could do some work more in that area. I know you've given it a good go, Carmen, but I think I'll give it another try. I mean seeing whether this family wants to do anything but live together while each is alone and working hard. . . . Could we try to meet for a few more sessions?

By now, the counselor has developed a clearer notion about the family process and Carmen's role in it. She sees the parents as sensitive, proud people whose feelings are easily hurt and who attempt to cover their vulnerability with a veneer of efficiency and hard work. Like many couples who marry so young, they seem to have been precipitously thrown into their adult roles and, in attempting to succeed as parents and in their own careers, their emotional life has lagged behind. Carmen's negative role in the family appears to provide enough conflict so that the parents can have some emotional contact with each other in their concern for her development. On the positive side, she has challenged them to lead richer lives.

With just this much information, the counselor made plans for a series of three or four interviews, as follows. One important topic was Carmen's feeling of neglect by her parents. The counselor decided to do some work on Carmen's low estimate of how her parents saw her. Then she would attempt to help Carmen see that she was old enough now—especially since she disagreed with many of her parents' values—to be her own judge. She would work toward Carmen's becoming more aware of how very hard she was on herself, with a view toward referring her to a teenage group if the problem didn't improve in the next few sessions.

A second topic was the parents' career-mindedness and their emotional distance from family activities. The counselor decided that she would work on this problem for a few sessions to see (1) whether the parents wanted to change toward spending more time with their daughter and (2) whether they were able to do so. There was a possibility that their fast pace was a symptom of estrangement between them. The counselor had seen several families where the strenuous social life and career of the parents served to give the couple a semblance of togetherness at a time when their own relationship was deteriorating. If this were the case, the counselor planned to make recommendations for marital counseling, because it would be unlikely that the long-term, complex issues involved would be solved in a few sessions.

The counselor's third strategy was to help the family to make short-term plans. At this stage of the counseling, the counselor had made a diagnosis and a general plan for three or four weekly meetings, but she needed to accomplish one more step with the family before the first interview was over.

Carmen had come to the counseling session after running away from home. At the time the session took place, she was living at the group home. During these initial interviews, the parents often make the assumption that, at the end of the interview, their children will return home with them, while the children assume that they will remain at the group home. This crisis, like most crises involving adolescents, represents a family's failure to live together successfully, as well as a failure to live apart. At the end of the interview, the family often finds itself back in the limbo to which they have become accustomed. The situation is hazy. No one takes a stand. Everyone expects to be disappointed. The counselor needs to address the family's living arrangements directly:

MOTHER:	Well, this has been a very nice talk. Better than I thought it was going to be, Carmen. How do you feel now, honey?
CARMEN:	It was okay. But I don't want to come home yet. Not yet.
MOTHER:	[*Looking crestfallen.*] You don't?
FATHER:	[*Somewhat angry.*] Well, you sure could have fooled me! I thought for sure you'd be coming right home with us. What do you want to do?
COUNSELOR:	Are you very disappointed? [*Looking at mother and father.*]
MOTHER:	Sort of. Well, you know, I like to have things looking up and as long as she's here . . .
COUNSELOR:	And you? [*To father.*]
FATHER:	No, she has to do what she has to do, that's all. She wanted to be on her own, now she is on her own. She'll . . .
CARMEN:	It's just that I . . . I don't. . . . Well, I thought another week here and I can get some more counseling, like about a job and stuff. . . .
COUNSELOR:	You don't want to hurt their feelings?
CARMEN:	No, I guess not.
COUNSELOR:	Tell them. You can tell them what you want.
CARMEN:	Well, Mom and Dad, I don't want to hurt your feelings, I really don't, I just don't want to get my hopes all up high and then crash, you know.
COUNSELOR:	So what I want . . .
CARMEN:	I'd like to stay another week and then meet like this again and then see.
COUNSELOR:	How would that be for you? [*To parents.*]
FATHER:	Like I said, she's on her own.
MOTHER:	OK. I agree, honey; I'd rather do it right than just fix it up and have it not work out. [*Mother still looks disappointed but is saving face.*]

Now the family is ready to leave. Four essential steps toward crisis intervention have been accomplished:

1. The family is no longer so resistant to counseling.
2. The counselor and family have learned something about this family's process.
3. An assessment of the family process has provided information sufficient to produce plans for further counseling sessions.
4. The immediate situation has been clarified, and a realistic short-term plan has been made.

Much has been written about the counselor's style in doing short-term crisis counseling. Students often wonder about whether the nature of a short-term relationship requires them to behave in a certain way, a way that prevents the family from becoming overly dependent in a situation that cannot last a long time. Should the counselor maintain a distant, objective manner? Other students are acquainted with the point of view that an authoritative stance provides comfort to a family in crisis, because it lends structure and provides an impetus with which any plan can be implemented. Should the counselor make an attempt to take charge in a more authoritative, sure, no-nonsense style during crisis counseling? How should she obtain a family history? Should she pursue the family history in the kind of detail that might turn up skeletons now safely stored in the closet—the unresolved issues around grief, depression, and addiction that lie behind many a seemingly innocent family situation—when there is so little time to deal with such disturbing issues? Should the counselor make sure that the family maintains at least a semblance of their social façade?

The assumption underlying such discussions is that the counselor has attained a personal style secure enough to allow him a choice about the manner in which he approaches his clients. He is so at home in the province of counseling that he can be warm and direct with one set of clients and cool and impersonal with another, without sacrificing his authenticity. The youth counselor, however, is often young and so lacks the experience that would let him play a specific role with any family without severely limiting himself. He has to be himself. He is just beginning to find his way through the maze of family process. He must present himself as a whole person in order to be sensitive to his own, personal reactions, which provide a major source of his understanding of family dynamics. If he is concentrating on being distant or objective or, indeed, adopting any attitude that is foreign to him, he will be role-playing a counselor, rather than learning to *be* one by using his own inner resources.

We will be stressing the view that the counselor's best resource is his own life experience. Like the family he is interviewing, he has grown up in a family; like his clients, he has experienced stress. To the degree that the counselor finds himself in the beginning stages of developing the techniques described here, it will be his humanity that bridges the gap between him and his clients when his professional knowledge fails him. Spontaneity frequently is associated with loss of control, and there is no question that the student who reacts to his clients by expressing his own feelings may risk blurting out something he would prefer to keep to himself. Such possibilities, however, need not be deterrents. (These questions will be discussed in some detail in Chapter 8.)

The problems that arise (between family and counselor) can be handled in the same way as the ones that occur among family members: by clarifying them, paying attention to both the counselor's and family's particular processes, and making plans that best fit the situation. This interplay between the counselor's life experience and his professional training, between the family members and the counselor, will be described in many specific situations in the following pages.

The last question about crisis intervention often relates to the kind of clients seen. Agencies that do a lot of crisis intervention see more individuals who have less income and education than clients generally seen in long-term therapy. There are many third-world families, many poor families, many families who are in no way prepared for counseling. The question of specific needs arises again for the counselor who wonders whether he can be included in a different cultural context without changing his behavior in some way. Once more, the author is strongly biased in favor of the counselor's authentic experience, as contrasted with adopting an unfamiliar stance, however appropriate to the clients' cultural background.

The counselor who finds himself working with a family whose background and present circumstances in no way match his own will need, of necessity, to explore his reactions in each particular situation. These will determine any necessary changes in his behavior. Does he feel superior? At a loss? Full of pity? Curious? Hostile? There is a vast range of possible reactions. If the student understands his own reactions, he will be able to work out an approach that will help him work in another cultural context. The counselor can take charge of his area of expertise without pretending that he is all-knowing in other areas as well. If he feels at a loss, he can profit by assuming the position of learner and ask the family to educate him about their ways. My own experience has taught me that the distance I often sense between myself and clients from another culture and/or race is bridged most easily if I acknowledge it and ask a lot of questions. I assume that a poor, black family, for example, knows that I'm going to be ignorant about their particular context and background. Just as they can help me to get to know their style, I can help acquaint them with my work, which may be unfamiliar to them. Rather than assuming that they are different from me in ways that specifically require me to behave in a style that may not suit me, I want to remain curious about the ways in which we are different and develop ways of accommodating each other.

Families from different cultures present vast differences in the details of their everyday existence. Any counselor who tries to change his approach and style in any major way to accommodate these differences will have to become a chameleon. This is not necessary, however, because there are issues that present problems for all human beings: rearing children, accommodating differences, facing fears, letting children grow, dependence, independence, loneliness, love. The problems of growing to adulthood, parenting, illness, working, success, failure, death, and grief occur in all cultures. Only the solutions differ, and there we all can learn from one another.

In conclusion, then, it is important for the counselor who is doing crisis intervention to accomplish a few minimal tasks. First, he must let the family overcome their initial resistance so they can begin to look at their process. He then can form a diagnosis that will help him to establish goals for short-term therapy and develop plans for the immediate crisis situation with the family. In my view, the counselor who accomplishes these tasks is successful to the degree that he can do his work in the style most congruent for him, whether as a consultant to the family, as an authority figure, or as a fellow traveler.

Suggested Readings

Beggs, Larry. *Huckleberry House.* New York: Ballantine Press, 1968.

Brown, Frank, and Madelon, Stent. *Minorities in U.S. Institutions of Higher Education.* New York: Praeger, 1977.

Conger, John. *Generation under Pressure.* Life-Cycle Series. New York: Harper & Row, 1980.

Golan, Naomi. *Treatment in Crisis Situations.* New York: The Free Press, 1978.

Haley, J. *Changing Families.* New York: Grune and Stratton, 1971.

Haley, J. *Uncommon Therapy, The Psychiatric Techniques of Milton Erickson, M.D.* New York: Norton, 1973.

Ketty, Joseph. *Rites of Passage, Adolescence in America, 1970 to the Present.* New York: Basic Books, 1979.

Langsley, Donald G., and Kaplan, David M. *The Treatment of Families in Crisis.* New York: Grune and Stratton, 1968.

Leveton, Alan, and Leveton, Eva. Children in Trouble, Family in Crisis. A series of 5 training films demonstrating a family counseling alternative. University of California at Davis, Administration of Criminal Justice, 1975.

Rabichow, Helen G., and Sklansky, Morris, A. *Effective Counseling of Adolescents.* Chicago: Follett, 1980.

Umana, RoseAnn. *Crisis in the Family, Three Approaches.* New York: Gardner Press, 1970.

5

Contracts and Cotherapists

Contract: a mutual agreement between two or more parties that something shall be done or forborne by one or both; a compact; convenient, bargain, esp. such as has legal effects . . .; a convention between states. [*The Compact Edition of the Oxford English Dictionary*, Oxford University Press, 1971.]

Contracts

Every family enters counseling with a lot of doubt. There is something comforting about setting up contracts in counseling or therapy. The client describes his problem; the counselor describes her work. They agree on a set period of time and/or the kind of symptom relief that will tell them the work has been accomplished. A fee is set. There is something comforting about such contracts, and there is also something misleading.

The word "contract" suggests an agreement where both parties understand the terms. When the contract involves the remodeling of a kitchen, both the contractor and the client come to an agreement about the desired result. He sees the same wall that his client sees. Both agree that it has to come down. When the client describes the kind of cabinet she wants, she and the contractor can look at enough samples to clarify exactly what is wanted. Together, they look at his drawing of her remodeled kitchen and, with negligible exceptions, see the same drawing. While the contractor is the expert on methods and the client knows little or nothing about how he will proceed to accomplish their joint goal, they have a common basis for judging his finished product. If anything in the contract seems unreasonable, his client can take her drawing to another contractor who will check on the terms the first offered. Here is a situation in which a contract is both comforting and useful. It helps insure against surprises regarding cost and quality of work. The contract to remodel the kitchen deals with the tangible.

Problems may exist even in the contract just described. The contractor may have lied about his license. His work may have been shoddy. He may not have kept to his bargain and may have worked far longer than agreed. The client, then, has one source of comfort: her contract. If worse comes to worse, she can take him to court.

Now, the realm of counseling and psychotherapy is very different from the world of the building trades. One belongs to the world of concrete, predictable, and measurable reality. The other, despite all of its efforts and pretenses to the contrary, remains part of a world of intangibles where certainty is rare and measurability hard to find. It is no accident that so few books on psychotherapy deal with the normal personality. Normality, or the absence of symptoms, is very difficult to define. Emotions, value judgments, and intuitions have to be taken into consideration in discussing symptoms and cures. There are times when both patient and counselor are convinced of the success of their work without being able to assign either a measure or an exact description to the success, much less replicate scientifically the methods that produced it. The client feels "better, relieved, like a new person, changed." The counselor feels he "worked hard, was lucky from the start, had good rapport." The vagaries of each individual dynamic, the complexity of the relationship, and the limitations of language provide solid barriers when it comes to assessing the results of counseling.

Returning to the analogy of the contractor and his client, clearly, there are few counselors who would be able to come to an agreement with their clients about the nature of the problem in the first interview. One of the generally accepted strategies of family counseling is that the counselor attempts to shift the focus from the person who is in trouble (the identified patient) to the entire family. Right away, the family and counselor disagree about the nature of the problem. In other words, when the family comes in and asks that the counselor help Irma, who got caught for stealing last week (please remodel the kitchen), the counselor answers, though she may not do so in so many words, that the entire family needs some help (no, the foundation of the house needs rebuilding).

Second, there is seldom any agreement between counselor and

clients about the meaning of the word "work." In the beginning, the counselor and her clients seldom speak the same language. The counselor knows what she means by work: Her client(s) will attend sessions for a certain number of hours a week, during which time she will apply a variety of strategies to help her client(s) to function more successfully. Successful counselors use many different strategies. Leaving aside differences due to varying theoretical convictions, let us examine only the family counselor who uses a systems approach to family therapy. There are radically different styles of family counseling, even among those who share a similar theoretical background. One counselor may work by having family members talk to her and clarify messages she wants other family members to hear. Another will de-emphasize direct talk between family members, refusing to act as a "go-between." (Going back to the remodeled kitchen, that's a bit like asking the client to do the carpentry work herself.) One counselor will be kind and supportive as he works with the family, so that they can use him as a source of comfort and strength when confronting painful issues. Others confront directly, seeming harsh or tactless at times. One counselor likes to hear about the family's history; another wants to work almost entirely in the "here and now." One counselor uses active techniques such as Gestalt and Psychodrama; another is content to hear family members relate problems in a narrative style. All of these counselors use a systems approach. All work differently. Each would find that explaining his way of working in a scientific, objective manner would be difficult, if not impossible.

The counselor knows something about the nature and difficulty of change and the kind of pain attendant on it. Family members, unless experienced in therapy, have little or no idea about the consequences of the process they're agreeing to. The woman whose kitchen needs remodeling knows that she will be inconvenienced because the walls will be torn down. The family member contracting for therapy doesn't know anything except that he wants to experience less pain. He often thinks in terms analogous to the owner of the house who wants a remodeling job while she and the family are on vacation.

In the world of counseling and psychotherapy, we are dealing with intangibles. It is true that there are a few behavioral approaches that attempt to work in a tangible way, helping clients alleviate clearly defined symptoms such as phobias and addictions. Most counselors, however, and especially most family counselors, deal with methods and products that are mysterious to the novice. Not only are they mysterious, but they may have to remain so for the period of time required for the clients to understand their counselor's language.

Why can't the counselor explain what she is doing when she meets the clients? Any attempt to explain methods or diagnosis seldom succeeds because the words used have a different meaning to the talker and the listener. If a family counselor were to state that she wanted to shift the focus from the identified patient to the whole family, she would very likely be met with a hostile, defensive response from family members who would feel blamed and ambushed. In attempting to explain her work, the counselor has to have recourse to theory, which, though familiar to her, is new to the family. In order to explain fully, she would need to give the family a short course in her training, a task not only time consuming but intolerable in the crisis atmosphere that brings the family to treatment.

Contracts for family counseling are bound to be misleading because the two contracting parties cannot be expected to share the same frame of reference when discussing terms. It is regrettable that this is so. It appears to be unfair to the client, and, in fact, it is. Aside from the most crude measurements of competence such as degrees, memberships in professional associations, sponsorship, or personal recommendations, the client has very little basis for forming a judgment about his prospective counselor. In most cases, moreover, the client has to pay for the time he takes to decide whether or not he wants to work with his prospective counselor. Who would ever consider paying a contractor for the time he takes to make his bid? The therapeutic contract attempts to reduce the anxiety attendant on beginning family counseling. Sadly enough, in many cases there *is* no way to reduce that anxiety, which is, in fact, an appropriate reaction on the client's part to beginning a risky venture.

If a contract cannot be written and a bargain cannot be struck, what can be done to help the client in this unfair situation? Obviously, one simple step out of the dilemma is not to charge for the first session(s). It also behooves family counselors to be aware of the clients' dilemma. The counselor can tell his clients that he is not the family's only choice. There are other counselors using a similar approach, as well as altogether different approaches. When he is referring clients for further treatment after an initial work-up or a short period of crisis counseling, he can emphasize that the client need not accept the first referral and, at the same time, encourage him to give the new counselor a chance.

Although a contract is impossible, in the conventional sense, an agreement is not. The clients' dilemma in choosing a counselor makes it imperative for the counselor to be clear about her limitations and the demands of the situation. If her job only permits her to see the family for a period of two or three months, for example, this must be clear at the outset. While the counselor may not be able to agree to a definite time for ending, she can agree to review the work at predetermined periods of time, such as every three or four weeks. These measures will help the family to express their worries and develop some strategies for dealing with them.

"How long do we have to come here?"

FATHER: How long's this going to take?

COUNSELOR: I don't know. What I'd like is that we continue to meet once a week for an hour like this to work on the problems we were just talking about.

MOTHER: [*Interrupting.*] But Bill has to work and Billy has to go to school; we just can't keep coming here forever.

COUNSELOR: I can understand that. I don't think I'd be able to do that anyway, and, if I would be able to, I wouldn't want to. Forever is a long time. You know this is a crisis center and I can see you for two or three months at the most.

FATHER: I'm not sure I could come that long.

MOTHER: That's what I was saying.

COUNSELOR: How about this? Let's meet a couple more times and then we'll all have a better idea of how we're doing and where we're going. We'll set some time aside in the third session for review. How does that sound to you?

FATHER: Well, I'd rather have the answer to my question, but if that's the best you can do. . . .

COUNSELOR: That's the best I can do.

FATHER: OK, then. OK with you? [*To Mother.*]

MOTHER: Yeah.

COUNSELOR: We don't have to wait until the third session to talk about how it's going, you know. Any time you don't like what's going on here or you have some question about it, I would like you to raise it, OK? It is important for me to know how it's going for you, positive *and* negative.

The counselor's last statement is important if the client's judgement is to play any part in the counseling process. She has given permission and encouragement for the client to comment on the process of counseling and indicated her willingness to take these comments into account.

In summary, it has been my contention that it is impossible for family counselors to make clear contracts of any complexity. It is difficult to define problems and describe procedures, let alone guarantee success in the generally accepted language of other contracts. At the same time, I have emphasized the counselor's need to present the client with a chance to comment on the treatment he is receiving, as well as give him clear indications about the limits of counseling in terms of time, hour, and fee. I also have stressed the need for the counselor to teach his clients that they have a choice of counselors and types of counseling.

Cotherapists

Sometimes one counselor is not enough. The family that enters family counseling often is seen by a cotherapy team. Many of the same processes will occur that characterize any family counseling, yet the relationships are different.

Usually, counseling relationships begin when counseling begins. Just as the counselor and his individual client develop a relationship together, so do group members meet each other and their counselor(s) at the same time. The power of the family system is felt by every family counselor and accounts for some of the difficulty and confusion befalling those attempting to learn their trade. The family enters counseling with a complicated and profound set of relationships already made. They know each other well; the only new person in the relationship is the family counselor.

Sometimes the counselor may find herself strongly handicapped because she is drawn into a family system where she forms an emotional alliance with one or more family members. Other families are practiced at the art of excluding outsiders, and the family counselor finds herself forever trying to find a way to join her elusive clients. Most families offer the counselor a combination of both processes—she feels included some of the time and excluded some of the time, and only seldom on an equal footing with her clients, free to comment and behave as she sees fit.

Cotherapy puts the counselors into a strong position vis-à-vis the family system. No longer is the individual attempting to relate to an already formed system, but rather there are two systems relating to each other. In all likelihood, the family system will continue to outweigh that of the counselors in terms of cohesive skills and traditions, but the cocounselors will have gained immensely in their ability to cope. This has to do with the problem of self-perception in new groups. To go far afield for a moment, it is well known that individuals alone have a hard time resisting group pressure, even in the most recognizably absurd situation. Such television programs as Candid Camera have demonstrated that an individual can be induced to behave in a way practiced by others before he joined the group, no matter how absurd. A doctor's waiting room, for example, is filled with "patients" who have been coached previously to remove silently their overcoats, then topcoats, then shirts and ties, as they sit and wait. The newcomer enters the waiting room, looks visibly uncomfortable, checks several times to see whether everyone, indeed, is behaving the same way, and, finally, joins them. When one person (not coached to undress) is present in the same waiting room, however, the newcomer finds an ally to help him resist group pressure and remains dressed, exchanging puzzled glances with the other person. The impact of the family on the counselor is similar. With some discomfort, but an increasing degree of compliance, she is induced into the family system. A cocounselor helps her to remain herself because, in a very basic way, he provides feedback that is different from that of the family.

Cocounselors form their own system, their own frame of reference. When one is reacting in an automatic, unconscious manner, the other can observe and, having observed, comment. Some counselors do this explicitly, as the session unfolds. For example, a counselor who noticed that his partner was interrupted by the father in the family and then seemed to be passive and resentful for awhile, commented, "Let's see, Lori, you're so quiet. It seems to me that awhile ago Dad interrupted you and you haven't yet got back to what you were saying. Is that right?"

Other counselors prefer to reserve comments about each other's feelings for later, after the family has left, when they feel freer to explore their own process. There may be times when commenting doesn't seem appropriate. Luckily, cotherapy also provides the counselor with the opportunity of taking over during a part of the work that rendered his partner ineffectual. In her partner, the counselor has an observer who can help her gain more awareness of her actions in the family setting. As the team becomes more "familiar" (!) with each other, comments can be made nonverbally and a quick glance may be enough to inform the other that a dysfunctional process is being repeated.

The counselor who feels she is losing ground in a family session does not have to wait for her partner's rescue, unless, of course, she has no awareness of what is going on. Often, she knows she is confused and needs to know more about what's happening. She can then address her partner directly and say, "You know, I'm really puzzled by something. First I got quiet. And now Mom isn't saying much either. I know I'm not being quiet because I feel fine about what's going on. I'm being quiet because I'm confused. I don't know what to say. Does that make any sense?" As Lori and her partner talk, they discover that a very obvious direction for the session has been neglected, or that Lori is wrong about Mom's lack of participation, or her partner may be able to connect her confusion with something specific that happened in the session. No matter what happens, Lori has regained the freedom to comment in her conversation with her partner and thus will be in a position to work more effectively.

The beginning cotherapist often is reluctant to talk to her partner in front of the family. Since the session is partly a social situation, it seems rude to exclude the family members. The more she practices this skill, however, the better she will understand that it benefits the family as well. One of the ways family members resist the counseling process is to oppose it. They already have talked about these issues, and it didn't help. They already have tried what the counselors suggest. They disagree with what the counselors are saying. This kind of resistance often has the effect of nullifying the counselors' efforts in the session by giving tit for tat. The family's perception of their own process gets reasserted in a way that seems to neutralize any changes the counselors try to bring about. If the counselors exclude the family as they talk to each other, however, the family is not able to oppose them. While the counselors talk, the family listens, a captive audience. The counselors then can engage in discussions of themes that are central to the family's process, tantalizing them with a dramatic presentation that includes both sides of a given issue, several outcomes, and provocative comments. This process is sometimes referred to as "splitting." It is illustrated in the following case example, which was a conversation between cocounselors, to which the family listened.

Peter: Should He Be Allowed to Move Out and Work on His Own?

JOHN: You know we've been over and over this territory. I don't think these guys are ever going to make up their mind. And I think the reason is that Mom isn't ready to let Peter go. She's been a terrific mother, and for that she needs a son.

LORI: Yeah. She has been a great mother. I don't know though. I think she's ready to start something new. In a way she's in the same boat as Peter. Maybe if he offered *her* that job in Redwood City, she could move in with those other guys. Just kidding. No, I think Mom's ready to do something new. She's a strong lady.

JOHN: Well, maybe that's the trouble. If Peter goes off and Mom is a strong lady, what about Dad? He'd probably start drinking again, and then we'd all be back to "go."

LORI: You are really pessimistic this morning! I say Mom could go to work part time for awhile and see how Dad felt about that. I think they're both strong enough to see her be less of a wimp.

JOHN: You mean she and Peter should just try it? Are you crazy? Do you remember what happened the last time anyone made a big change in the family?

As the counselors talk among themselves, the family reacts. The conversation highlights many sore points, but there is no arena to oppose or censor what is being said. When the counselors are ready to include the family members in the discussion, enough emotion has built up to insure that the material can no longer be neutralized. Cocounselors can make use of the same process the family uses. They too can include or exclude the family with powerful effect.

Cocounselors also can comment briefly to each other on the family's process. If a family persists in returning to blaming and shaming each other, for example, the counselor can say to her partner, "Can you believe it? We let it happen again! Every time I relax just a little because I think we've stopped these guys from bickering, they start up again!" This kind of talk permits the family to gain a little distance from their process without being engaged by the counselors in a blaming or restrictive way—they are simply musing out loud about their work.

Cocounselors also can discuss strategies with each other during family meetings. When some work has been completed—an argument settled, a plan made—one counselor may say to the other, "I'd like to go back to something we haven't heard about for awhile—the family rules. Is that okay?" If the partner agrees, the path is clear. If not, the counselors may wish to discuss different possibilities: "I want to get back to that, too, but I still don't understand why Mom looked so sad when she came in today. Could we look at that first?"

In all of their discussions, the counselors provide a role model for the family. They show family members how to comment on process, how to settle differences, how to find out whether someone wants to help, how to make room for each other in terms of thoughts and feelings. Another way in which cocounselors may wish to work is to split functions. In this way, each is free to pursue a different line with the family and model a different way of behaving. In the Billy interview, for example (see p. 27), it became clear as we worked with the family that my cotherapist, Alan, made most of the conceptual interpretations of the family system, helping the family to understand what was happening, while I made emotional alliances with various members, helping to draw them out and become more trusting and modeling a more spontaneous, intuitive style. Other cocounselors divide the work with one being more active than the other; one commenting more on the system, the other on the individuals; or one more rational, the other more emotional. Many counselors shift their division of functions according to their own needs and the needs of the family they are seeing in each session.

Cocounselors are a source of information for each other *outside* the family therapy setting as well. After the session is over, they can discuss what happened and formulate new strategies for working with the family, finish up any unfinished business in their own relationship, and give each other much-needed support and validation. Cocounselors should meet together following each family session, whenever possible, or at regular scheduled intervals. These meetings provide an opportunity to solidify and develop the relationship of the counseling team, just as the family's life together gives them time to reassert old family processes and practice new ones. Since identification is such an integral part of any learning situation, it is not surprising that family processes seem to be catching, in the sense that the counselors often find themselves duplicating an aspect of the family's struggle in their own relationship. Although this malady is seldom as serious as it is for the solo counselor, family conflicts always stir old memories and emotions in the observers, who then frequently find themselves reenacting an old conflict that resembles that of the family. Comparisons between the counselors' process and that of the family should provide useful information for further work.

Who will become the best cotherapists? How should a cocounselor be chosen? Human processes seldom, if ever, lend themselves to clear-cut questions and answers, and there is certainly no definite answer here; however, there is a variety of issues to be raised in the selection of a cocounselor.

The family system's powerful advantage vis-à-vis the counselor has already been discussed. It is not surprising, then, that many family counseling teams have been formed by married couples, such as my husband and myself. Not only is system pitted against system, but family against family! There are many advantages to such teamwork. There is usually more time available for discussion of problems; the cocounselors often share, or at least understand, each other's point of view; they have a shared verbal and nonverbal vocabulary that usually facilitates communication; they have a lot of time to work on their own relationship, unrelated to the family in treatment. The problems that occur are related directly to the quality of the marital relationship. The more dysfunctional it is, the more problems are added to the work-load, which now includes *two* dysfunctional systems. Working together with a family is not advisable for any husband and wife in the throes of their own family break-up. It is possible, but will require a good deal more time and complicated commenting and searching on everyone's part to remain comprehensible, let alone helpful. On the other hand, if the marriage is good and permits commenting on the normal stresses and strains as they become relevant, much will be gained by other families. Working together seldom comes naturally to any husband-and-wife team. It is not necessarily related to other skills demanded in a marriage and has to be learned separately. In the beginning, and at times of stress, husband and wife will be vulnerable to issues affecting their sense of self. They may fear judgments from the other person and sometimes hear them when they haven't been uttered, they will struggle to establish themselves as potentially equal partners, and they will need to evolve a system for working on the problems as they arise. None of these stresses need be a handicap; in fact, the more they can be discussed in the family setting as they relate to a family's growth and development, the more these struggles will prove an asset to the work.

The question of role-modeling suggests that, when possible,

differences among cotherapists are welcome because they allow the modeling of a wider range of behavior. Cotherapists may well be male and female, old and young, experienced and inexperienced, introverted and extroverted, talkative and silent. Cotherapists who bring different life experiences to their work necessarily widen its scope, as long as their relationship remains functional and neither eclipses the other.

The most important clue to whether a cotherapy team can be effective is the quality of their communication. The nature of family counseling demands that the cocounselors develop an understanding of each other's language, enough mutual trust to allow the exploration of personal issues touched off by the work, and enough respect to continue working together at times of stress. It may take time for cocounselors to develop enough confidence to explore their own relationship during a family session, and some therapy teams never achieve this skill. However, when the family can observe cocounselors handling the kinks in their own relationship, the demonstration of process is more clear and powerful. Cocounselors who allow each other to comment on differences and hurt or angry feelings not only demonstrate their own humanity to the family, but also, we may hope, show a way to deal constructively with the same difficulties that lead the family to counseling. On the other hand, just as a husband-and-wife team gets into trouble as their own relationship becomes dysfunctional, so does any cocounseling team. If the therapist team members are defensive, denying their own difficulties, and pretending to feel better than they do, the family probably will attempt to deal with the confusion and pain that results. This process seldom leads to a cure of either system. More often it leads to frustration, anger, and the family's departure from therapy.

The foregoing discussion leads to the conclusion that two counselors are invariably better than one. Where inexperienced counselors are concerned, I believe this to be true. Experienced counselors also sing the praises of cotherapy because of the undoubted reduction of stress on many levels. Some, however, prefer to work alone, and not just because they can't get along with a cotherapist or don't wish to share their fees. The experienced family therapist has developed a mental shorthand that helps her identify family problems and decide on the methodology she will use and the pace the situation requires. Her work with families has developed an aesthetic pattern. She has developed her own language. Her relationship with the family grows at a predictable rate. In this situation, a cotherapist might be experienced as an intruder, as someone interrupting a smooth process, who talks when the therapist would be silent or interprets something the therapist wants to disregard. These are the hazards of cotherapy for anyone, but for the experienced therapist they may be the deciding factors leading her to use cotherapy only on specific occasions, such as getting consultation on a difficult family, bringing a new part of the family to the sessions, or other situations in which therapist or family stand to gain something specific from the use of a cocounselor.

In summary, cotherapy offers benefits and relief in direct proportion to the amount of stress experienced by the individual family counselor. Much depends on the quality of the relationship developed by the counseling team. Discussion and review outside of the family sessions are of the utmost importance, as is supervision at times of stress in the cocounseling relationship. When the cocounselors work toward having as much fun together as possible and the work develops a light, easy quality, the goal of teamwork is realized.

Suggested Readings

Abroms, G. Supervision as meta-therapy. In F. Kaslow (Ed.), *Supervision, Consultation and Staff Training in the Helping Professions*. San Francisco: Jossey-Bass, 1978.

Anada, Gerald. *A Guide to Psychotherapy*. Washington, D.C.: University Press of America, 1983.

Berne, Eric. *Transactional Analysis in Psychotherapy*. New York: Grove Press, 1964.

Boyer, Pat, and Jeffrey, Ron. *The Family, A Living Kaleidoscope. A Guide for the Beginning Family Counselor*. Cheyenne, WY: Pioneer Printing and Stationery Company, 1981.

Ewalt, P. (Ed.). *Mental Health Volunteers*. Springfield, IL: Charles C. Thomas, 1967

Framo, J. L. Chronicle of a struggle to establish a family unit in a community mental health center. In J. L. Framo, *Explorations in Marriage and Family Therapy: Collected Papers*. New York: Springer, 1983.

Knapp, Michael. *Non-verbal Communication in Human Interaction*. New York: Holt, Reinhart and Winston, 1972.

Lazare, A. The customer approach to patienthood. *Archives of General Psychiatry, 32*, 553–558, 1975.

Leveton, Alan, and Leveton, Eva. Children in trouble, family in crisis. A series of 5 training films demonstrating a family counseling alternative. University of California at Davis, Administration of Criminal Justice, 1975.

Montalvo, B. Aspects of live supervision. *Family Process, 12*, 343–359, 1973.

Napier, August, with Whitaker, Carl. *The Family Crucible*. New York: Harper & Row, 1976.

76

Process, Techniques, and Challenges

Palazzoli, Maria S., Checchin, G., Prata, G., and Bescola, L. *Paradox and Counter Paradox*. New York: Jason Aronson, 1978.
Papp, P., and Aponte, H. J. The anatomy of a therapist, paradoxical strategies and counter-transference. *American Journal of Family Therapy*, 7, 11–12, 1979.
Robson, Elizabeth. *Getting Help: A Woman's Guide to Therapy*. New York: E. P. Dutton, 1980.
Whiffen, Rosemary, and Byng-Hall, John. *Family Therapy Supervision: Recent Developments in Practice*. New York: Grune and Stratton, 1982.
Whitaker, Carl, and Keith, D. Symbolic experiential family therapy. In A. Gurman and D. Kniskern (Eds.), *Handbook of Family Therapy*. New York: Brunner-Mazel, 1981.
Wilmer, H. A. In M. Berger, (Ed.), *Video-tape Techniques in Psychiatric Training and Treatment*, New York: Brunner-Mazel, 1978.

6

The Active Techniques

Once the family has become involved, the counselor often wonders how to keep the work going. Is talking enough? Is there a way to expedite matters?

Here on the West Coast, family counseling developed in an era when psychotherapy was changing its focus, not only from the individual to the group, but also from techniques largely based on talking about events in the client's life, to techniques involving the client in a variety of activities. Family therapy developed concurrently with other active techniques such as Gestalt therapy, sensitivity training, body awareness therapies, and art therapy. Many of the early family therapists developed a lasting commitment to the integration of the active techniques and family therapy. This commitment was brought about by a growing distrust of therapies that relied heavily on content, sometimes described as the "grocery list of last week's events," or referred to as "about-ism." The mere recounting of a client's life began to be regarded as having a dead—or at least rehearsed—quality. The active techniques transformed the counseling setting from one of merely sitting and talking about important events, to one requiring active participation and spontaneous expression of feeling. The counselor's role changed from that of listener to one in which he directed and observed his client's activity. The active techniques seemed to add a dimension of spontaneity and vitality to the counseling session.

The risk for the counselor using the active techniques lies in their thoroughly unconventional, and therefore unexpected, quality. Families in crisis expect to talk to the counselor about their problems and get his advice; when he asks them to speak directly to each other, they are puzzled. They do that all the time! Why here? There is an element of self-consciousness to be overcome if they are to behave as though the counselor is not there, when he really is. Families in crisis expect to spend their time focusing on material relative to what has gone wrong. They do not expect to be asked to draw pictures, sculpt each other into a monument, or reenact scenes from their past. How, then, is the counselor to convince them to begin?

First, the counselor must examine and attempt to overcome his own resistance. He can talk with a supervisor or other counselors about his problems in risking the families' dislike, for example, or appearing unconventional. In order to develop a feeling for the experiences he is asking his clients to undertake, it is helpful for him to immerse himself in the active techniques. Books, films and videotapes help the inexperienced counselor to learn. Participation in workshops and consultation groups that use the techniques will provide an arena where he can become personally acquainted with the various techniques, in a supportive environment.

The active techniques—sometimes called experiential techniques because they rely on experiences the client has during therapy—require the counselor to take charge, if they are to be successful. These activities—drawing together, speaking directly to each other, and the like—are the counselor's idea, not the family's. He cannot expect the family members to know what to do. He must be willing and able to become active himself, to guide his clients from one part of the activity to the next; to demonstrate, if necessary, or help the family begin, by being a model. If the task requires that, instead of addressing the counselor, family members speak to each other directly, he can move his chair back a little and look down or straight ahead, demonstrating his unavailability. If the activity requires the family to stand, he can begin by standing up himself, inviting the others to follow him.

Beginning an active technique means bridging the gap between what the family expects and what the counselor has in mind. It often helps to formulate the activity as a novel experience: "Now I want you to try something you may not have expected." "Now I want to try something new." "Now let's do something very different." Labeling the newness of the process can help the family to overcome any beginning awkwardness or self-consciousness.

As the counselor develops his skills in the area of experiential techniques, he will find that he can become more and more spontaneous in their use. In the beginning, however, it is well to plan ahead carefully, thinking through exactly what he expects from the family, so that his instructions to them can be clear and direct. He will return to his familiar role only after the task has been completed, when the work is reviewed and compared to what already is known about the family process.

The following exercises and illustrations are given with the intent of demonstrating some of the active techniques commonly used in family counseling. The descriptions are limited to the techniques themselves. In actual clinical practice, they will be enlivened by the ongoing process of each counselor and family, some requiring more in the way of support and introduction, some overwhelming their counselor with material, some beginning with self-consciousness and withdrawal, others challenging the counselor with their playful spontaneity.

Talking Directly to Each Other

During family counseling, talking about problems often seems to add a gossipy quality to the session. Father says, "Johnny never did well in school, doctor. They thought he was kind of slow but we knew it was just that he's lazy!" Meanwhile, Johnny is sitting there, simultaneously included and excluded from the conversation. The technique of requesting clients to speak directly to each other was emphasized both by the sensitivity training groups and by Fritz Perls, the founder of Gestalt therapy, as part of an effort to make the therapy hour more than just talk about the past. The family counselor, of course, has not renounced the recounting of history entirely. When historical material is relevant, it is necessarily included in the counseling session. Most of the talking done by family members, however, involves talking directly of current material.

Why should family members be requested to talk to each other, when they want to talk to the expert whose advice they were seeking? Because they have to talk to each other whenever they are together, and because they have not found a workable way of talking together to solve problems, or they wouldn't have needed counseling. As the counselor begins to coach family members in talking directly, they experience what is going wrong in their process and often spontaneously evolve ways of doing something about it. A direct statement has a hundred times more emotional impact than a statement about someone else. A client talking about his father to the counselor, saying, "My father never thought anything I did was right," experiences something very different from the one who actually faces his father and says, "I felt I could never please you, Dad." The first example remains an often-told abstraction about childhood; the second is an experience in the here and now, a process developing before the counselor's eyes, demonstrating how father and son interact when confronting an emotionally loaded issue. Both counselor and family can learn as they let the process unfold.

Johnny: "He's Always Late for School."

FATHER: Johnny never could get to school on time.

THERAPIST: Why don't you say that to Johnny?

FATHER: Okay. Well, Johnny, you never get to bed no matter how many times we ask you.

THERAPIST: Could you also tell Johnny how that makes you feel?

FATHER: Frustrated.

THERAPIST: Tell him.

FATHER: I really feel frustrated in the mornings when I'm trying to get you up and you're just lying there. I hate to see you get in trouble with your teacher.

In this interaction, the counselor is no longer in the middle, translating communications from one family member to another. The family members relate to each other as usual, with the counselor available to comment and coach when necessary. This way of working also helps shift the major part of the responsibility for solving the problem from the counselor to Dad and Johnny, where, of necessity, it belongs.

Training family counselors reveals that it is sometimes difficult for the student counselor to switch his orientation from talking with families to asking them to talk directly to each other. The counselor expects to act as the go-between for family members. The family expects to talk to the counselor directly. When the counselor takes himself out of such a central role, however, he is at an advantage. Not being directly involved in the interaction means gaining distance from which he can watch the family's verbal interaction. Family members, with their common history, soon forget the counselor's presence when challenged by a direct interchange. Without the demand of a constant response on his part, the counselor can listen more carefully while the process of the family unfolds before him. The student of family counseling often fears the family's resistance to an unexpected request that makes them self-conscious. He is afraid the family members will wish to avoid speaking directly to each other. Watching experienced therapists use the active techniques may help the student to overcome his own initial resistance. Seeing the change in a family that is actively engaged often is enough to give the student confidence to begin to try the newer ways of working. Role-playing different family counseling situations also helps acquaint the student therapist with these active techniques. It also is important to remember that there is no need to be rigid in asking the family to perform any new task, including talking directly to each other. There will be times—many times in some families—when talking at length *about* something or someone is necessary. However, with some firmness and consistency on the part of the counselor, most families do learn to talk directly to each other in the counseling session, helping the therapy to intensify.

Family Drawing

Family drawing is pure gold for the family counselor who enjoys active techniques derived from art therapy. It is an activity most families enjoy because it has an element of play. Materials are few and directions simple. It is a technique that can be repeated as often as necessary.

First, the counselor introduces the task as he would any other active technique, by explaining to the family that they are about to do something a little different, something that will require all of them to participate, adding, "We're not going to talk at all while we do this." The counselor then shows the family a large pad of drawing paper and a box of crayons. "First—and remember this all has to be done silently—I want each of you to select a crayon which is a different color from anyone else's in the family. Second, I want you to work together on this piece of paper. After you've worked for awhile—again, without saying any words—you may decide you've finished and you want to work on another piece of paper. There probably will be time for that, too. I'll give you a little warning before the time is up. Go ahead."

The counselor then steps back, giving the message that he will not be involved in this task, except as an observer. Most families complete at least one drawing in about five minutes. If the family remains actively engaged and chooses to do more drawings, the counselor may wish to give them more time. A warning is given about two minutes before ending the task: "You have just a couple of minutes left to finish whatever you're working on. I'll tell you when the time is up."

Family members often resist the instruction to be silent, especially in families where talk is used to reduce anxiety. They often want to ask for more information, asking questions like, "Should the whole family make one drawing together?" "Should each person have a separate piece of paper?" "Should we make a picture or a design?" The counselor who encourages the family with his own nonverbal gestures to make these decisions without talking will find that their solutions present him with a graphic illustration of the family's process. Clearly, many modes of the family interaction will be revealed in this simple task. If Father feels that he has to be the leader in the family, he will show it by the way he nonverbally takes over the theme of the drawing and gives direction to the others as to where and how to draw. If one of the children feels excluded, there is no doubt that this child will draw less than the others, and the counselor may observe what efforts the others make to exlude him.

Some of the following questions may prove helpful in talking about the family's process:

1. How did the drawing get started? Who decided to start, and why? Does that person often take this kind of responsibility? How did the others react?
2. How did the family members divide the paper? Did each stay in his own corner? Did they interact, gradually making a common space? Did anyone feel excluded? Intruded upon? Did anyone try to join anyone else? How did that go? How is the family's use of space on paper similar to the family's use of space at home?
3. How did the family communicate? Were there times when anyone sent any specific messages? Were there messages about the kind of drawing it was to be, when to stop, something someone didn't like? How was the communication received? Were there any similarities to the way the family usually communicates?

The counselor has the job of observing the family closely while they are drawing and then to use the discussion, together with his observations, to make analogies to the family's process at home. The material is immediate and relevant, a useful catalyst for exploration and change. The following example is drawn from Billy's case, which we began exerpting in Chapter 2 (p. 27).

Billy: "I don't belong here."

Billy's family drawing was begun by Dad and Michelle, as might have been expected from these leaders of the family. Billy left himself out much of the time. On a piece of paper covered by vigorous drawings, Billy drew only the slats of a fence and a few vague scrawls representing birds. He looked subdued and quiet, watching the others most of the time. Other family members made no attempts to include him.

After the first drawing was completed, we wanted to give Billy a chance to contribute more forcefully. Giving the family specific instructions to help Billy accomplish this task, we asked them to do a second drawing. Our instructions were followed easily. Billy drew more and the family allowed it. Thus, in a very short time and with only minimal efforts on our part, Billy got a taste of positive self-assertion while the family got support and praise for encouraging him.

The recent death of the mother came up as the family discussed the drawings. Michelle had made an attempt to draw the whole family using stick figures. In talking about it, she discovered that she had only drawn five members, not six, as she intended. In other words, she had drawn the family as it really was, leaving Mom out. But the family was not yet ready to face the reduced number; so Danny, with Dad's support, quickly cooked up the story that he probably had been away at camp during the drawing, and Michelle hastily drew a sixth family member. At least in the drawing, the family was whole again.

As this case illustrates, family drawing can be used for a variety of specific therapeutic purposes. Families may be encouraged to fight and then make up, using only the family drawing as communication. The counselor may want to rotate leadership among the different family members. Families who get stuck on representational content (what to draw, who drew the right thing, who the wrong) may learn something new by limiting themselves to an abstract drawing or a design. The family drawing, like other experiential techniques, has the advantage of being adaptable to the specific needs of each therapeutic session.

Family Sculpture

Developed by Virginia Satir, this method lends itself to exploring family process in a great variety of ways. No materials are required. The counselor begins by saying, "We're going to do something a little different to help us learn what's happening in the family. First of all, it involves everyone getting up out of their seats. (The counselor rises first as an example.) Now we need someone who will make a family sculpture (general confusion). What I mean is, I want someone— without talking—to arrange the family into a grouping that, if I were walking through the park and saw you, would tell me something about the kind of family you are. Who is close to whom and who is far away might be a way to start. The rest of the family has to let the sculptor sculpt. That means being as much like clay as possible. Some sculptors have sculpted the kids and Mom together as a tight group, with Dad as the outsider. Another had teenage kids sitting on their mother's lap. You get the idea? Who wants to try it first?" When small children are present, the counselor may add, "It's like using play-dough. They're play-dough and you can make them into what ever you want."

When someone volunteers, the counselor proceeds by reinforcing the directions, reminding the sculptor to proceed without words, family members to be quietly cooperative, and so forth. If no one volunteers, the counselor can decide who is to start by choosing the family member who seemed most interested while she was giving the directions. In large families, it is sometimes difficult for everyone to hold his pose until the sculptor is finished. If the counselor notices that family members are uncomfortable in their physical positions, she can add, "You can relax, for the time being, but be sure you remember your exact pose, so you can take it up again when the sculpture is finished." Family sculptures not only reveal the family process in the way the task is accomplished, but in the final product as well. The family sculpture is a frieze of the family process.

Once a person has molded the first family member, the rest follows easily. The counselor can help by making sure that her instructions are followed, underlining the need to act without talking. Talk promotes distance in this technique, whereas touch is one of its positive byproducts. When the sculptor has included all the other members of the family in his sculpture, the counselor directs him to fit himself into the picture, thereby completing it.

The sculpting is followed by a discussion that begins with an inquiry conducted by the counselor while the family members remain in their sculpted positions. (Those in awkward positions may need a moment or two to stretch before resuming their assigned places). The counselor says, "Let's see if each of you can tell me something about what it feels like to be in the spot you're in." She first asks the person with whom the sculptor began and continues in sequence, "What's it like to be where you are? Comfortable? Uncomfortable? Whom can you touch? See? Who is far away? Does this position resemble the way you feel in the family? How?"

Completing the first inquiry may take up an entire session with a family. The counselor may choose to stop and work on a particular comment by one or two family members, or she simply may proceed from one to the next, to round out the whole picture before working on any particular part with her usual techniques.

A sensitive sculptor will place his family in positions that evoke poignant comments. A father who had been placed outside the family circle, facing away from it, for example, said, "This feels so lonely. I never realized how cold it is out here." The counselor worked with him for awhile, encouraging him to express his feelings to other members of the family and exploring their reactions. Further work included a sculpture in which the father sculpted the family as he would have liked it to be, with him and his wife in the center of the family, holding hands with each other and the children.

Like the family drawing, the family sculpture is a flexible technique. It does not even have to remain static; once completed, the sculpture can be set into motion. The counselor may wish to find out what would happen if everyone took one step forward, or if a particular person left the family, or if a new member were to be added. In a family where the youngest child recently had grown old enough to leave, the mother's report of feeling "empty-handed" when the child was taken out of the sculpture led to a touching discussion of her fear of this next step in her development.

The family sculpture often is used as a diagnostic technique when the family first enters therapy. At this time it can be done in the context of the present, past, and future, with instructions to sculpt the family in terms of "how you see the family now," and "how you would sculpt your husband and yourself as you were when you were first married," and "how you picture the family in one year." The context can vary from ideal to the most feared circumstance: "Sculpt the family as you would like to see it," or, "Let's see you sculpt the family as you are afraid it would look, if worse came to worse." Like the family drawing,

the family sculpture, once taught, can be adapted to any family problem that would benefit from exploration with an active technique. For a
case example, we will have another look at Billy's family.

Billy: "I'm lonely in this family."

Almost before we had finished the instructions, Michelle volunteered to sculpt the family. Like the little mother she was, she
concentrated on sculpting the fights that the three boys got into
and showed herself as the peacemaker. When Billy volunteered to
do a sculpture, he placed himself outside the family circle, looking
in. Using a variation that allowed him to assign each person a
sentence to say to him that typified their relationship, he complied
by painting a word picture consonant with the isolation he seemed
to experience so intensely. All the sentences were critical. "I hate
you." "You're stupid." "Can't you do anything right?" He
answered each person with the same words, "I feel I'm not
wanted in this family." Billy came to the interview with the reputation of being one of the family brats, possibly the worst offender.
The sculpture helped the family see his inner self, the self he had
hidden by running away.

Doubling

The double, as a technique of psychotherapy, was originated by J. L.
Moreno, the founder of Psychodrama. The technique is immensely
valuable as an adjunct to individual, group, and family therapy.

Basically, the double is someone who represents a part of another
person, speaking for that person, saying things he may be thinking or
feeling but isn't saying. The counselor can introduce the technique
simply by taking a seat next to the person for whom he wishes to
double and saying, "I'm going to be another part of you now and say
some of the things you might be thinking or feeling but not saying." In
order to set the patient's mind at ease, the counselor may wish to add,
"You don't have to agree with what I say. Remember, I can only guess
at what might be going on with you. So if I'm on the wrong track, let
me know, or if you feel like it, argue with me. We often argue opposite
sides of the same question or opposite feelings about one issue in our
own minds. This is another way of doing that. Okay?" One more
direction helps to clarify the process in the family setting: "Our rule is

going to be that only you can hear me because I'm part of you. The others can't hear me or respond to me. If you want to use any of the things I say to respond to the others, you have to say them yourself." Without this direction, the question of who is talking to whom in the conversation can become quite baffling. The rule also stimulates the client to take responsibility for his own thoughts and feelings because it prevents him from continuing to be silent while his double speaks for him. Not all of the directions mentioned so far need to be given immediately. They can be fed into the process as it develops. It is sometimes helpful to touch the client lightly while doubling.

There are many varieties of doubling. A counselor may limit his doubling to one sentence in which he endeavors to help his client express a certain emotion, or he may work as a double for an entire hour, helping the client work out an inner conflict. The counselor can double for different members of the family at different times. In families, the counselor may begin by being the only one to use doubling, but he will find that family members pick it up quickly and add it to their list of skills.

A double can reflect a family member's feelings quietly (Double 1) or play a loud counterpoint (Double 2) to his client's tight, inhibited demeanor:

CLIENT: I don't want to go out with you, Lenny.
DOUBLE 1: I feel uncomfortable saying this.
DOUBLE 2: I can't stand you! Go away! Quit bothering me!

Learning Exercise 1

Doubling depends on the skill and sensitivity of the counselor. Two exercises are helpful to learning this technique. The first requires that the double comment by asking questions. Instead of asserting that his client is thinking about something, he represents the client's asking himself what he is thinking.

CLIENT: I don't want to go out with you, Lenny.
DOUBLE: Don't I?
CLIENT: No, I really didn't like it last time.
DOUBLE: But don't I kind of like his asking me, all the same?
CLIENT: No, I wish he'd go away.
DOUBLE: Then why am I talking to him?
CLIENT: Go away!

Using this technique, the counselor steps out of the role of adversary. He joins his client in the search for a solution to his problem. The technique is quiet and relatively undramatic. Since it is close to the counselor's usual method of procedure, it has the advantage of allowing him to begin to double without taking big chances. His client's feedback will guide his steps.

Learning Exercise 2

Another technique is to verbalize extreme versions of what might be happening:

> CLIENT: I don't want to go out with you, Lenny.
>
> DOUBLE 1:   I think you're a creep!
>
> DOUBLE 2:   I'm frightened of you.
>
> DOUBLE 3:   I hate you.
>
> DOUBLE 4:   Please take me out, no matter what I say. I really love you, Lenny.

The counselor must be prepared to risk being dramatic and emotional. His own abilities to express feelings spontaneously and strongly will encourage family members to do the same. As an example of the doubling technique, let's take the following case.

Virgie: "I'm not as good as the boys, I guess."

> Virgie is a 15-year-old girl who was seen for a family interview at her probation department after she had run away from home to live with a man, 15 years older than she, and his children. Virgie and her mother attended the interview.
>
> Virgie, a very pretty girl with long, brown hair, behaved in a kind of quiet, agreeable manner that seemed to be in direct conflict with her situation. When I began to double for her, I was aware that she had just been brought back home involuntarily. Her mother was glaring at her. Virgie responded sweetly, as though the two had just got together for a chat. Sitting next to Virgie, I caught several deep sighs, and I guessed that the sighs were related to her feelings about her mother. As I put these thoughts into words, Virgie responded quickly, as though she had been waiting for permission to express her feelings:

VIRGIE:	[*Answering her mother.*] I don't know what I want to do now.
DOUBLE:	I mostly feel like you don't care about me.
VIRGIE:	I really *do* feel you don't care about me!
DOUBLE:	You seem to care about my brothers, but not about me.
VIRGIE:	You always favor the boys, Mom. *Sometimes I thought you hated me!*

The vehemence with which Virgie said the words suggested by her double was surprising. Through doubling, the transition from a superficial, social exchange between a mother and daughter in crisis had been accomplished and the work could begin.

Doubling is a peculiar technique in that it introduces a new dimension of reality to the counseling session. A client has not usually had any experience with another person speaking for him, using the personal pronoun, "I." Once he accepts the counselor as another part of his own thoughts and feelings, the client, acting without the usual interpersonal defenses, often moves very quickly to material that is central to his problems, in an intense, emotional way, just as Virgie did. If that happens, the counselor must be ready to switch from his role as double to the role of counselor in order to help his client integrate the experience.

Psychodramatic techniques have the advantage of immediacy to the counselor who familiarizes himself with their use. They require no extra materials and very little in the way of structure, and they enable the counselor to transform any part of a session into an active experience.

Role Reversal

Most families conduct their lives in such a way that few if any of their members have any ways of exploring the rich detail of each other's lives. Even in families where empathy is stressed, what is known about another's inner state is often limited. Role reversal, another psychodramatic technique, addresses this problem. Using this technique aids the counselor to help two people in conflict to begin to develop mutual empathy. The directions are simple. After observing a conflict of the type that will end predictably in an impasse, the counselor interrupts the process and tells the couple to switch chairs and role-play the other person, continuing the conversation. A description of an actual case will illustrate the process.

*Tom and Jewel: "Sometimes I just feel like
a thing in this marriage."*

Tom and Jewel are the parents of Gloria, a 16-year-old girl who was seen at the probation department after running away. The family is black. Tom is a thin, quiet middle-aged man who works only sporadically. Jewel is energetic, efficient, and works full time. Her full, rich voice stands in marked contrast to his soft, barely audible tones.

During the interview, Tom and Jewel repeatedly had brought up their conflicts about who was responsible for housework, without apparent compromise or resolution. Jewel seemed willing to blame Tom endlessly, and Tom equally willing to listen. We used role reversal to help break the repetitive routine of these fights and to help each understand something about what the other was experiencing.

It was difficult for Tom to get started. He seemed unable to imagine himself in his wife's shoes. Some reminders in the form of the therapist's addressing him directly gave him the necessary support to play his role! "You're Jewel now. What do you have to say to Tom over here? Jewel, what do you think of him?"

As both Tom and Jewel warmed to their roles, it became clear that neither felt valued by the other. "I never do anything right for her," said Tom, played by Jewel. "All he likes is my cooking," said Jewel, played by Tom. They switched back again. We commented on their apparent awareness of each other's feelings of worthlessness. They stopped their bickering and let sadness come through. "Sometimes I feel just like a *thing* in this marriage," said Tom and Jewel listened.

It is important to ask the participants actually to switch chairs when using this technique, to help structure the role-playing. "In this chair you are yourself. In Jewel's chair you are Jewel." If people don't actually change places, they often become confused as to which role they are playing.

The timing of role reversal often is determined by an impasse in which two people keep repeating the same dialogue. The counselor's request to reverse roles may be preceded by picking up a sentence typical of an impasse: "Harry, I want you to start role-playing Violet by saying, 'Well, where do you think I was?' just the way she just did. And, Violet, answer him by saying, 'Don't pressure me.' "

In addition to the exploration of conflict, role reversal is used frequently to explore a new event. A new mother and father may do well to switch roles after the birth of a child, for example, or a mother and daughter may switch after the daughter has announced her plan to move out of the home. Role reversal, like doubling, can be used for small or large portions of any counseling session and is extremely flexible in its use.

The Empty Chair

Fritz Perls, the founder of Gestalt therapy, developed the use of the empty chair, another technique originated by J. L. Moreno, to drama-tize internal conflicts. Like the double, the empty chair is used to discover and make explicit hidden aspects of an internal dilemma. Different from doubling, while using the empty chair the client works out each part of the process alone. This technique requires the pre-sence of a counselor who directs the action; a client who provides the problem; and the empty chair, which can represent any adversary, imagined or real—in short, any entity the counselor and client wish to confront. For an example, we will return to Jewel and Tom's case.

Jewel: Her Mother's Daughter

During the counseling session, Jewel's recurrent theme was the one we already mentioned—her hard-working, suffering martyr-dom in working for a family of ungrateful, lazy dependents. We used the empty chair in an effort to help Jewel see her internal conflicts and to avoid her negative, martyred monologues. When Jewel talked about her mother's role in raising her to be hard working and overly responsible, we pulled up an empty chair, placed it directly opposite her, and asked her to sit in it, to show us how her mother had talked to her when she was a little girl. Jewel had no trouble following our directions. She portrayed a busy woman who didn't seem to realize that her little girl wanted to spend some time playing. She placed one responsibility after another on Jewel. "Take care of the house; take care of dinner; take care of your little brother." Jewel then was asked to switch back to her own chair and reply to her mother as the little girl would have. Jewel switched chairs, and, for the first time in the hour, limited herself to a few shy words: "Yes, Ma'am." We asked her whether that was all she would have said. She indicated that her mother did not permit any backtalk. When we asked her what she would have wanted to say instead, she answered, "I'm so tired, Mama." Her voice heavy, her body quiet, these words had a ring of truth that had been absent in her earlier conversation. We asked Jewel to repeat the sentence, looking at her husband, Tom, and then her daughter, Gloria. Jewel's voice had a deep quietness as she repeated the sentence that she had worked so hard to suppress, a sentence that opened the door to another choice for her: to take better care of herself rather than blaming others for her overworking.

Later in the interview, Jewel talked about her painful ulcer. We used the empty chair once more and asked her to sit in it and speak for her ulcer, to personify it, give it a voice with which to address her. "Pay attention to me," said the ulcer, "You can't ignore my pain." Jewel had found another way to ask for something for herself; through her ulcer, she had found the words to demand attention—the opposite of the self that was eclipsed by her working for others.

The directions for the use of the empty chair are simple, as we have seen. Like much of Psychodrama, the learning comes from doing, not from explanations. Asking the client to sit in the empty chair, encouraging him to represent another person or thing, and discouraging any of his attempts to explain or "talk-about" are all that is needed.

The empty chair can be used to characterize aspects of dreams. "Be the car that was about to run over you. Talk for it." "Sit in the empty chair and fly as you did in the dream. Close your eyes if it helps. Tell your other self over there how it feels to be in the air." The empty chair can be used to act out parts of the self: "Do you hear yourself giving yourself orders? Go and sit over there and give those orders. 'Do this; do that; don't make mistakes.' Now come back and answer. Put your whining part over here. Let's hear you really complain and carry on. Show us how helpless you are to change things." The empty chair can be used to dramatize the internal conflicts relating to objects:

"Be your house demanding you to take care of it." "Be your car refusing to work." The object in the use of this technique is to allow the family member to experience his conflict in a new way that lets him confront himself and his projections and actively work out a new integration.

In using this technique, the counselor stays in touch with his client in order to give further directions. Jewel, for example, told us that her "Yes, Ma'am" to her mother really covered her desire to say the opposite: "No. I don't want to do what you tell me. I'm tired of working all the time." We used that information to work further with Jewel's relationship to her husband and daughter, for whom it was equally relevant information. Clients often present conflicts that are repetitions of the battles they fought in their original families. It is often helpful for the counselor to ask someone engaged in a dialogue with his conscience, some other person, or a part of a dream, "Does this part of you remind you of anyone else in your life?" If the answer is his mother or father, for example, the counselor can then ask the patient actually to play that role in the empty chair and continue from there. When the client's conscience is unreasonable, chances are that there was an unreasonable parent, as demonstrated by Jewel. To begin to resolve the conflict, the client has to confront the unreasonable parent, using her adult experience and the counselor's help to take a new, stronger position than she could as a child. Jewel, for instance, will realize gradually that she is no longer a little girl who must fulfill limitless responsibilities because she does not dare to argue with a mother on whom she depends. As her picture of her own helpless, trapped position changes, she can learn to speak in a less aggressive and more genuinely caring way and to make room for her playful, relaxed side. She can shrug off impossible burdens and resign from being "Mama's best little girl."

The Active Fantasy

What if? What if I lost my job? If I didn't take care of the children? If I made a mistake? If I just dropped out and went to a desert island? Fantasies—catastrophic, fanciful, paradoxical, romantic—play a role in everyone's life. The dream of the perfect marriage, with two children, a boy and a girl, a house with a lawn and/or white picket fence, for example, is still responsible for many a life decision made by the young. The fantasy of poverty looms behind the commitment to hard work; the fantasy of losing control causes many a fragile, vulnerable person to adopt a stoic, implacable exterior. Fantasies help some individuals to escape to a better existence. They often are used to punish others. "If I'd only married Joe instead." "I should have been an actress." "I should have had children." "If we only lived back home where we came from." Everyday routines often are based on fantasies and dreams long forgotten.

Troublesome, repetitive behavior, daydreams, fears, future plans, and hopes can be explored with the active fantasy technique. The counselor, recognizing that his client is driven by something other than material or interpersonal circumstances, begins by asking, "What if?" "What if the client stopped working so hard?" "What if his dreams came true and he became a millionaire?" "What if his fears were realized and he found himself without a penny?" Once the theme of the fantasy or catastrophic expectation is established, the counselor helps his client explore it with further questions. "What would life be like as a millionaire?" "How would the day go?" "Where would he live?" "What about friends? relatives?" "What would be the biggest change?" "What would change for the worse?" As the fantasy existence is explored in detail, the client frequently experiences confusion, surprise, and a new freedom that results from his confronting a fantasy that he had imbued with magic powers; his options are increased.

Jewel: "Mother wants to run away from home."

Gloria's mother, Jewel, is known already to the reader for her constant preoccupation with housekeeping. When we asked her to explore the catastrophic expectation underlying her ceaseless efforts to keep her home neat and clean, she was reluctant to begin. Looking up at the ceiling, then looking at us as though we had asked her to perform a walk on the high wire, she said, helplessly, "Oh, I wouldn't even know where to begin. Oh no!"

Having begun, however, she was equally reluctant to stop. What if she didn't do all that housework? The mess in the house lent itself to long lists of problems, which Jewel rattled off enthusiastically as her husband and daughter smiled self-consciously. Dirty dishes, filthy laundry, radios and television sets blaring, dust everywhere, bits of old food in the kitchen—Jewel relished the description of the chaos that would be produced by her absence. What if she walked into the house in the state she'd just described? Her answer came without hesitation: "I'd check into a motel." She smiled broadly. It was a possibility she had not considered before. For the family and for us, her hard work became more understandable. Her martyrdom had a purpose beyond that of accomplishing her mother's high standards. Jewel, like her daughter, Gloria, wanted to run away from home. With her hard work she was bonding herself to a family that depended on her, and whom she needed.

In another use of the active fantasy, the counselor suggests a theme to the client, choosing material that could be helpful to him in accomplishing the next step in his growth or in facing a difficult problem. A counselor working with an adolescent facing his graduation from high school without plans, for example, could suggest that they might explore a story together in which a young man is traveling along a stretch of road and finally arrives at a crossroads. What lies ahead if he takes one direction? What if he takes the next? Carefully exploring each road will help explore the boy's real-life choices.

Seating Arrangements

Family counselors often are trapped by family homeostasis. The family functions in its own way and goes on repeating the same patterns in the counseling room and outside. The techniques discussed here are intended to help the counselor upset the family homeostasis to create a momentary imbalance out of which new, more functional patterns can emerge.

Since the family's rigid patterns will be expressed on every level of their behavior, the way the family chooses to sit in the counseling room is important. Like any family behavior, it can help the family resist change. For example, the oldest sister sits between Mom and Dad, separating them and enabling each to talk to the others through her. In another family it is clear that the primary relationships are between Mom and her son, who sit together on the couch, and between Dad and his daughter, who sit opposite them.

Changing the seating arrangements may help the family to observe its own process and thus begin to change. If, in the first example, the counselor moves the oldest daughter's chair out from between her parents, she may be facilitating two new processes in her family. First, the parents now can be asked to confront each other directly. They face each other, rather than the oldest daughter. Second, the daughter can examine her usual place from a new vantage point. The counselor may wish to explore the new situation in some detail: "How long has it been since the parents have faced each other?" "What is it like?" "What are the advantages and disadvantages of having the daughter in the middle? of talking directly?" "What is it like for the daughter to be sitting with the other kids?" "Does she feel like a parent or like one of them?" "What are the advantages and disadvantages of being in the middle? of not being in the middle?"

On the other hand, the counselor may want to change the family's seating arrangement without comment, in an effort to produce a change in the family process, as in the following case.

Cindy and Mom against Tammy

Cindy sat between her sister Tammy and her mother. During the stressful talk that ensued, Cindy was quick to support her mother by attacking Tammy whenever Tammy started to present her own point of view. When we asked Cindy to change places with Tammy, she did so under great protest, muttering, "I might as well leave the room." However, her changed position and her preoccupation with her anger at having been moved kept her out of the conversation that ensued between Mother and Tammy, who were able to complete their exchange.

In this chapter, a variety of experiential techniques have been discussed. All of them serve as active processes in which the family and the counselor can learn more about how the family relates. All of the techniques are flexible; they can be used at many different times and in many different ways.

Counseling is hard work, both for the family and the counselor. Talking about family problems often becomes a burden to the family and helping difficult and unrewarding for the counselor. The active techniques lighten the family's burden by providing a structure. At the same time, they help the counselor develop a sense of play, exploration, and adventure to counteract the bog of his own seriousness vis-à-vis the family's troubles.

Suggested Readings

Blatner, Howard. *Acting-In: Practical Applications of Psychodramatic Methods.* New York: Springer, 1973.

Boyer, Pat, and Jeffrey, Ronn. *The Family, A Living Kaleidoscope. A Guide for the Beginning Family Counselor.* Cheyenne, WY: Pioneer Printing and Stationery Company, 1981.

Jung, C. G. *Man and His Symbols.* Garden City, NY: Doubleday and Company, 1964.

Kempler, Walter. *Experiential Psychotherapy in Families.* New York: Brunner-Mazel, 1981.

Knapp, M. *Non-Verbal Communication in Human Interaction.* New York: Holt, Rinehart and Winston, 1972.

Leveton, Alan. Elizabeth is frightened. *Voices, 8,* 4–13, Spring 1962.

Leveton, Eva. *Psychodrama for the Timid Clinician.* New York: Springer, 1977.

Leveton, A., and Leveton, E. Experiential techniques. In A. Leveton and E. Leveton (Eds.), Children in trouble, family in crisis. A series of 5 training films demonstrating a family counseling alternative. University of California at Davis, Administration of Criminal Justice, 1975.

Perls, Fritz. *The Gestalt Approach: An Eyewitness to Therapy.* Palo Alto: Science and Behavior Books, 1965.

Rhyne, J. The gestalt approach to expression, art and art therapy. *American Journal of Art Therapy, 12,* 237–248, 1973.

Satir, Virginia. *Peoplemaking.* New York: Basic Books, 1972.

Whitaker, C., and Keith, D. Symbolic-experiential family therapy. In A. Gurnan and D. Kniskern (Eds.), *Handbook of Family Therapy.* New York: Brunner-Mazel, 1981.

7

The Challenge of
Strong Emotions

The counselor of adolescents often finds herself caught in an emotional tornado. Adolescents, in fact, represent one of the rare subgroups in our Anglo-Saxon-based culture, for whom the expression of intense emotion is not taboo. Most of us feel a measure of reluctance to show ourselves weeping uncontrollably, yelling with anger, or speaking in a voice that declares deep and tender love except—if at all—with those we know intimately. The family session challenges the family to show intimate behavior to a stranger, the family counselor. Naturally, the clients are reluctant to break a strong cultural taboo. The counselor, usually raised in the same culture, cannot be blamed for having difficulty insisting that family members comply with her demand. She may not want to encourage the expression of strong feelings before she feels that the family has come to know and trust her more. Or, in fact, she may be reluctant to press the family to show strong feelings at any time; aware or not, she may fear her own helpless embarrassment.

Moreover, the counselor has a specific reaction to each family she sees. Many counselors dread the expression of strong feeling that recalls personal pain. For one counselor, for example, the expression of grief may be a special problem because he has as yet been unable to grieve the recent death of his mother. He may experience anxiety and confusion as he is forced to confront a family member's unrestrained tears of grief, which bring his own repressed feelings closer to the surface.

For another counselor, grief may present no problem, but anger may. This counselor was a peacemaker in her own family. Any angry family scene triggers her into action. She distracts, she soothes, she quiets. She is not aware that she is afraid of angry feelings. When a family member is provoked, anger remains largely unexpressed and the interview continues with a quality that appears friendly and pleasant, while underneath it is frantic and tense. The counselor is helping the family and herself to deny essential aspects of the process. If a family session is going well—especially in a crisis-intervention setting—strong feelings will emerge. In order to be effective, the first question the counselor must ask herself is, "Can I tolerate strong feelings?"

Does counseling families mean that one has to be able to tolerate feelings? I think it does. The counselor who feels unready must do all she can to equip herself. First of all, she must become aware of the problem. As she talks cases over with her supervisor, she will get a picture of her own process with families. She may discover that she steers the family away from certain areas. With her new awareness, the counselor can check herself in further family sessions. If her own reluctance to enter the arena of grief, tenderness, despair, or rage continues, she may want to work further with a counselor of her own in this area, which undoubtedly contains some material of great importance to her personal development. This may be a long-term process, providing the counselor with little help in seeing her cases at the time she becomes aware of the problem. One solution to this is for the counselor to work with a cotherapist who is aware of her difficulty and who can step in and help when necessary. One of the advantages of cotherapy is that, if and when one therapist gets caught in the family system or misses an important point, the other therapist can take over.

Grief

Like any strong emotion, grief evokes a strong response. When it is evoked in a counseling session, the counselor usually experiences some turmoil related to her own past grieving. If the counselor is unable to tolerate the expression of deep grief in the families she sees, chances are she will use her authoritative position to keep the family from expressing it. In working with Tina, for example (whose case we will study in more detail in Chapter 12), the counselor might notice Mother begin to cry and perhaps ask a question requiring the mother to use her head: "How old was your brother when he died? Was he living at home then? Were you?" Only a few seconds are necessary to suppress Mom's tears. Or perhaps Mom's crying would cause the counselor to change the subject: "What's your reaction to Tina's cutting school?" This enables Mom to gather herself together. Or the counselor simply may clear her throat and hand Mom a kleenex in a way designed to let Mom know that she is to dry her tears. The family also comes with a sense of embarrassment and shame about the problem. That is why they need help to express their feelings. If the counselor communicates her negative anticipation, chances are Mom won't express her feelings at all.

We must look as well at the other side of the interaction, namely, whether the client can tolerate the expression of strong emotions. The counselor must ask, "Is Tina's mother ready to tolerate her feelings of grief?" "What if she just collapses? or starts to become so depressed in the session that she's worse when she gets home?" "What if she becomes suicidal?" Since the emotion is grief, we seldom face such negative consequences. For most of us, the expression of grief is healing. Even if it seems as though the tears will never stop, there is an accompanying feeling of relief. Tears of grief are tears that must be cried.

Tina's case makes excellent reading for the student who feels that both he and his client are ready to work with a grief reaction and would like some help. Barbara, the counselor, used the "empty chair" technique in order to help Tina's mother confront her grief. The other students in the consultation group had mixed reactions to the use of this technique. For example, those familiar with the technique showed surprise that it had worked at all, commenting that it seemed artificial and difficult to apply.

The counselor also could employ a combination of interpretation and direct questioning. For example, on learning that Mother's brother died when he was about Tina's age, she could comment that it wouldn't be surprising if Mother had some feelings of fear about Tina that dated back to her brother's death. It is important to be slow and gentle in making this interpretation, lest Mom feel blamed. It is not easy to talk about someone close who died a sudden, unexpected death. The counselor must be aware of this difficulty and be ready to support and encourage the mother in venturing forth into this private territory. If the mother agrees that some of her feelings for her brother are, indeed, mixed with her cautious attitude about Tina, the counselor can go on and ask some of the same questions that are elicited in the empty chair technique: "Tell me about your brother; what did he look like?" "What was he like?" "How did you get along with him?" "What was it like for you when he and your mother did not get along?" "Tell me about how he died and how you and the rest of the family reacted." "Perhaps there are some things you could think of now that you would have liked to have told him."

It is often helpful to give the client some homework as well, asking her to do some writing about the person who died, to think of a ritual to say a final good-bye, to look over old letters or photographs—all with the goal of bringing to the surface feelings that have affected the client's behavior strongly. The counselor herself may want to take the role of the deceased person, in order to help Mother express her feelings. There is a wide range of techniques to choose from. The greatest test of the counselor's ability to work in this area rests in her sympathy and understanding of the client's experience and her adaptation to her client's inner pace.

In the rare case where the counselor encounters a person who is so rigid that any show of emotion may cause both deep embarrassment and an exacerbation of the symptoms, the family will provide her with clues. For example, they may make allusions to a previous nervous breakdown in the family, or the fact that a relative had a heart attack after an emotional scene. The counselor can say to the family, "It's been a long time since Mom's brother died. What happened since?" "Have you cried at all, Mom?" "Why not?" To the others, she may say, "You looked concerned about Mom the minute she had a tear in her eye. Are you worried about her?" Tina may answer by telling a story about an event in her mother's past that worried her, such as a hospitalization, a suicide attempt, or an indication that Mom was afraid to lose control. Mom also could respond by suddenly leaving the room, showing the counselor that she could not tolerate an allusion to her grief. The counselor cannot be certain, of course, but if she keeps the range of possibilities in mind—the social taboo; particular fears of counselor and family; specific, serious problems affecting one family member—she will be in a position to decide on the most effective way to work with grief.

Anger

The expression of anger is problematic in many a civilized society. In our world, the more "civilized" we become, the more rules and inhibitions we have regulating behavior; thus, the more difficult it becomes to find ways of expressing anger. It is a rare counselor who comes from a family where no conflict existed regarding the expression of anger.

Just so, the client and his family almost always experience some stress around anger.

Anger is disquieting. It is one emotion known to bring possible harm to others. In our society, we sanction direct expression of anger on but a few occasions and only in specific social contexts. Parents, for example, may spank a young child (a privilege teachers once enjoyed but for which they now must obtain parental permission), or adolescents may fight for superior rank in or out of gangs, or, very occasionally, a man may challenge another to pay for an insult. Aggression is permitted in organized sports and on the playground. And, of course, there is the right to self-defense. Our society sanctions it if life is threatened, and the expression of anger is executed with the intention of protecting of the self or other person. Even here, the road cannot be distinguished easily from the blind alley. Our courts are filled with arguments about what constitutes a proper definition of self-defense.

There are special professions that permit a hostile, aggressive response; for example, the military, the police, and some sports. By and large, however, the middle-class purveyors of our society's values not only disapprove of angry actions but also punish them by law. Only one method of expressing anger is generally acceptable: the use of words. "Sticks and stones can hurt my bones, but names can never hurt me." Our society appears to have learned its lesson. We allow names but no sticks and stones and no breaking bones. For most of us, the only acceptable rule to teach children about the expression of anger is that it is all right to feel angry; it is even all right to express that feeling in words, but it is not all right to give expression to anger through action.

Clearly, this is a difficult lesson to teach a child. The use of words is man's most sophisticated tool. Resorting to action to express anger is one of our most primitive impulses. We all have smiled as we watched a two-year-old kick the door that he ran into. Further, the United States still encompasses many cultures in the old melting-pot tradition; among them, cultures whose rules do not agree fully with those generally promoted in our schools and by our police departments. Problems occur in families where there is much cause for anger but where expression with words has not been successfully learned. The problem can range all the way from the lack of awareness of anger (the proverbial cartoon of the person who snarls, "Who? Me? Angry?" comes to mind) to a lack of ability to control the expression of anger, resulting in rages that harm persons and/or objects.

There are families in which anger is simply not permitted to come to fruition. When a frustrating situation occurs, the family quickly diverts the arising feeling into another arena. Thus, a potentially angry father is distracted by his wife's headache, for example, or a potentially angry child is taken for an ice cream by an older brother. The angry person learns to become confused rather than angry. He is dimly aware that something is wrong as he attends to the headache or eats the ice cream, but what it is he can't say.

In other families, anger is experienced, but its expression is forbidden. Everyone in the family knows that Dad's neck turns a flaming purplish red when he gets angry, but neither Dad nor the other members of the family say anything about it. "What's the point of arguing?" the mother likes to say. In another family, the father is labeled as "violent" because he is in the habit of raising his voice when talking politics. Signs of irritability, no matter how small, are nipped in the bud by shaming tactics. In these families, the angry person also may be confused and not quite sure about what is going on; very often, however, he knows he is angry and that he must not express it. He often has extensive and complex fantasies in which he avenges wrongs and tortures wrong-doers. He feels the world is unfair to him. He may develop physical symptoms such as headaches or stomachaches as the anger "eats into him."

There are families in which there is a tradition of expressing anger by exploding into immediate and often violent action, where the threat of harm always exists. Here the angry person often feels quite justified and congruent in his behavior, while the others in the family live in anxiety and fear. Depending on the culture of the attacker, there also may be a measure of guilt expressed by the angry person, which enables the rest of the family to make him the scapegoat for all of their own problems. "I could make something of myself if I weren't so worried about my husband all the time." "How can the boys learn what is right when their father hits me in front of them?" "I can never do my homework because my parents fight."

Most families experience one or another of these problems some of the time. In most families rules regarding the expression of anger change with the growth of the parents and the children. What is appropriate for a family with young parents and small children changes for older parents with teenagers. Difficulties arise when dysfunctional rules are rigidly held in a family.

In this chapter, I cannot hope to cover the complex subject of anger and the techniques of counseling that apply. Reading further in the area of personality and family dynamics and development, as well as continuing to study counseling techniques, will be necessary for the interested student. Our aim is to raise those issues relevant to the young clients and their counselors.

Anger challenges the counselor personally much in the same way grief does. A counselor is not in a position to be effective who has a theoretical conviction that he should promote the expression of anger but becomes fearful or disapproving the moment there is an angry outburst. It is vitally important that the counselor know himself well enough to anticipate his own reactions to the anger of his clients. He must be able to tolerate the expressions of anger he promotes and to control his own reactions.

Anger evokes a very different response from grief, where the counselor can give himself full permission to grieve along with the family he is seeing. A counselor who impulsively joins a fight or tries to stop it without understanding what he is doing more often than not adds to the family's confusion. A counselor may find he is afraid of a member of a certain family, or tries to divert potential anger in order to make himself more comfortable, or becomes angry when a family member is angry, or becomes confused about what is going on in a family where much anger has been expressed. In such cases, he needs to work with his supervisor to understand the nature of his feelings.

Two issues regarding the counselor's role in angry confrontations were raised frequently in my consultation groups. The first is what I call the polarization of counselors in relation to anger. On one end of the continuum we have that most common breed of helping persons, the counselor who wishes to avoid angry feelings. We already have described the family rescuer who becomes a counselor in order to help her clients avoid pain rather than solve problems. She is apt to over-look angry feelings in herself and her clients. She often will take a stand against the expression of angry feelings, calling them intrinsically unproductive. For this counselor, anger has a negative value. On the other end of the continuum is the counselor who values anger above other emotions. When the threat of violence is in the air, when his clients are yelling at the top of their voices, this counselor feels most successful. He values the energy that attends the expression of angry feelings as productive and life giving. As often as not, he has some difficulty with the quieter emotions, such as tenderness and grief, and manages to circumvent them by challenging his clients to confront each other.

Many staff disagreements are fueled by polarization. Anger is portrayed either as a skeleton to be avoided or a cure-all. My view is that, as long as the counselor finds herself at either extreme, she will be handicapped in the range of her possibilities. Working with her consultant, with her supervisor, and her peers, the counselor will become more flexible the more she becomes aware of her own reactions and limitations concerning anger, so that she can plan her strategies according to her individual clients, rather than in concert with an extreme position.

Women counselors frequently have particular difficulty with the anger their clients express, and that brings up the second issue. In these days of struggle for the ERA and women's liberation, much has been written about the way our middle-class society trains women to extinguish assertiveness in conflicts with men, in fact, to avoid conflicts altogether. Men fight; women weep. Men shout; women whisper.

The reader may have noticed that our previous example of the "anger avoider" was female while the "anger promoter" was male. This reflects my own experience, which is filled with more women in the first category and more men in the second. This in no way suggests that the categories don't cross—and it would be wonderful if we could dismiss such stereotypes as meaningless—but the truth is that women counselors more often than men find themselves timid, confused, and helpless when confronted by a client's anger. It is important to pay attention to this problem. Women are often afraid to talk about their fears because they risk being branded professionally incompetent. Youth services abound with people whose thinking and goals are progressive and who therefore expect women to have risen above the problem of fear in response to threat. For this reason, the woman counselor is apt to be manipulated easily by the patient who threatens violent behavior when he wants to avoid talking about something that makes him feel vulnerable. In several of the centers where I have worked, women staff members have formed a separate group to help them address specific issues—anger and its expression being a major one—and begin to work on them. Consultation, of course, also can be of much help here. A cotherapist, more comfortable with the expression of anger, can help train a more timid counselor and be of help to the family at the same time.

Men, on the other hand, often meet the angry patient's challenge with anger and later regret it. When an active technique called "structured fighting" was used in several therapy groups that I attended, several male students sustained minor injuries because they appeared unable to design a structure in which a safe fight could occur. Discussion of these injuries would often reveal an unwillingness to appear cautious or weak. In one family, a member challenged a male counselor to a political argument, which the counselor answered so directly that he found himself yelling his opinions, helplessly trapped in an unproductive process.

There is much to be said about the treatment of the angry client. Without going into detail about the diagnostic categories involved— these can be studied elsewhere—we want to proceed by reviewing some of the problems typically faced by the counselor of teenagers and their families.

Anger can be a problem when it is expressed in words that threaten another's self-esteem, when it is expressed without awareness, when it is unexpressed, and when it is expressed by threats of physical action, or, in fact, acted out. One of the more frequent problems the counselor faces is the suspicion that anger is being expressed to him indirectly by the family that avoids a session. On the face of it, there is no anger at all: No unfriendly words have been spoken, no threats made. Yet the family is not returning to the counseling session. Often this can be explained by the family's resistance to treatment. At times, however, there is more than general resistance; there is withheld anger about a specific situation.

The following cases illustrate our discussion on anger.

Emmy: The Joneses Have Been Too Busy

Dzena, the counselor, had seen the Jones family just two times when she asked for consultation. The family consisted of Mr. Jones, an attorney, his wife, Mrs. Jones, who worked as his legal secretary, and their 14-year-old daughter, Emmy. Emmy had run away from home after many family disputes about her overeating. She was, in fact, considerably overweight. She was presently living in a youth center housing facility. The first of the family interviews was preceded by some trepidation on the counselor's part. She felt that her lack of college education would keep her from impressing this educated couple sufficiently to control the session. She soon took a liking to Emmy's parents, however, and, forgetting the discrepancy in education, worked easily and comfortably with the whole family. In order to avoid the foreseeable family struggles about Emmy's weight at least long enough to become acquainted, the counselor made a rule early on that Emmy's weight was not to be discussed except by Emmy's initiation, to which the parents agreed. The interview was spent reviewing some of the changes that had occurred in the family during the past few months. It appeared that Mother had gone back to work for the first time since Emmy was born. She and her husband had agreed that she would not work during Emmy's early childhood. Now that Emmy was a teenager, the mother felt that she should be able to return to work, but showed evidence of enormous guilt. Both father and daughter seemed to feel that mother would be better off working and put pressure on her both in the session and at home to continue. The session ended with Emmy's statements that she hadn't anticipated being able to talk about her mom in this interview and that she gave her mom her support, while Dad expressed his surprise at how quickly and pleasantly the time had passed. "This isn't half as bad as I thought it was going to be," he said, as the family left the room. The mother had responded openly during the session. She left looking thoughtful.

Dzena told the consultation group that she had looked forward to the second meeting. She was hoping that Emmy would feel confident enough to talk about her weight problem. She was quite surprised, therefore, when, after greetings had been exchanged, the interview quickly developed a very different flavor:

COUNSELOR: So what do you want to work on today? [*A general hesitation, some self-conscious smiles.*]

DAD: Well, I thought we'd kind of done our work already, I guess. [*To his wife, somewhat sarcastically:*] You just stay at work, honey, and we'll all be OK.

COUNSELOR: [*Feeling uncomfortable with Dad's tone.*] Oh, I hope you're mostly kidding . . . well . . . I . . . I know you know I meant it when I said everyone has a part in what goes wrong in any family. Was I clear on that?

DAD: Oh sure, just kidding; just kidding.
[*Dzena feels off balance. Something is going wrong. She can't pinpoint what it is. She decides to wait for more information from the family, whose members have fallen again into an uncomfortable quiet.*]

MOM: [*Attempting a light tone but not quite successful.*] Well, I don't want to be on the spot again, that's for sure.

EMMY: Mom! You weren't on the spot! We were trying to help you!

MOM: Well, why don't you talk about your weight, then?"

COUNSELOR: Oh, oh; I need to remind you of the rule we made last time.

FATHER: Well, how long do we have to wait? She'll never talk about it!

At this point, the counselor had a sinking feeling. Things had gone from bad to worse. Not only had she been unable to clarify what was going wrong, but now she found herself in a solid alliance with Emmy, an alliance that further increased the distance that had developed between her and the parents. She felt she was losing the family. The interview continued without notable improvement.

In talking with the consultation group, the counselor described both the mother and father as deliberately uncooperative. She had felt unjustly accused by both of them, and, at the same time, the bantering tone they had used had confused her. Emmy, too, presented a problem. The counselor knew that it would have been advantageous to switch the focus of the interview to Emmy in order to get away from the uncomfortable feelings that had developed between her and the parents, yet she also felt bound to stick to the rule she had made, especially since it seemed unfair to attempt to use Emmy's weight problem to rescue the three adults. The interview had ended with the scheduling of another meeting. The counselor was not surprised that the family had canceled with what seemed to her to be a lame excuse. She had asked the mother, who had called in to cancel, whether there was anything wrong, but had been told that the family was just too busy with other things. The counselor had offered the family another appointment, but, a week later, that too had been canceled at the last minute. The counselor felt frustrated and upset. These people, she said, just weren't giving her a chance.

The discussion with the consultation group raised the following points:

1. The counselor was reminded of her earlier defensive reaction to the Jones' educational background. It seemed to the group members that perhaps Dad's banter had reawakened her feelings of inadequacy.
2. The group members pointed out that the counselor had engaged in a power struggle with the parents in which, rather

than giving the family a chance to vent whatever feelings had arisen after the first interview, she was defending her work and her rules. She had been inflexible, vying for ultimate rightness. The family had no choice but to be wrong.

The counselor used the group to work further in the area of her own feelings of inadequacy. The others validated her efforts to further her own education. She soon realized that her confused, depressed feeling during most of the second interview had been produced by her inability to admit her own disappointment and anger about the Jones' failure to fulfill her expectations. She suspected that the Joneses had been angry as well—their oblique references to the previous session had suggested that some of their former enthusiasm had covered inner resentments. The parents probably had been angered further by the counselor's lack of receptivity to their complaints. The group suggested a technique to bridge the gap between the counselor and the family, which was for her to say, "I felt upset and a little angry; did you?" In this way, she could model a way to talk about difficult emotions. The counselor in a phone call to the Joneses:

DAD: Hello.

COUNSELOR: Hello, Mr. Jones. This is Dzena. I'm calling to make another appointment . . . but . . . well, before I do that, I had some thoughts about the last meeting I'd like to talk to you about. Is this a good time? I could call back later.

DAD   No this is fine.

COUNSELOR: Are Mrs. Jones and Emmy home?

DAD: Yeah, sure, which one do you want to talk to?

COUNSELOR: Would there be a way for me to talk to all three of you? Do you have an extension?

DAD: Sure. They could sort of share the one upstairs. They've done it before. I'll call 'em.

COUNSELOR: [*After greeting Emmy and Mrs. Jones, hoping that she will find the right tone:*] Well, I just wanted you to know I felt that last interview wasn't one of my best ones. I . . .

MOTHER: Oh, it was all right . . . really . . . I don't . . .

COUNSELOR: No, I really think that some things went badly. Here's what I figured out after I thought about it for awhile and talked to some of the other people that work here, too. I think I felt differently about the first meeting than some of you did. Here I thought it had gone really great . . . and then, when we got stuck right away the next time, I wasn't ready for it. This is hard to admit, but the fact is I was mad at you guys for not being really enthusiastic, do you know what I mean? And I was mad at myself for not being able to make it better.

EMMY: Yes, I see.

DAD: Oh, now [*still using his bantering tone*], don't feel like too much of a failure on our account. We aren't that bad, are we?

MOTHER: Honey, she's serious. I think I know. Well, I just thought . . .

DAD: Okay, okay. I know what you mean there.

COUNSELOR: Thanks. I appreciate that. I had one other thought I wanted to tell you. I thought you all came to the interview a little mad because Mom had been the main focus the time before and I wouldn't listen. Is that right?

EMMY: That's right, but I wasn't mad.

COUNSELOR: I guess I meant to ask your mom and dad, Emmy. Was there anything to it?

DAD: You got me there. We got home and we got to thinking, we didn't go there for Jane, we went for Emmy!

COUNSELOR: That's what I didn't let you say. . . .

MOTHER: I mean, it wasn't . . . it was all right to talk about me, but *just* me, seemed too much.

COUNSELOR: I can understand that.

DAD: I wouldn't have said it!

MOTHER: Honey, she's trying to . . .

DAD: I know. I know. I really kid too much.

COUNSELOR: Well, I feel better; I don't know if you do.

MOTHER: I do. I'm just surprised. I thought counselors didn't feel that way. I . . .

COUNSELOR: Well, I didn't plan for you to find out this way but counselors are the same as other people. They make mistakes. How would you feel about coming in later this week?

MOTHER: I'd like to; would you, honey?

DAD: Sure; we've got her on the ropes now. . . .

The counselor set a date and time for their next meeting and ended the phone call. When she reported back to the consultation group, she was greatly relieved. It had not been easy for her to take the first step—counselors seem to get used to asking questions rather than making statements—but she had felt rewarded by the family's reaction. She had experienced twinges of her old defensiveness when the father had continued to tease her, and especially when the mother had registered her complaint. But she had stifled her desire to explain, realizing that it would not further the cause by helping the family express negative feelings.

The counselor presented a case of mild, suppressed anger, both hers and the family's. It is undramatic with little or no explosive potential, yet, left unexpressed, it would have been enough to prevent the family from attending further meetings.

Rachel: "Rob, I can't let you hurt your own children."

Frank, one of the more seasoned counselors at Youth Advocates, asked for a special meeting with the consultation group because he felt thrown off balance by the events that had occurred in his first meeting with Rachel's family. Rachel, 15, her brother, Payne, 13, and her parents had come in because Rachel had run away from home. Rachel had told the counselors that she no longer could live with her father's violent outbreaks. She had said that he had hit both her and her mother for "no reason at all." She had been willing to have a meeting with her whole family, only to see what the next step could be. The counselor had the impression that her apparent resolve to leave home hid a good deal of ambivalence; Rachel seemed eager to prove that her dad had wronged her, but not to leave home.

When the counselor started to explore the family process in the first session, Rachel started to cry:

RACHEL: Its just always the same. I say I'm going down the street to see my girlfriend and he starts yelling and screaming . . .

DAD: Oh boy! I sure know what you're going to say, young lady, and it is a load of . . .

RACHEL: [*Starts to yell.*] It is not! You're always saying that! You're always saying I lie!

DAD: [*Looking to his wife and seeing that he was not going to get any support from her.*] Oh, yeah! What about the time I caught you with Johnny in the truck? That time you were at your girlfriend's, too, weren't you?

RACHEL: Well, I'm not taking it any more! That was *one* time. *One* time and I'll never hear the end of it. I've just had it! [*She's yelling.*] I'm definitely getting out of here.

DAD: Oh no you're not, young lady!

RACHEL: Oh yes I am!

DAD: [*Obviously furious and shouting, gets up and starts over to where Rachel is sitting.*] We'll just see who is the stronger one here!

The counselor had been following this escalating fight with a great deal of apprehension. Several times, he had made a start at intervening but had not succeeded in getting anyone's attention. He told the group that he was as surprised as everyone else when, after Dad rose up out of his chair and was walking toward Rachel, he quickly got there first, standing in front of Rachel with both his hands on the father's shoulders, pushing him back, saying, "Rob, I can't let you hurt your own child."

Everyone at the meeting had appeared to be shaken. After an embarrassed silence and some false starts, the father started for the door saying that there was no point in these meetings that he could see. Rachel echoed his pessimism. Mother and Payne stayed quietly in the background. The counselor, still somewhat confused and upset about what had happened, had not wanted the session to end so abruptly.

COUNSELOR: I hope you can stay just a little bit longer. I'm not sure about all that just happened. I know it was scary for everybody, but I also know it was nothing new. This is what you guys were talking about, right?

ROB: [*Pausing and leaning against the door.*] Yeah, that's right.

COUNSELOR: [*Realizing that there was no point in getting into a power struggle in order to keep Dad at the session, decided to*

> *concentrate on getting him to return.*] Okay, so now I
> know what it's like, how about coming in day after
> tomorrow so we can figure it out? We'll all be able to
> talk better by then.

With a lot of support from the rest of the family, the father agreed
to come.

The counselor told the consultation group that he was most disturbed about the fact that he had acted just as impulsively as the
father. The group had listened to his story with a good deal of
surprise. The counselor was known as calm, rational, and mild
mannered. While there was nothing inappropriate in his response—there had been a threat and he had reacted protective-
ly—the others could understand that he might be upset by it. The
counselor did some work in the group in trying to understand the
incongruity between his mild-mannered, rational self and the
angry, active self he had just described. He learned that he valued
his anger more than he had known; that, in fact, by attempting to
hide that part of himself, he had been depriving himself of a
valuable source of energy. Why had he hidden it? He wasn't quite
sure, but he thought it was because he had always been much
larger than his peers physically and had developed a fear of
hurting others. Was he afraid, then, of losing control and hitting
someone? Frank thought not. He had been surprised by his quick
reaction, but in thinking back on it, he felt it was appropriate. He
had, in fact, never hurt any other person. He had no real fear that
he would lash out and hurt anyone now.

Then the group helped the counselor to turn what he had considered a liability into an asset in his work with the family. The feeling
that he, too, had been out of control emotionally put the counselor
in the best possible position to understand the father's experience.
The group suggested that he make a temporary coalition with
Rachel's father, using their common experience to open the door
to exploring this explosive feeling. This could produce some positive consequences from getting caught in the family system in a
crisis.

The counselor was glad to see the family arrive for the second
meeting. He had been afraid that the father might feel too

ashamed to come, or that the others might need to protect him by giving reasons of their own for not continuing.

MOTHER: We've been okay since we saw you. [*Giving a little smile.*]

RACHEL: Yeah, but it's only been two days.

PAYNE: Well, it's better than nothing!

COUNSELOR: I agree with you, Payne. [*He had noticed the apparent coalition between Payne and his mother in the first session.*]

FATHER: Well, come on; I've gone for two days without hitting anyone before, you guys. [*Looking a little sheepish.*]

COUNSELOR: Oh, I didn't mean it that way; just accentuating the positive, you know. [*He decides to talk about what he's been thinking about.*] Listen, you're not the only one who looked a little dangerous there for a minute, you know. I was up and on my feet before I knew it, too. I was really surprised when I found myself standing there with my hands on your shoulders, shoving. I still don't know exactly what it triggered inside me. Was anyone else surprised?

MOM AND
PAYNE: Yeah . . . wow; it all happened so fast . . . and then both of you were up. . . . I was afraid of a fight.

RACHEL: I didn't know *what* was going on. [*Some disgust in her voice.*]

MOM: [*To Frank:*] I didn't know *you* were surprised. I thought you knew exactly what you were doing, I guess.

COUNSELOR: Well, gee, I wish I could say that was true, but it isn't. I'm a person just like you except that I do have some special training in counseling. But sometimes the way things happen catches me by surprise, and there I was, just another person, reacting. It doesn't happen often, but I can't imagine that it wouldn't happen sometime to most anyone working with people. . . . [*Switching to the father:*] Is that what happens to you? You're up and on your feet before you know it?

FATHER: [*Still sheepish but smiling in recognition.*] Yeah. I'm up there hittin' before I know it.

COUNSELOR: Do you know what triggers it?

FATHER: Rachel. That's the answer, Rachel, pure and simple.

COUNSELOR: Rachel, do you know how to get him mad?

RACHEL: I guess I know something about it, but I'm not the only thing that makes him mad.

COUNSELOR: Sure. Can you tell me how you act or what you do that's sure to get him mad, though?

RACHEL: Anything I say about leaving home, or maybe about boys . . .

COUNSELOR: Is she right? I can see she is; the whole family is nodding yes. What happens inside you when she talks about those things, Rob?

At this point in the interview, the counselor felt assured that the session would be productive. The transition between commenting on his own sudden anger and that of the father had been accomplished. The work of taking Father out of the role of family scapegoat had begun. The explosive process between father and daughter was open to comment and exploration.

Janet: "My stomach hurts. I'm losing a little weight.
But we all feel wonderful."

Terry, the counselor, had been seeing Janet and her family weekly for some months. Janet had been referred by her school counselor, who had noticed that Janet had been losing more and more weight, and also that she appeared at the nurse's office whenever there was any sign of conflict between her and her teachers or classmates. When the counselor presented Janet's case to the consultation group, she showed a great deal of exasperation. "They're so frustrating," she said. "Here's Janet, clutching her stomach, and both her parents are just smiling and telling her everything is going to be all right. I know in my bones that it's not all right, but I just can't get anyone to talk straight about anything except the weather."

She told the group about her last session with the family, which now included a fourth member, the mother's mother, who also lived in the home. The counselor had decided to include her because she apparently wielded a lot of influence in the family. She also had entertained a small hope that some conflict between mother and grandmother might lead the family to behave more spontaneously.

The session began with the usual bright, hopeful reports from everyone in the family. The counselor had tried to avoid a power struggle (in which she would play the role of accuser, telling the family that she was overwhelmed by evidence that things were not all right) by telling the family she was glad some things were going well. She then had asked family members to give her more details about what was going well, hoping to make a start at getting the family to describe its process. The counselor's voice rose as she described the family's reactions. "They beat me every time!" she said. The grandmother had answered her request by praising Janet's ability to tell Bible stories and then had proceeded to ask Janet to tell several, accompanied by many "praise the Lord's" from the grandmother. It seemed to the counselor that Janet felt resentful and exploited, but, when she asked, Janet said that she enjoyed learning from the Bible. The counselor noticed that Janet had lost even more weight and said so, but Janet replied that it was only her clothing that made her look that way. The counselor unhappily reminded the group that she had spent the last 15 minutes of the session lecturing the family about the importance of expressing feelings verbally, lest they be expressed through physical symptoms. The family had appeared to listen, but the counselor knew enough about counseling process to question lectures as a technique of choice. She felt she was making no impact at all on this family.

The counselor described Janet's family. They were not well off, in contrast to so many of the other teenager's families who came to the center. The family was black, and on welfare, living in a small town where everyone knew one another, surrounded by communities better off materially. The whole family was devoutly religious. The Baptist background provided the many biblical quotations that accompanied their glowing reports. The counselor spoke about how familiar Janet's family was; their cultural background resembled her own. She knew about the resentments that simmered between the mother and her own domineering mother, about the family's frustrated material hopes and dreams, about the father's recurrent bouts of unemployment. She had asked to be the counselor for this family because she had felt that she would be in the best position to help them. "It should be so easy," she said to the group. "For once, I understand what it's all about. I'm not confused about the process. But it's so hard! I get so angry with them!"

The consultation group helped the counselor with her problems by first examining her paradoxical feeling of closeness and distance to Janet's family. The counselor learned that coming from the same background doesn't always help; a close personal understanding of a family can be a hindrance as well. When a counselor feels very closely identified with a family she is seeing, she often neglects to examine the differences between her own family and the one she is counseling. The counselor had developed unrealistic expectations of both herself and the family from the outset of counseling. The group pointed out that the counselor had been overly confident in the family and had developed unrealistic expectations of both them and herself in treating them. She had made a serious error in her initial strategy: Although Janet had complained of stomachaches and had shown evidence of severe weight loss, the counselor had not consulted a physician, who could have given her some valuable information about the extent of Janet's problems and the appropriateness of family counseling as the exclusive method of dealing with them.

With the group's help, the counselor learned that, although her own family resembled Janet's superficially—a poor black family living on welfare with a maternal grandmother—her own family showed some qualities that were missing in Janet's. The counselor's mother and grandmother had fought openly. Her family had argued a lot and laughed a lot, too. Her grandmother also had offered to study the Bible with her, but she had refused. She had stopped attending church at 16 and left home at 18. She could see that her own family had expressed emotion directly, whereas Janet's family operated with a rule of blanket denial. No wonder her repeated invitations to express feelings had fallen on deaf ears. No wonder she felt so frustrated!

Finally, the group helped Terry the counselor to see that her angry frustration was a signal that she, in fact, was not able to handle the symptoms the family was presenting. This had to do partly with her overidentification, but, perhaps even more important, with the severity of the symptoms of the family. The symptoms were physical, consistent with the picture of emotional suppression that the counselor described. The symptoms also were quite serious, suggesting the diagnosis of anorexia nervosa or self-starvation. The group suggested referring the family to a psychiatrist, who could take charge of the medical aspects of the problem, and who could plan to see the family over a long period of time, to help them shift gradually to a more open and spontaneous manner of communication.

Through the preceding three cases, we have discussed some of the more frequently mentioned problems counselors of teenagers face in dealing with anger in themselves or members of the families they see. The reader will have noted that anger often provides an opportunity for the counselor to learn something new about himself. Our first two cases provide examples of therapy bogged down until the counselor could come up with enough personal information to start the process off again. The counselor often needs to take the first step in repairing a situation hindered by anger because, so often, the family's embarrassment and shame prevent them from being able to go on. In taking the first step, the counselor makes a bridge for the family to reenter counseling by modeling a way to deal with the anger and reframing the situation. This removes the focus from embarrassment and shame and shifts it to a perspective where family members can see that they have been provided an excellent opportunity for understanding a basic part of their process.

Tenderness

The evocation of strongly positive emotions also poses a problem for the counselor. With its strongly Anglo-Saxon base, our society—especially its large and powerful middle class—relegates the expression of strong positive emotion, such as joy, laughter, warmth, love, and delight, to restricted corners, just as we do with aggression. Motion pictures show us how to express romantic love, but there is little permission to express it in public. Intense joy and delight are reserved for special occasions—the birth of a child, a promotion, a gift, a surprise—but there is little room for them in the workplace and little occasion for them in many everyday life situations. Warmth is expressed freely in affectionate gestures toward children and pets, but in many adolescent and adult groups the physical expression of affection is problematic, at best. Counseling itself is definitely a work situation, and there, too, the expression of strong positive emotions poses dilemmas.

As with the other strong emotions, the counselor must be able to give permission for the expression of tenderness or warmth. If he feels particularly deprived in this area, it may be difficult for him to permit others to show warmth to each other. He may give double messages of the sort that encourage open expression of warm feelings in words, accompanied by a clear show of discomfort on his part when the feelings emerge. For example, one counselor, having worked for weeks with a couple on their marital conflicts, experienced their demonstrativeness with acute embarrassment. He reported to his supervisor that, when the husband and wife reached agreement, she got up from her chair and went over to her husband's, whereupon he drew her head down, and kissed her. The counselor had been surprised by a mixture of emotions: pride that he had helped to bring this moment about, embarrassment, a feeling that he shouldn't watch, and an intense desire to leave the room. He had stayed. Afterwards, the couple also reported experiencing some embarrassment. In supervision, he talked about the roots of his feelings, roots that lay in a family life where there was little expression of affection, and none in public.

The same inhibition exists on the side of the clients, and for them it may be exaggerated by their understanding of what the situation requires. An Italian family, for example, told one student counselor that they behaved quite differently at home—shouting and embracing much more frequently—but had held back for weeks because they expected the counselor to misunderstand this behavior and label it pathological. After this discussion, their expression was, indeed, filled with a much greater variety of intense emotional expression.

Warmth is an emotion feared by many individuals who have renounced any hope of finding a relationship in which they can be loved or trusted, but still yearn for it. Many times, an affectionate remark on the part of the counselor may provoke tears on the part of the client, tears that contain a mixture of hope that affection is, after all, possible, and despair that it has been so long in coming and may soon leave again. The counselor who can face the extreme existential loneliness of his clients, without "catching" their hopelessness at the same time, can give himself and them permission to express positive feelings.

One of the greatest inhibitors of warm feelings is the fear that they will get out of control and transform the therapeutic context into a sexual encounter. There are times when such a transformation is wished for by both counselors and clients. Aware of such a wish, a counselor may become more and more guarded. The inhibition of warm feelings, however, does nothing to make the counseling situation "safe" from sexual transgression. In fact, like many general inhibitions, it may fan the particular desire by labeling it so clearly as "forbidden fruit." Like any other emotion, sexual desire can complicate the counselor–client relationship. The counselor who allows himself to consider the possibility of his or his clients' experiencing sexual feelings will be able to work them out by understanding their meaning in terms of his and his clients' needs, and then finding a way to formulate that understanding, possibly by using the help of his supervisor. Without the possibility of acknowledging sexual feelings, however (and a commitment to the kind of "professional" manner that inhibits the expression of warm feelings often promotes such denial), the counselor is in the position of adding to the unspoken stresses that beset any counseling relationship.

Throughout this book the reader will find references to counseling as a form of parenting. Parenting without warmth, without an openness to the expression of intense joy and pleasure, leads to symptoms in the family. The counselor must learn to develop his tolerance for these feelings, which, despite his efforts to release them, frequently remain absent from the counseling session. Once the counselor can tolerate the expression of strong positive feelings, he can learn to facilitate their expression by using the active techniques (see Chapter 6).

Powerful feelings, powerfully expressed, can represent a highpoint, or they can become a feared test for the counselor. The metaphor of parenting will stand him in good stead, as he watches his clients grow through their various stages of existence. He can be an eager coach at one point, reticent at another, warm and affectionate, inhibited, angry. As long as he is willing to use these emotions to help his clients express their own unexpressed feelings, he can develop (with the help of his supervisor if necessary) a strategy that will allow him to increase his range of tolerance and his range of expression.

Suggested Readings

Ackerman, N. *Treating the Troubled Family*. New York: Basic Books, 1966.
Bowen, Murray. *Family Therapy in Clinical Practice*. New York: Jason Aronson, 1978.

Gehrke, S., and Kirschenbaum, M. Survival patterns in family conjoint therapy. *Family Process, 6,* 67–80, March 1967.

Kempler, Walter. *Experiential Psychotherapy in Families.* New York: Brunner-Mazel, 1981.

Kübler-Ross, E. *On Death and Dying.* New York: Macmillan, 1970.

Langsley, Donald G., and Kaplan, David M. *The Treatment of Families in Crisis.* New York: Grune and Stratton, 1968.

Levenkron, S. *The Treatment and Overcoming of Anorexia Nervosa.* New York: Scribners, 1981.

Leveton, Alan. Time, death and the ego chill. *Journal of Existentialism, 6:* 21, 69–80 1965.

Leveton, Alan. Elizabeth is frightened. *Voices, 8,* 4–13, Spring 1972.

Leveton, Eva. *Psychodrama for the Timid Clinician.* New York: Springer, 1977.

Messinger, Lillian (Ed.). *Clinical Approaches to Family Violence.* New York: Aspen Institute of Humanistic Studies, 1982.

Palazzoli, Maria S. *Self-Starvation.* New York: Jason Aronson, 1978.

Perls, Fritz. *The Gestalt Approach: An Eyewitness to Therapy.* Palo Alto: Science and Behavior Books, 1965.

Redl, F. *The Aggressive Child.* New York: The Free Press, 1957.

Rosenheim, E. Humor in psychotherapy: An interactive experience. *American Journal of Psychotherapy, 28:* 4, 584–591, October 1974.

Satir, Virginia. *Peoplemaking.* New York: Basic Books, 1964.

Schutz, William J. *Expanding Human Awareness.* New York: Grove Press, 1967.

Searles, Harold F. *Collected Papers on Schizophrenia and Related Subjects.* New York, International Universities Press, 1965.

Searles, Harold F. *Counter-Transference and Related Subjects: Selected Papers.* New York: International Universities Press, 1965.

Siggins, L. D. Mourning, a critical survey of the literature. *International Journal of Psychoanalysis, 47,* 14–25, 1966.

Snell, J., Rosenwald, R., and Rolley, A. The wife-beater's wife: A study of family interaction. *Archives of General Psychiatry, 2,* 107–113, 1964.

Tatelbaum, J. *The Courage to Grieve.* New York: Lippincott and Crowell, 1980.

Umana, Roseann. *Crisis in the Family: Three Approaches.* New York: Gardner Press, 1970.

Whiffen, R., and Byng-Hall, J. *Family Therapy Supervision: Recent Developments and Practice.* New York: Grune and Stratton, 1982.

Whitaker, C., and Keith, D. Symbolic–experiential family therapy. In A. Gurnan and D. Kniskern (Eds.), *Handbook of Family Therapy.* New York: Brunner-Mazel, 1981.

Winnicott, D. W. *Therapeutic Consultations in Child Psychiatry.* New York: Basic Books, 1971.

8

The Challenge to the Counselor's Use of Self

In this chapter, the therapeutic use of the counselor's personal and emotional life will be discussed in two categories: self-awareness and self-disclosure. There is general agreement about the value of self-awareness: almost all schools of counseling require that the student undergo a form of the treatment she is studying. On the subject of self-disclosure, or the introduction of actual personal experience or spontaneous personal reaction into the therapy hour, there is a great deal of debate. Many therapists agree with the analytic schools that self-disclosure only will interfere with the patient's work on his own psychological problems, that the patient needs a blank screen—the analyst—on which he can project his own conflicts in order to work them out. Others, especially those in the more recently emerged group therapies, hold varying opinions on the kind and degree of self-disclosure that can be helpful and appropriate.

Like many other family therapists, I believe self-disclosure can be helpful. In fact, there are times when the lack of it can increase the intensity of symptoms. Both self-awareness and the ability to share personal material are necessary to counsel families. Without self-awareness, the counselor not only will fail to understand the families she is seeing, but she also will be drawn into their system and become a part of its malfunctioning. Without the ability to comment on her own behavior and express her feelings, the counselor will find herself modeling poor communication, mystifying family members with her puzzling reactions while teaching them not to question or comment.

Essentially, without the ability to report her own experience, the family counselor deprives her clients of a vital source of information.

Self-Awareness

"What I can see in myself, I can see in the family I'm working with. What I don't know about myself, I can't see in the family." This maxim, drawn from the early years of family therapy training at the Mental Research Institute in Palo Alto, does not delimit the counselor's understanding of family dynamics, but suggests that her self-awareness forms the basis of her understanding of others. When the foundation is shaky, the building will not stand; that is why every student of counseling also learns to know herself. Whatever the counselor's education, she can absorb only as much as her self-awareness will allow. By self-awareness, we refer to more than a superficial, intellectual acquaintance with personal strengths and weaknesses. Here the term is used to refer to deeper experience, intellectual as well as emotional, leading to self-knowledge.

It is generally agreed that family therapy presents a different emotional challenge to the counselor than individual or group work. The family challenges the counselor by acting out its dramas directly, in her presence. She is not faced with mere descriptions of difficult situations or memories of old wounds; instead, she often witnesses the wounding. In group sessions, members often represent an aspect of another's personal history; in family counseling, the personal history is actually unraveling and the counselor becomes a part of it. The counselor's personal growth must be able to encompass the range of feelings she encounters so that she can use her own emotional responses to help inform herself about the family process.

Students frequently want to know whether the counselor will be more effective if she joins the family system—becomes a part of it in some way—or whether she should remain the objective observer, outside the family process. Although her personal style may evolve later toward a stance more in one place than the other, I encourage students to learn to function both inside and outside the family system. The counselor joins the family in order to "familiarize" herself with their process, to empathize, to get the feel of the family. She steps outside to think about what is going on, to comment on it, to observe the family with more distance and objectivity. For the part of the work that takes place inside the family system, self-knowledge is crucial.

Without knowing herself, the counselor will inadvertently become a part of the family she is seeing. She will find herself reacting as the system stimulates her to react, and she often will do so unconsciously. If the family requires another failing parent, they will accuse her of doing a bad job of counseling them, and she may find herself guiltily dismissing them from treatment. If, however, she knows herself well enough to sense her temptation to take the blame for what's going wrong with the children in the family, just as the parents do, and withstands it, she may be able to continue to see the family and help them work through their fear of disappointment.

Problems in the diagnosis and treatment of psychosis are often directly related to the counselor's lack of self-awareness. Many helping professionals begin their careers with hopes of handling situations with which they are familiar and in which they can be helpful. In centers treating adolescents, counselors often begin with a background of work on a playground, or in a drug counseling program at a high school, where their "knack" in handling teenagers was recognized. The average beginning counselor is not prepared, for example, for the intense feelings of helplessness and rage stirred in her by psychotic themes as they arise in family sessions. When her patients bring up material that relates to insane fantasies or the fear of going crazy, the counselor often is unaware of her own fears and doubts relative to the entire spectrum of psychotic behavior. Her lack of awareness leads her to behave in an inadvertently controlling manner, ensuring that her client will stop talking about these themes. She may be aware that something is going wrong, but fails to recognize the seriousness of her client's symptoms. The following example is a case in point.

Joey: "I'm afraid I'm going to hurt my child."

Bob, a pediatrician who also saw families for short-term counseling, had seen Mrs. Brown for several weekly sessions with her two children, a daughter, aged two years, and a boy of three. Mrs. Brown had a frazzled appearance, was slightly overweight, and dressed in clothes that seemed to date back to her pregnancies, with her hair and makeup usually askew. The children were amiable, healthy-looking toddlers, who displayed the usual indomitable energy of their age levels. The counselor had enjoyed his early contacts with Mrs. Brown because he felt he was able to give her something the family needed desperately: a kind of fatherly authority. He had been surprised that Mrs. Brown seemed so completely at sea in terms of structuring her day with her youngsters, but recognized her as a woman in the throes of the isolation that her youngsters' early childhood demanded, without friends, and without a husband (he had left the family during her first pregnancy). She was a woman who tried to cope from moment to moment and failed much of the time. He could sympathize and make suggestions about the children's need for naps or the kinds of meals that might work out more easily. Mrs. Brown had accepted his advice gratefully. Thus the first few weeks of therapy had passed.

Bob told the consulting group that things began to bog down during the second month, when his client began to talk about her difficulty in accepting help. This theme had been somewhat puzzling to the counselor, who interpreted it as a further need for support and reassurance. Despite clear evidence to the contrary, Mrs. Brown often returned to the theme of her total isolation. When the counselor started to ask questions about the nature of these feelings, however, he experienced Mrs. Brown's withdrawal and found himself returning to giving her advice, repeating in a mechanical way what had earlier seemed vital and important. As he played a tape from a recent interview, it became startlingly clear that he was missing some of Mrs. Brown's most important communications: "When Joey didn't go to sleep last night, I got so upset I thought I was going crazy. . . ." "When I went in to see him for the third time, I had to hold that child on my lap to keep myself from hurting him." "Do you ever take a dislike to any of the children you see? I think I feel that way about Joey sometimes, but I know it's crazy; I really like him a lot." "If they didn't have daytime television I'd be in the looney-bin right now."

The counselor not only had failed to note the importance of these communications, he actually had labeled them as having no importance. Asked what he made of this material, he replied that he saw Mrs. Brown as emotional and overly dramatic some of the time.

The group replayed the sections of the tape where Mrs. Brown had spoken of her deep fears, where the counselor's response had consisted of more advice. The interviews had focused, not on Mrs.

Brown's anguish and fear of going crazy, but on ways to help Joey stay in bed, on television programs mother and child could watch together, on suggestions for more activities for mother and child. In other words, whenever the mother voiced her fear, the counselor would address another, more apparently soluble aspect of her problem.

When the group first confronted the counselor with his evident defensiveness, shown in his need to avoid talking about the mother's fears, he reacted—predictably—with more defensiveness. He argued that these feelings were normal and not really important; all young mothers experience such fears, and they could be made worse by his taking them seriously. He was convinced that Mrs. Brown was not really afraid of losing control. Group members commented that the counselor was denying the mother's problems instead of helping her express them. They described her apparently increasing intensity of feeling and her bewilderment at her counselor's response.

The group discussion switched to the more generally applicable theme of dealing with problems of losing control. Some students empathized with the counselor's difficulty in addressing these feelings, describing their own fears of anything related to "going crazy." They talked about fearing that the patient would become dangerous or even kill herself, relating their own sense of helplessness in such a frightening situation. One student described fantasies and projections he had experienced long ago when his mother had been "put away" in an institution. As the students haltingly described relevant experiences and explored misconceptions, it became clear that "going crazy" had been a taboo subject in the consultation group as a whole, not just for the counselor. Group members were able to bring into awareness some of their own fears of losing control. The counselor learned that he could work differently with Mrs. Brown.

The fear of losing control is a common and dramatic example of a theme often unknowingly distorted by the beginning counselor. Needless to say, the range of themes potentially threatening to the counselor spans the range of human experience. In another case, for example, a student was puzzled by the recurring theme of the wife's jealous examination of her husband's whereabouts.

Jane: "You betrayed me, and I'll never get over it."

Irma brought the following problem to the consultation group: She had been seeing a couple for the past three months, apparently without getting anywhere. Both were office workers, a well-dressed and well-spoken couple in their late forties who had been married 18 years and raised two children. The counselor had been happy to get a chance to do some marital counseling with these two people, both of whom she liked immediately.

When Jane and Michael McKinley had first come in, they had described their problem as "empty nest" syndrome. As the sessions continued, it became more and more apparent that the real problem was Jane McKinley's jealousy. Michael complained that he was no longer free to do what he wanted to do because his wife demanded an accounting of every minute he spent away from her. The counselor had made many efforts to distract the couple from this tedious theme, but she was caught again and again in the middle of the couple's endless blaming. The counselor found out that the origin of the quarrel dated 15 years back, when Michael had had an extramarital affair. She told the group that exploring the history had not had a salutory effect. It had, in fact, added fuel to the fire, reenergizing the same old script.

Once again, the McKinleys had left therapy furious at one another, the wife feeling justified in her vindictive suspicions, the husband martyred and put upon. The counselor was most concerned about her own reaction, however. She was beginning to wonder whether she should continue working with this couple, because she was beginning to find them tiresome and unlikable. In the last session, she had retreated into silence much of the time because her inner reactions had been too moralistic and judgmental to be of use.

The group's discussion with the counselor proved to be painfully touching in terms of her own personal life. Only a few months before starting to treat this couple, the counselor had discovered that her own husband had started an affair. While giving her the necessary personal and emotional support, group members helped her to see that her reactions to the couple had been based on her own situation, that her silence was designed to keep her from confronting her own pain. The consultation session ended with her making plans for obtaining counseling for herself and her own husband and for including a cotherapist in the sessions with the McKinleys.

Unconsciously, the student usually is trying to help both herself and the family when she avoids a major issue that threatens her. She is afraid of losing control of her own feelings and attempts to maintain control by avoiding threatening themes. She usually defends her stance with rationalizations: She discourages a certain theme because discussing it would disturb the family needlessly; or, exploring a couple's differences could lead to separation; or, exploring fantasies of losing control could lead to the actual loss of it.

When the counselor is unaware of an intolerance of a given human dynamic in her own life, she often will overlook it when it occurs in a family she is treating; moreover, she frequently will work to prevent the dynamic from coming to the surface. Once brought to awareness, her fear may continue, but she will be in a position to comment on it, ask for consultation, or get help from a cotherapist. Much of the work of the supervisor or consulting group, therefore, has to do with finding out what is *not* going on in a given session. Bob's interview with Mrs. Brown was proceeding along lines that naturally would lead to an exploration of her fear of going crazy. Once the group learned that this was *not* happening, they were in a position to help Bob uncover an area that he had been avoiding; in fact, the group process itself became a model for his working with Mrs. Brown. The McKinleys, Irma's clients, were returning over and over again to the subject of jealous distrust because Irma was keeping them from expressing their deeper feelings. The expression of rage, betrayal, and grief was *not* occurring in the sessions any more than in the real-life situation of the couple, whose process of constant complaining had left their deeper feelings unresolved. Once Irma could face her reluctance to touch on material so close to home, she could ask for help in the form of a cotherapist who could help her, should she again withdraw from the couple's pain. Perhaps even more important, once she found out about what she had *not* been working on, she began to face the fact that she needed to confront these issues in her own life, with the help of her own therapist.

The counselor's lack of awareness of her own process can hamper her in many different ways. Clearly, we cannot discuss them all here. They must be the subject of each individual's investigation into herself.

There is one other area, however, that has general applicability for those who see families. That area has to do with the counselor's role and process in her own family.

Anyone who works with families must be committed to learning about her own family process. Each family in treatment creates a powerful atmosphere. Families, as we all know, can be loud, silent, emotional, dry, witty, sober, kind, or cruel. There can be weak fathers and strong mothers, strong fathers and weak mothers, a united front, or children ruling the roost. Families can show concern or disdain for the symptoms that bring them—there is a very great variety of styles and processes. The more the family's process, or even some part of it, resembles that of the counselor, the more likely she is to play the same role she played at home. Family counselors are often reformed or unreformed rescuers in their own families. Reformed, or partially so, they now confine their rescuing efforts to professional endeavors; unreformed, they still are trying to save their own families, often under the illusion that their professional training entitles them to take responsibility for others. In her own family, the family counselor was often the child who understood. Perhaps Mom could talk to her about her difficulties with Dad, or, when the family faced a stressful situation, she could be depended on to restore good feeling. Possibly, she ran interference for Dad, who couldn't stand to be involved in anything emotional. In short, the family rescuer was the person the family depended on to make things better somehow, to keep the pain from getting unbearable. She was not the Identified Patient; she was the Identified Therapist.

Undoubtedly, the family rescuer is a good candidate for the job of family counselor. She has been training all her life. She genuinely wants to help people and has a tremendous storeroom of information about family process ready at her fingertips. Unfortunately, there are also disadvantages to be considered. The family rescuer grew up committed to the goal of lessening the immediate pain in her family. She is convinced that she has the power, the ability, and the duty to help. As a child she devleoped extraordinary skills in detecting family pain and in healing it. As a grown person, her radar system will be very useful in diagnosing family problems; however, her desire to lessen pain often will cause her to be in conflict with herself. As a counselor, she will want to establish deeper, more meaningful contact between the parents, even if it involves exploring painful material. The more the child she once was recognizes her own father in the parent she is seeing, the more she will want to prevent any conflict from erupting. The counselor will want to discourage her six-year-old client from staying home from school to keep Mom company in Dad's absence, but the child in the therapist will support the six-year-old's efforts.

Family feelings run strong and deep. They stir many of the same loves and hates felt during the counselor's struggle to grow in her own family. To the degree that she is unaware of her own process, she will keep families in the dark about theirs.

Once the family counselor confronts one of her blind spots, she can begin to do something about it. If she feels comfortable with the family, she can comment, "I just noticed that I lined myself up with you, Mom, against the kids and Dad, and I'm thinking that this isn't the first time I've done that. Has anyone else noticed it?" "Does anyone else in the family get into that spot of protecting Mom when things get tough?" "What gets you into that spot?" "I'll tell you what gets me into that spot, or at least what I think gets me into it" "You get a sort of hurt look in your eyes, Ann, when the kids complain; it looks almost as if you might respond by crying. We've talked about that before. What I think gets to me about it is that you remind me a little of my own mom, when you have that look, and when I was little I think I would have done anything to keep her from crying. And sometimes I get back into that. I don't mean to, because, as an adult, I know that you could take it, and, more important, that I could take it, if you cried. So, if any of you notice me protecting Mom, let me know—I don't want to give you that kind of protection." There is no necessity, of course, to deliver this entire speech to the dumbstruck family. The actual comment probably would be restricted to one or two of these sentences, to be developed further by the family's reactions. The counselor must keep switching back and forth between her awareness of her own experience and the process of the family she is seeing.

Self-Disclosure

Self-disclosure of any type was frowned upon by the traditionalists of psychotherapy. Although Freud was a friend, host, hiking companion, and even financial advisor to some of his analysands, his followers came to the conclusion that such practices were harmful to the work of therapy and developed a rigid code in which even the most conventional of therapeutic interpretations was supposed to be made in an impersonal, "professional" manner. The patient brought his own past to the therapy, it was reasoned, and, if his analyst was a blank screen, he could project that past onto the therapist in the classic transference relationship. The therapist would be perceived as the patient's father, mother, siblings, or whatever. The more the therapist appeared as a real person, the less the patient would be able to project. Further, the analyst needed to remain impersonal to perform his own work best, to maintain a high level of objectivity in relation to his patient. A thorough discussion of transference, of course, would require far more complexities than we have just cited; our discussion here has the simple aim of summarizing something that accounts for a code of therapy that was—and is—practiced by many professionals for whom psychoanalysis was a major influence.

The psychoanalyst is, of course, the prototype of an objective therapist. He does not deny that he has problems of his own. He has undergone a thorough training analysis and sees his consultant for ongoing work on the countertransference, during which his own feelings and reactions to the patient are analyzed in order to be rendered harmless to the patient. The patient, however, knows little or nothing about his analyst's feelings or experiences. The analyst is the unquestioned expert. The patient talks about himself. The analyst talks about the patient. The analyst questions the patient and expects to be answered. If the patient questions the analyst he will not be answered; rather, the expert will help him understand why he asked the question. The therapist tries not to intrude as a person in his patient's life.

In sharp contrast to this is the relationship practiced by many therapists influenced by systems theory and the experiential techniques. While there is no question that the therapist remains an expert who has knowledge and experience which the patient doesn't have, he attempts to equalize the relationship between himself and his patient. He negates the possibility of behaving as a "blank screen" and asserts the proposition that the therapist inevitably joins his patient's context and becomes a part of the system in treatment. In other words, during those moments when he does not feel "neutral" about a client's story, the analyst may think he is presenting a "blank" screen, but the systems theorist believes he communicates bias. As part of the system, the family counselor is open to questioning about his own reactions, experiences, and methods of proceeding. He sees himself as a human being whose struggles and emotions affect his relationship to his patient. When these parts of his character remain closed to examination, they can *produce* symptoms, make the situation worse through the therapist's modeling indirect communication, and deprive the patient of an opportunity to test reality.

For example, a patient notices his analyst's tired and distracted look and says so. To the degree that the analyst really is exhausted, evading the question will puzzle his patient. He doesn't know whether to pay attention to his analyst's obvious tiredness or to the implicit message that the analyst's life is irrelevant to this discussion. If he follows the analyst's request and talks about himself, he will feel some guilt and handle it in a defensive manner, such as by restricting himself to material he deems easy and pleasant for his analyst or by challenging and provoking him in order to make him appear more vigorous. Undoubtedly his chosen defense will be meaningful for his own understanding of himself. As he and his analyst talk, however, the patient continues to be deprived of an opportunity to test reality, that is, to check his own perceptions against what really is going on, and to react to the real situation with kindness, resentment, or whatever. The family counselor in a similar situation may answer his client's observation by saying something like, "That's true. I am tired. I had a very rough hour with the last family and I'm still getting here." The client's response now will be based on two reassuring factors: (1) his perceptions were correct, and (2) his counselor trusts him sufficiently to tell him something about herself. The client's history will continue to determine whether he handles his counselor's tiredness caringly or with resentment, but the therapeutic situation itself will not have added to a history of miscommunication.

When there is a rule against self-disclosure, or when the counselor fails to take into account the importance of the contribution of her own reactions and experience, self-disclosure continues to occur but it becomes inadvertent. One of the maxims developed by the communication theorists was, "You can't not communicate." Extended to our subject, the maxim would read, "You can't not communicate something about your unique self." If the communication is not explicitly made, it is made implicitly and, rather than being potentially clear and understandable by the client, it becomes murky, mystifying, and tantalizing. We have talked already about the therapist who communicates her tiredness through her personal appearance. A more malignant miscommunication is represented by the counselor who, although she declares she has no opinion on a given subject involving moral conduct, becomes more and more moralistic in the tone of her voice as she pursues what seems like a cross-examination of her client. The client is inevitably frustrated in this situation. He is being attacked by someone who not only denies the attack but declares herself to be neutral in feeling and to be acting on his behalf. There are times when a client's life experience has such powerful reverberations for the counselor that seeing or hearing it throws her into an associative distraction that virtually causes her to be absent from the room. If she can be challenged to report her experience, she will have enlarged the client's frame of reference. Unexplained, the situation leaves the client alone and mystified.

The most obvious interference in the treatment of others is caused by the arousal of the counselor's violent, or at least disturbing, feelings of anger or grief, which, no matter how hard she tries to suppress them, become immediately apparent to clients who observe her flushed face and tense body or her growing sadness and tears. Explained, the situation can help the client's understanding of himself and his counselor; swept under the rug, the process will disturb the client and hinder the treatment. Sometimes the counselor's inadvertent self-disclosure appears in her driving intent to concentrate only on one subject; the subject that is most problematic in her own life. There are counselors who persist in quizzing families about anger when it is clear to the most casual observer that the only one whose voice betrays hostility is the counselor herself. Others ask plaintively and repetitively to be told something that goes right in a family where conflict is fairly boiling under a ruffled surface. One of the more dysfunctional choices family members make in such a dilemma is the attempt to please the counselor by cooperating, that is, fabricating angry material to please the angry counselor or being "nice" for the one who needs cheering up. Some counselors are so inexplicit in their communications about themselves that their clients waste valuable energy becoming finely tuned to minute changes in the furnishings of the room or the clothes of the counselor, or watching her so carefully that they notice and attempt to account for a change in her rate of breathing.

The family counselor has a special reason to permit self-disclosure. Her systems approach convinces her that, during the session, she will become a part of any family system in which she is counselor. Her feelings and emotions, her alliances and antagonisms, and her personal style will become a part of the family she is counseling. To the degree that she can be explicit about this process, she will be helpful to the family. The work done by such authors as Don Jackson and Virginia Satir on communication theory suggests that the family counselor functions as a model for communication in the family. The counselor also is a source of information to the family as another human being, a peer, with her own strong relationships and life events that may well have relevance to the therapeutic process.

Experience in the realm of self-disclosure in family therapy has shown that two processes can be counted on to be active in any family: (1) the need and drive to grow through learning about the family process, and (2) the need to learn and grow through a kind of reparenting or friendship that promotes identification with the counselor.

These processes can and do coexist without one interfering with the other.

The most difficult questions about self-disclosure are, of course, "when?" and "how much?" Clearly, they must be answered over and over again by each of us for a staggering variety of personal reasons. However, a discussion of some guidelines may be helpful.

The question of the timing of self-disclosure can be addressed in a variety of ways. The most useful guideline is the degree to which an event in her own life or a personal reaction changes the counselor's behavior in the session. Great life changes usually bring about equally great changes in behavior. An upcoming marriage, pregnancy, the birth of a child, a bitter quarrel, a plan to move to another city, oncoming illness, convalescence, death in the family—all such changes in the self or family structure of the counselor will cause her to behave differently with the families she sees; therefore, they deserve comment. The counselor may wish to save her clients the detective work of ferreting out the reasons for her changed behavior by bringing up the reasons for her change of mood, or she may want to wait to talk about her own experience until it becomes relevant to the work she is doing. Her timing always will depend on her clinical judgment; there is no question, however, that some discussion of a major change in the counselor's life is necessary.

Students often react with a mixture of shyness and delight to the prospect of sharing an event in their own lives with families in treatment. It is difficult, at first, to know just how to say what is necessary and how much. The questions that arise are much like those of parents wishing to inform their children about major events in the family, and the solutions are similar as well. The counselor's goals are to help her clients to know her, to model open communication, and, whenever possible, to use what is happening in her own life as a bridge to what is happening in the family she is treating. Just as the parents in a family cannot explain the complexity of their grief about a loved one's death to a five-year-old toddler, so the counselor cannot expect the families she is treating to understand and remember the details of her experience. Becoming the focus of the discussion should not be confused—except in really extraordinary situations—with becoming the patient. The counselor attempts to communicate what is going on in her own life in order to become congruent in her expression and help her clients both see her more clearly and make a bridge to their own experience:

COUNSELOR: I'm getting married tomorrow, and my head is full of a thousand details and excitements. I think I can work and I want to, but if you catch me looking vacant, call me off my cloud, OK? How was that for you, hearing me say what I just said?

or:

COUNSELOR: I may seem a little different to you today. It's because I'm really somewhat confused. My husband just called me to tell me we might be leaving this area next year. I want to tell you a little about my own feelings before we start our work, to help me get myself here. . . . Have any of you experienced similar feelings? Has anyone here been uprooted anytime in the past?

Issues of lesser consequence permit use of the same guideline. If a given feeling or reaction changes the counselor's way of working, it needs to be addressed:

COUNSELOR: You know, I got so angry during the staff meeting that I was at just now. I really read them the riot act, but I seem to have something left over still. . . . Will I ever learn that things won't always go the way I want them too? No! . . . Well, how do you feel about that outburst? Did you expect better of me? I did! . . .

or:

COUNSELOR: I feel a little funny today. I noticed it in the last session. I don't have a temperature, but I think I might be getting the flu, so, if you notice anything different about me, I think that's what's happening.

The counselor's own history frequently impinges on her work. Human existence everywhere encompasses similar struggles of growth and emancipation, marriage, childbearing, illness, death, and complicated relationships in the family and community. For the counselor, working with families means listening to echoes of her own life history as the family struggles with a given problem. There are many times when the echoes are subtle and barely heard—these have no relevance to the problem of self-disclosure. But when the reverberations are strong and the counselor finds herself projected backward into the midst of her own reminiscences and emotions, she usually needs to say something to the family in treatment. She may make a general reference to having had a similar experience, for the purpose of helping herself make the separation between her experience and that of the family's, or she may need to speak in more detail to accomplish the same goal:

COUNSELOR: I'm nodding my head when you talk, Dad, because I'm remembering the time my first daughter got married. I felt a lot like you did. . . .

or:

COUNSELOR: I think I know something of how you feel in coming to a new community. I came here when I was 11 years old, from Germany. I felt like a stranger for a long time because the kids seemed so different from the German kids and I didn't speak the language. . . . Well, some of that probably applies to your situation, but not all. Or does it?

Another reason to bring the counselor's personal history into the treatment is to illustrate a point, as a teaching story. Family therapy, at such times, becomes a kind of group therapy where the counselor is a contributing member. When there are common areas, such as child rearing, the counselor can reminisce, for example, about how she reared her own children in similar circumstances. This can be done both to teach a specific solution, or simply to enlarge the family frame of reference. A self-conscious, serious parent, for instance, often benefits from hearing references to practical jokes in a counselor's family, although he actually may never resort to similar behavior.

It is difficult for the counselor to decide how much of her own experience to recount to a family in treatment. The shy counselor feels more and more vulnerable as she contributes personal material and therefore tends to restrict herself to a minimum. The extroverted, chatty counselor may find herself talking so much about her own situation that she loses the focus of what she is doing and begins to be in doubt about whether it is she that is in treatment or the family. As she begins to use personal material in her family sessions, the counselor will use her intuition about the appropriateness and amount of what she is saying. The situation is spontaneous; she is not often in a position to stop and think about the nature of her choice. As she develops her skill, however, she can become more adept by using some guidelines.

Perhaps the most important standard for personal contribution in treatment is that the focus of the treatment process is the family, not the counselor. In other words, no matter what is said, or how much time it takes, it is important that the communication occur in the context of working with the family, rather than simple self-exploration on the part of the counselor. In this context, the counselor often makes the mistaken assumption that, in order to treat the family, she must be in perfect control. That is not one of our guidelines. In fact, the counselor who approaches a personal subject in a vulnerable, gingerly way, or finds herself moved to tears during a family session, can communicate a very helpful message to family members, namely, that it is not necessary to wait for a moment of mastery to address a difficult subject and that the expression of spontaneous emotion is valued. The following cases illustrate some of these guidelines.

Cathy and Paul: "It's their therapy, not mine."

Cathy. The counselor is Cathy, whose aunt died the day before the family session. She was feeling tearful and vulnerable as the family came in. As she watched them seating themselves, she had the following thoughts: "Let's see; I wonder if they notice I've been crying. I see Mom looking at me. I guess she does. Well, I guess I'll just say I've been feeling sad and give my reasons briefly and then we'll just go on with the session. . . ." So, Cathy explained her situation, then thought, "Well, I did tell them, but now I feel worse. I feel like crying and I don't want to. . . . Why not? I tell them to be open about their feelings . . . but . . . I'm going to tell them how important she was to me and if I cry, then I cry. . . ."

Cathy told the consultation group that she had cried with the family, and, as a result, felt a great deal closer to them. The mother had listened warmly and spoken with a lot of empathy, while the kids had waited until she felt calmer and then returned to discussing some of their own problems. She felt pleased that she had taken a chance. In the rest of the session, to her surprise, she had felt comfortable and energetic.

Paul. This counselor, who had been divorced for a number of years, told us about seeing a family consisting of a recently divorced mother and her three children. He reported that, when she initially had addressed some of her feelings about her divorce, they had done a lot of sharing, during which time he recounted many of the relevant experiences in his life. When, in a subsequent session, he again thought of an experience he could describe, he began to wonder whether it wasn't time to shift the focus more exclusively back to her family's material. Interrupting himself, he asked the mother and children whether, once he got going about his own life, they would ever try to stop him and tell him that they wanted to talk. The family's reaction let him know that it would be difficult. He then promised that he would check out more carefully whether family members needed to talk, before talking about his own life.

Except in the instances we discussed earlier, where lack of self-disclosure interferes with the counselor's work, guidelines about what and when to talk about the counselor's own life experience will center around the family's needs. There are many occasions in family counseling where the rhythm and tempo of the family's contributions to the session are working so well that the most relevant personal experience on the part of the counselor would become irrelevant. Some stories about the counselor's life describe unresolved conflicts where there are villains and victims. If she chooses to tell such a story, she must consider who in the family she is treating might be offended by her description. Although the counselor frequently wants to give a message of kinship by telling a family member of a similar life situation, she must be careful not to overdo it, lest she become so thoroughly identified with the client that she confront him with the same challenges and demands she makes on herself. Personal stories can be used to make a bridge when the flow of conversation has halted, but they also can interrupt a family concentrating on their own process. The counselor must be sure that she is not introducing personal material in order to block a communication that is arising in the family itself.

The final decisions in these matters depend on the subtle combinations of the counselor's style and the family's process. Most of our examples have dealt with situations that rise in most counselor's lives, situations that have relevance to most families and result in emotions that the average student can share. To round out our discussion, here is an example in which the counselor, his experience, his manner of sharing it, and the family's reaction were all unusual to an extreme degree, yet the results are the same. The family benefited from the experience and made positive changes.

Mr. and Mrs. Jones: "I can't stop crying."

Jack was a white psychiatrist in an advanced training group in family therapy, in which each member worked with a family, while the others watched through a one-way mirror. Before starting with his first family, the counselor had undergone his third divorce and was convinced that he was losing his children in the settlement. He was experiencing intense grief and hopelessness. None of his marriages had worked out. His children would be in another state. He felt they were dead to him. He felt desolate and alone.

The family he was seeing was the family of a black janitor and included the mother and four children ranging in age from seven to 15. The family clearly had come to consult an expert on the matter of their oldest youngster's school failure. Both mother and father had a self-abnegating, obsequious quality in which they humbly asked the expert for advice. The counselor experienced his feelings of grief and aloneness most acutely during the third session with the family. He shared them with the family, who sat dumbfounded as the renowned doctor sobbed.

The next four sessions were identical. The counselor would greet the family, look at the children, become overwhelmed with his own feelings, and begin to cry. His grieving took much of the hour. The observers, watching from behind the one-way mirror, experienced a mixture of fear, embarrassment, certainty that the family wasn't getting what they were supposed to be getting, and envy because they couldn't imagine themselves in such a scene. As the weeks went on, a curious series of events took place. The parents became more comfortable with this new image of the expert and began to comfort him. Their obsequiousness began to disappear. They became more sure of themselves in relation to their counselor, and, more important perhaps, more sure of themselves as parents to their children. When the counselor ceased his crying in their sessions, they tackled the work of their own therapy in an aggressive, energetic manner that would have been inconceivable earlier on.

Jack's is an extreme case. He risked a great deal and won. It is just as possible to risk and lose. Some of the most exciting learning in family therapy goes on in this exchange between the counselor and the family, as all parties become better able to risk more personal contact. The serious family counselor has taken it upon herself to explore whatever she can fathom emotionally and intellectually in the realm of family life. Learning about the families she sees will teach her about herself. Her knowledge of herself will teach her clients about themselves.

Suggested Readings

Bowen, M. Toward a differentiation of a self from our own family. In J. L. Framo (Ed.), *Family Interaction: A Dialogue between Family Researchers and Family Therapist*. New York: Harper & Row, 1972.

Brill, O. (Ed.). *The Basic Writings of Sigmund Freud*. New York: Modern Library, 1938, 1966.

Chapman, A. H. *Harry Stack Sullivan: The Man and His Work*. New York: Putnam's, 1976.

Ford, F. R., and Herrick, J. A typology of families, five family systems. *Australian Journal of Family Therapy*, 3, 71–81, 1982.

Gardiner, Muriel (Ed.). *The Wolfman, by the Wolf-Man*. New York: Basic Books, 1971.

Haley, J. *Uncommon Therapy: The Psychiatric Techniques of Milton Erickson, M.D.* New York: W. W. Norton, 1973.

Jung, C. G. *Man and His Symbols*. Garden City, NY: Doubleday and Company, 1964.

Koehne-Kaplan, Nancy. The use of self as a family therapist. *Perspectives in Psychiatric Care*, 14:1, 29–33, 1976.

Kramer, Charles H. *Becoming a Family Therapist: Devising an Integrated Approach to working with Families*. New York: Human Sciences Press, 1980.

Laing, R. D., and Esterson, A. *Sanity, Madness, and the Family*. New York: Basic Books, 1964.

Leveton, Alan. Family therapy as play: The contribution of Milton H. Erickson, M.D. In Jeffrey K. Zeig (Ed.), *Ericksonian Approaches to Hypnosis and Psychotherapy*. New York: Brunner-Mazel, 1982.

Leveton, Eva. *Psychodrama for the Timid Clinician*. New York: Springer, 1977.

Leveton, A., and Leveton, E. The use of the self. In A. Leveton and E. Leveton, Children in trouble, family in crisis. A series of 5 training films demonstrating a family counseling alternative. University of California at Davis, Administration of Criminal Justice, 1975.

Luthman, S., and Kirschenbaum, M. *The Dynamic Family*. Palo Alto: Science and Behavior Books, 1973.

9

The Challenge of the Family's Resistance

Everyone wants to change something about himself. Everyone resists change. Models of the ideal self are served up daily by newspapers, magazines, television, to say nothing of books especially tailored to self-improvement. The media usually take a "positive" view of change; implied in the new concept of self-improvement is that it requires little or no effort. Gone are the days of the pioneer, or the self-made man who earned his way to the top through years of hard work. Improvement arrives in a short time—anywhere from a weekend at the right place to 10 lessons with the right person. It is no wonder that helpers, whether they appear in the guise of doctor, minister, family member, neighbor, friend, or counselor, often react with puzzlement to the frustrations of those they are trying to help, unable to understand how someone apparently motivated to change can be so stubborn in clinging to the patterns that prevent it.

"Resistance" is the term used in the psychiatric literature to describe the process of frustrating a desired change. Since all therapists are engaged in the process of helping someone change, all forms of resistance are, of course, widely discussed. In the following pages, rather than discussing resistance in general, those resistances peculiar to family counseling will be described, along with strategies for dealing with them.

In the context of family therapy, change refers to behavior the family counselor expects from family members who need to develop new ways of relating to one another to get out of trouble. Our society provides no model for family therapy. Individual therapy can be likened to heart-to-heart talks with a friend, an older member of the family, or a respected authority figure. Implied in such a relationship is confidentiality and privacy. No tradition exists for families to talk to another person about how they are doing with each other. Only a very few families have ever experienced or heard about family get-togethers with a minister or priest or, perhaps, a grandfather, where serious matters were discussed. Most people are at a loss when they try to imagine what family counseling might be like. Not knowing often leads to projection, fear, and a reluctance to attend.

From the beginning of family therapy, counselors have been seeing clients who did not necessarily elect to enter treatment. Many of the early research projects in family therapy dealt with groups of hospitalized patients whose families were asked (and sometimes coerced) to cooperate in the treatment of their children by attending family sessions. Even now, most families are referred by an outside authority—a doctor, schoolteacher, or counselor—who decided on the basis of a child's behavior that there was something wrong in the family, and persuaded them to seek help. Unlike the individual who seeks counseling help, the family seldom has reached the decision to enter counseling unaided.

Resistance to family therapy occurs on many different levels. Both family and counselor come to the first counseling session with backgrounds that have prepared them to resist the process. Including the counselor in the family setting is the first level of resistance that each family must overcome. The counselor brings his own expectations to family counseling. The way a particular session unfolds frequently disappoints him, and negative reactions on his part will reinforce the family resistance. On a deeper level, both family and counselor have their reasons to both desire and resist change. The family dreads the consequences of changing from a known behavior—however painful—to an unknown, unpredictable way of life. They resist the embarrassment of confronting painful issues in front of each other and the counselor. The counselor, who wants to be liked by the family, not only dreads being the agent of changes the family resists, but brings his own personal history to the sessions. The range of resistance to family therapy will be discussed in this chapter, with a view toward addressing problems that occur for both counselor and family members when change threatens to upset the homeostasis.

Resistance to Counseling: The Phone Call

The initial phone call brings the first level of the family resistance to bear on the counselor. We already have discussed the fact that our society expects problems to be solved rapidly and painlessly. Families with symptoms usually feel a sense of failure; they feel guilty and ashamed for not having solved their own problems. Seeing a family counselor often seems like an added burden. "Family counseling? Why should we want to do something like that?" the family seems to be asking. "That sounds like washing our dirty linen in public. Our family is our own affair. We mind our own business. Why don't they just let Johnny talk to one person? It's probably something the rest of us shouldn't know about anyway. But in front of the whole family? Forget it. We won't go."

The family counselor, sensing the family's resistance when he first contacts them on the telephone, frequently reacts with a mixture of confusion and surprise. Family counseling is difficult work; he was willing to do his best to help a family in trouble, and now the family seems set against him from the start. It must be remembered that the counselor, too, approaches family counseling with a bias. Possibly, he comes from a family that strongly espouses open communication and thus he would have little difficulty inviting his own parents or spouse to attend an interview with him. Such a background would make empathy with a family's initial resistance difficult. More likely, however, the counselor comes from a family that was conflicted about open communication. Perhaps he chose to be a counselor partly because he strongly values confronting issues that his own family urged him to hide. He may be aware of experiencing opposing sets of feelings when confronted with a resisting family: On the one hand, he experiences a desire to persuade them to risk more open communication; on the other hand, he empathizes with the family's need to keep feelings under wraps. The counselor who is relatively free from conflicts about openness will find himself tempted to moralize, to express in disapproving terms his sense of frustration about the family's seeming unwillingness to enter therapy. The counselor who, in part, empathizes with the family's resistance, will find himself tempted to support their negative feelings. He may wish to protect his clients from painful experiences with which he himself is only too well acquainted.

The beginning counselor may need to use role-playing to rehearse several phone calls to a prospective family, in order to acquaint himself with this new territory. In consultation with his supervisor or fellow staff members, he can explore various problems that arise and his reactions to them, and he can learn new ways of dealing with both.

The following is a common example of an initial resistance in family counseling. The mother tells the counselor that the father would never come in for counseling, so there would be no use in her asking him. The supposed resistance of the absent father gives many clues to the family process and provides rich material for examining telephone strategies.

The Brown Family: The Resistance of the Absent Father

The first question raised by students in a beginning family therapy course frequently is, "How do you get the father to come in?" In all but a small percentage of families, our society places the primary responsibility for child care on the mother. Dad works; Mom takes care of the children at home. She also usually is responsible for getting the children to school, lessons, recreation, and doctors' appointments. Counseling is like a doctor's appointment; therefore, Mother is prepared to attend counseling sessions, while Father is not. Some of the most cogent reasons for including Dad in family counseling are suggested by the process just described. In some ways, many fathers remain strangers in a family to which they are deeply attached. A father has a very special relationship to his child, different from all others in the family, and important. Chances are that he has felt at a loss in the crisis that brought the family to consider treatment. At the same time, the counselor can guess that the mother has felt heavily burdened with responsibility. Family sessions will begin to ease the pain attendant on the process as soon as Dad is included and both parents can begin to work together. The counselor who excludes Dad, on the other hand, promotes the family dysfunction by giving his implicit agreement to the rigid division of roles set up by the family. One strategy for including Father in the sessions is to avoid allowing Mother to be the sole spokesperson for the family. This can be handled on the phone as follows.

MOM: Hello.

COUNSELOR: Hi. Is this Mrs. Brown, Ron's mother?

MOM: Yes.

COUNSELOR: Great. My name is Connie. I think Ron told you the other day that I'd be calling you up to invite you to come to our unit for a family session. Did he do that?

MOM: Yes, he did. I was just wondering; what about those . . . I mean, when are they and all that, because . . . well, I don't work but my husband does, and unless you could do it on Saturdays, and even then . . . [*She trails off.*]

COUNSELOR: Gee, that's great that you're ready to come. [*Wishing to remain positive as long as possible.*] How about Ron's brother? We'd really like to have him there also.

MOM: Well, it might be kind of hard because he has soccer after school, but, I could try and ask him.

COUNSELOR: Good. I know it sounds hard, but we'd like him to come even if it meant missing part of soccer practice one afternoon a week. The kids here usually do that. When do you think would be a good time for you? We could see you Thursday at 3:30 or Friday at 4 o'clock. I thought those hours might fit your schedule because they're after school times, and those are hard to get. [*A bit of a sell, here.*]

MOM: Well, let me think a minute. Well, I think maybe Friday at 4 o'clock. That sounds like we could all make it. But I still don't think Ron's dad would come, I really don't. He just isn't the type, you know?

COUNSELOR: Well, I'd sure like to include him. I'll tell you what I'd like to do: I'd like to talk to him about it. Is he home?

MOM: No, he doesn't usually get home until after 5:30.

COUNSELOR: OK, I'll call back later this evening. OK with you?

MOM: Sure. Why not?

COUNSELOR: And I'll get back to you after I've spoken with him.

MON: Yes, I think that'll be fine.

COUNSELOR: OK. I'll talk with you later, then. Good-by.

MOM: Good-by.

The counselor, Connie, has made her first important point. She will not let Mom take responsibility for Dad by speaking for him. She also has conveyed the message that she expects the family to change some of their habits. She expects Dad to attend as part of the family. Next, she needs to make good on her promise to speak directly to Dad.

MOM: Hello.

COUNSELOR: Hello. This is Connie from the Youth Unit; we spoke earlier and I said I'd call back to talk to your husband. Is he there now?

MOM: Oh, yes. Just a second. [*Calls him.*]

DAD: Hello. This is Ron's father.

COUNSELOR: Hi. My name is Connie; I work at the Youth Unit. Did Ron or Mrs. Brown speak to you about my calling about making an appointment for a session?

DAD: As a matter of fact, my wife did mention something about it. But I don't think I'll be able to come. I work, you know.

COUNSELOR: What kind of work do you do?

DAD: Oh, I punch a time clock. I work building autobodies at the factory down here.

COUNSELOR: Well, I can see it might be hard, but, you know, we've had other fathers from your place come here, so I know it's not impossible. Anyway, do you know what this is all about?

DAD: Well, sure, I guess; I mean it's a family session. I guess it's where we all get together and find out what went wrong with Ronnie that he's running away all the time, right? . . . And so we figured my wife would be going, because she's the one he's with most of the time anyway.

COUNSELOR: Uh-huh. That's right. But it's not really to talk about what's wrong with Ronnie. It's more to talk about how the whole family functions. How the family handles the problems. Right now, Ronnie's a problem, but what we're interested in is the whole family—what part you each play, how you work together. And you're very important in that. You're the father.

DAD: Well, I can't deny that. [*Laughing.*]

COUNSELOR: And nobody can tell us about your part except you. That's very important.

DAD: Well, it's just that it's hard to get away. When are these meetings?

COUNSELOR: We do have a time that maybe you could arrange for, maybe you could switch shifts with someone or something. Friday at 4:00 o'clock? How would that be?

DAD: Well, I do work then. I don't know. I might be able to get a guy to trade with me. I might.

COUNSELOR: Would you try, and then call me to tell me what happened? Because if you can't make that time, I want to schedule the appointment at a time you can come in.

DAD: Yes, I guess I could do that.

COUNSELOR: Terrific! OK, I'll be hearing from you, then. When do you think you'll be calling? Tomorrow night? We'll be at the unit until 7 o'clock.

DAD: Yeah, I'll call then.

COUNSELOR: OK. Thanks a lot; I'm sure we'll work something out. Good-by.

DAD: Good-by.

Given such an invitation, the counselor thought the father very likely would call her back with a positive response. A large part of the problem, after all, lay in the fact that he had been ignored thus far as a potentially active, helpful contributor to his child's education and growth. The counselor, through her phone call, had included him. She had made a point of addressing Dad in a warm, validating manner, reiterating her positive expectations of his contribution to family meetings.

Like most students, the counselor had had little training in making the initial phone call, an area vital to family counseling, so she was a bit surprised when Mr. Brown did not call back. Initially, she felt rejected by the father's lack of response. In a session with her supervisor, she asked for help, knowing that, if she called the father again while feeling upset with him, she would not succeed. Her supervisor pointed out that she was giving Dad—a guy who, when all was said and done, seemed to be a good Joe without any notion of therapy, except that he was afraid of it—the power to reject her. She remembered Dad as she thought about him: his awkwardness, his desire to appear to be thoroughly in control of the situation. Why help him avoid something that might be good for him and the family? Why not take one more step in encouraging him to come? She decided to give it one more try.

DAD: Hello.

COUNSELOR: Hi, Mr. Brown. This is Connie from the Youth Unit. How did it go? Could you arrange to come to our meeting? I sure hope so!

DAD: Well, hi, Connie! Yeah, well, I was going to call you earlier but I just didn't get to it. I talked to the supervisor and he said it would be OK, but not on a regular basis, you know what I mean? I mean, most guys don't want to work Friday afternoons either and it's not easy to get a man to replace me, you know what I mean there?

COUNSELOR: Sure. Well, that's terrific that we'll see you Friday, then. Maybe we can go from there in planning a better time if you feel like the family would benefit from more sessions. Anyway, we can talk about it then. I'll see you Friday at 4 o'clock, OK?

DAD: Yeah; we'll all be there.

COUNSELOR: OK. Good-by, then.

DAD: Good-by.

The counselor overcame her feeling of rejection and found that, with just a little more support on her part, Father was willing to come in. Let us suppose, however, that the counselor's second call to Dad has a less positive outcome:

DAD: Hello.

COUNSELOR: Hi, Mr. Brown. This is Connie from the Youth Unit. How did it go? Could you arrange to come to our meeting? I sure hope so!

DAD: Well, see, . . . No. I mean, I asked the boss and all that, but they just can't change something just like that and . . . [*Voice trails off.*]

COUNSELOR: So it sounds like Friday isn't going to work out. How about another time?

DAD: Naw . . . I mean, I can't do it; it just wouldn't be right. I got to tell you, I don't know about this stuff anyway. And I have to be at work.

COUNSELOR.   OK. I got you. This isn't a good time. Listen, we'll meet on Friday anyway and we'll be missing you. So if there's any chance you can come, now or another time, just come ahead, OK? We'd sure like to have you be there.

DAD: Well, no. [*Laughs self-consciously.*] No. Thanks.

COUNSELOR: OK. Good-by now. I may even call you one of these weeks just to check.

Many counselors would consider this the limit in extending help to Dad to join the family sessions; however, the counselor is keeping in mind that the initial interview is not Dad's last chance. As the family gets to know the counselor, the situation will change. Dad will have a great deal of information about what went on in the family sessions. This information may serve to increase his resistance. He will feel excluded, as usual, and upset that the family is talking behind his back. On the other hand, what information he has about the sessions is tantalizingly incomplete. He will be curious and possibly regretful.

The counselor who still wants to engage Dad in the counseling sessions can continue to develop imaginative strategies. He can, for example, schedule a home visit at a time when Dad is sure to be home. Or, he can write Dad a note, urging him to do something, such as behave in a novel, surprising way in a particular situation, spend an hour with a particular child, or whatever. The counselor who misses Dad during the family sessions can include him symbolically by adding an extra chair to the session and asking the family to address it as "Dad." This, too, may have the effect of eventually stimulating the real father to attend the sessions, through the family's communication at home. The counselor can use his imagination to think up novel ways to engage any particular individual; once he feels free to use it, resistance in general will hold less of a threat for him.

Resistance to Counseling: The Initial Interview

The first time the family assembles in the counselor's office is frequently difficult for all. The family is on unfamiliar territory. Often, this is their first experience with counseling of any kind, and they come equipped with very little in the way of realistic expectations. Frequently, they are prepared to be judged harshly for their failures in family life; they regard their prospective counselor with a mixture of apprehension and defensiveness. Their attitude may be critical, shy, angry, smooth, awkward, eager, or recalcitrant, but the counselor can expect evidence of discomfort in the family members as they sit down to find out what it is all going to be about.

The counselor, especially if he is relatively new in his work, also will come to the first session with some apprehension. Family counseling is known to be more difficult work than many other forms of counseling, just because it means dealing with a cohesive group. His primary concern is whether he will be sufficiently effective to take charge of the interview. Second, he wants to inspire confidence and trust. He is usually quite anxious to be liked by the family. Third, he is worried that he may not know enough to understand what is going on in this family. His teachers usually make it seem so easy; yet, he often finds himself thoroughly confused.

Often, all of these feelings are played out by family and counselor with a good deal of subtlety, as the interview continues smoothly, gradually dispelling some of the anxieties that colored its beginnings. When, however, the awkwardness in the room seems so strong that it all but occupies another chair, it often helps to talk about it. The family may be recalcitrant, each member following father's lead by answering the counselor's eager questions with one or two words. The counselor may feel like he's pulling teeth instead of helping the family express its problems to him. At this point, it may be helpful to redefine or reframe the family's resistance as something more acceptable.

Shyness, for example, is a quality that is usually acceptable to both counselor and clients in relation to negative behavior in a new situation. Shyness relates to the awkwardness of a new context, rather than willful avoidance:

COUNSELOR: I know it's hard to talk about family issues. Everybody feels a little shy in the beginning. Would you say that the word "shy" fits for how you're feeling? . . . It does for me.

Concepts such as privacy or pride also are helpful in such redefinitions. The counselor who attempts to argue with the resistant family member, on the other hand, soon finds himself contributing to the problems rather than helping to solve them:

COUNSELOR: I don't know how I can convince you, but talking really makes things better. . . . I was hoping you'd be willing to take this risk.

Family members also may be explicit about their resistance. The parents may tell the counselor that they are afraid that discussing troublesome events will only lead to more trouble; or they may say that such discussions usually end with someone leaving and everyone else being upset. In that case, the counselor may be able to give some support to the family in a variety of ways that recognize and address his clients' objections:

COUNSELOR: We'll be talking about what's been happening in the family. I imagine you each will have a different viewpoint about the situation. I want to know how each of you feels about being here.

and/or

COUNSELOR: We'll be talking about what you think is important in the family. The point of the work is to help you all relate in a more successful, happy way, not to re-create the bad scenes you've been telling me about.

and/or

COUNSELOR: I hear you telling me that the family values privacy. I understand that. It's important to your sense of family pride. If any of you feel that something is going to be talked about that you'd prefer to keep private, say so, OK?

and/or

COUNSELOR: I will try to proceed at a pace that feels right to most of you. It's true, things get uncomfortable some of the time. We are talking about problem areas. But if you feel strongly that you don't want an issue discussed, or that you want to discuss it differently, let me know and I'll do my best to give you support.

The key to handling the initial resistances is to remember that, whenever something about his own reaction or a family member's behavior puzzles the counselor, his first hypothesis should be to consider the fear of the unknown. Resistances may be expressed in many different ways. The family may want to disqualify the counselor, for example: "What exactly is your training for this work? Do you have children of your own? . . . How old are they? . . . We have teenagers and we really need an older person for a counselor." Some families avoid coming to the first session through lateness, forgetting, or finding a more important event to attend. All such resistances are handled more effectively by the counselor who remembers that, no matter how confident and controlled the clients sound, their resistance is largely motivated by fear.

The Family's Resistance to Change

Just as the individual often believes his neurotic defenses are responsible for his health (if he didn't wash his hands seven times a day, he'd get germs on them and become sick), so families often labor under the delusion that, without their neurotic defenses, the family could not survive. If the family broke up—for example, if Mom and Dad split up, or if Junior left, or if Sis were placed in a foster home—one or more family member might not survive or would become crippled. Mom might commit suicide if Dad left her. Dad would be a hopeless alcoholic without Mom. Junior would become a criminal if he left home. Sis would get pregnant and end up on welfare.

Catastrophic expectations such as these often lead a family to rigidify their ways of dealing with one another. Whether or not their fears are based on an actual incident, the process is the same. Timmy's parents, for example, seemed unable to overcome the attitudes they developed after he had a severe rollerskating accident when he was nine years old. Although he had recovered fully by the time he was 10, the parents remained frozen in their feelings, with Mother frenzied and overprotective and Father countering her worries with an incautious, devil-may-care attitude. The family repeated the same scenes over and over: The father was ineffective and courageous, the mother was cautious and frightened, and the boy was nine forever, although in reality he was now 15. A family such as this one must face and eventually conquer its dread of change if any significant growth is to be accomplished. Families with rigidified patterns act like any group of animals aware of being observed; they sniff the air and prepare to cover their tracks. They suspect change is lurking in every corner. Strong prohibitions are developed against just the kind of behavior the counselor wants them to try.

The family's resistance to change will ebb and flow throughout the counseling sessions. As the family trusts the counselor more, subjects hitherto banned from discussion, possibly even from awareness, will be opened up. As such subjects arise—drinking problems, thoughts of separation, long-buried crimes or accusations—the counselor can support the speakers by making sure that the old patterns of blame do not rekindle the family's hopelessness. After such a risk, the counselor can point out to the fearful family member that he is still alive, that no walls have tumbled down, that, in fact, the family is still together and on speaking terms. There are families who continue to skirt their most dreaded issues. The counselor must be careful, in such a situation, to avoid a power struggle, especially one he can't win. It is far better to assure family members that there is no need to discuss anything that still seems difficult to attempt, that there will be time enough to do so at a time the family feels more at ease, than to fall into the trap of coaxing the family to produce a potentially painful and unresolvable scene.

The beginning counselor often is surprised by a family's resistance behavior, especially when things appear to be going well. A counselor complimenting a family on their hard work, for example, is often surprised by their apparent backsliding at the next session. If he can rid himself of the notion that families welcome change, he will be more prepared for their mixed emotions. Change, after all, means risk, and risk usually is accompanied by some anxiety about the unknown. Change may portend a loss of integrity to someone who has clung stubbornly to a painful process that he believes to be productive. Change means facing the same old situations and not being able to do the same old things. Families usually take one step forward and follow it by a backward slide. The counselor needs to recognize their need to contact old, familiar territory.

Direct verbal resistance usually is expressed in negative terms: "We don't like the way it's going." "You aren't helping us." "We don't want to come any more." "Talking doesn't do any good." There is another way of resisting, however, that often takes the counselor by surprise. Aptly named, "flight into health" by the psychoanalysts, this refers to the maneuver of using the counselor's goal of curing the family to keep him from doing so: "You've been so wonderful and it's helped us so much." "I think we're ready to be on our own now . . . we've worked so hard, we're ready for a vacation." "We love to come, but we have no time." "We've never felt so good; we're going to leave." Spoken in the context of work completed, those words are balm to a counselor's ears, but when he feels that a lot of important work remains undone, he knows he is facing another form of family resistance. Working with this type of resistance usually means that the counselor must be ready for a temporary loss of affection from family members. If he is dependent on their praise, he is in trouble, because he must overlook it and remind the family that all is not necessarily well that ends well.

Mark: The End or the Beginning?

> MOTHER: You've been really terrific; I think we're about ready to quit, don't you?
>
> COUNSELOR: Thanks. I've enjoyed the work, too, but I'm not sure about something. Are you telling me you're feeling good today? Or that the discipline problems with Mark are all cleared up?
>
> MOTHER: Well, they're not all cleared up, but I think we've got a handle on it.
>
> COUNSELOR: Well, that's good. Let's hear about how it went last week. Wasn't he on curfew?
>
> MOTHER: Oh, do we have to go into that?
>
> COUNSELOR: Yes.
>
> MOTHER: [*With a good deal of anger.*] Don't you think sometimes a positive approach might be a little more helpful?
>
> COUNSELOR: Sure, but not if it means ignoring something important.
>
> MOM: [*Looks defiantly at counselor; silent for some time.*]
>
> COUNSELOR: Okay. I'm still interested in how it went with the curfew.
>
> MOM: [*Flushed with anger.*] Well? . . . Oh, I get so darn fed up with this sometimes, I just really don't know if it wouldn't be better to be doing something else entirely.
>
> COUNSELOR: It's a hard time.
>
> MOM: [*Starting to cry.*] I just think it isn't going to work. He did keep to the curfew the first few nights but then he missed three in a row!
>
> COUNSELOR: Well, let's see what we can do to improve that situation, Okay?

The counselor has deflated the balloon of Mom's false optimism. Mom has charmed her way out of many a difficult situation, not unlike her son, the client, whose curfew is being discussed. Like her son, she wants to avoid negative feelings and hard work; she doesn't want limits either. Faced with a counselor who is not willing to be charmed, her initial reaction is one of anger and frustration. The counselor dealing with this type of resistance must anticipate his client's deep disappointment at the moment he fails to go along. If he is drawn into the client's disappointment, he won't be able to help. He will feel apologetic, and his clients will be on their way out of treatment. If he recognizes this particular resistance, however, he also will understand the importance of helping the client to accept limits. He will know that, if he were to agree with Mom that the family is ready to quit, Mom would be secretly disappointed. She knows she wants to run away from something important. She knows it doesn't work in the long run. Armed with an understanding of the process, the counselor can help Mom with momentary frustration and anger—the explicit expression of a resistance hitherto covered by false optimism— and the work of the family sessions can continue.

The Counselor's Resistance to Change

Ideally, the family counselor creates a safe place for the family to talk. Since she usually is dealing with families whose discussions have bogged down, she attempts to provide an educational time during which each family member learns something about his own experiences, wants, and needs, as well as how to go about talking to other family members without blaming or threatening them. As this education progresses, wounds begin to heal. Each family member gradually feels stronger. With growing strength in the family, the need to avoid pain becomes less dramatic and the resistances less felt. Why should this process be so difficult, not only for the family but the counselor as well?

To answer this question, the theme that underlies most family resistance must be reconsidered, namely, the fear of the family's disintegration. If it is true that the catastrophic fear that underlies the family's resistance to change relates to the fear of its disintegration, then it must be true that the counselor's most profound problem in relation to a family is her reaction to it. The family brings an unspoken agenda to the counseling session: "We will do as much as we can as long as the family's survival is assured. If counseling threatens the family as a whole, or any member of it, our first obligation is to ourselves, to defend against the process that brought that about." When the counselor reacts to the family's fear with her own, she answers, "You are right. We have gone too far. I had hoped that talking would help, but, the way this is going, it could lead to divorce or somebody could really get hurt. This isn't working. I'd better stop this process. If you want to leave; leave. If you want to change the subject, we'll change the subject. This is too scary."

Once this kind of implicit agreement is reached by the family and the counselor, counseling has stopped. On a feeling level, the counselor has validated the family's worst fears. She, too, believes that the pain brought about by further talk would be unbearable and threaten the family's survival. Her conviction, like theirs, is the result of her personal experiences. When she finds himself joining a family's resistance, chances are very strong that she is reenacting a drama of her childhood in which she played a similar role. Supervision, therefore, is of primary importance to the counselor who wishes to overcome problems such as these. Once the counselor has gained some awareness of her own fear of the family's stepping into unknown territory, she will become free to help them. She will be able to talk about her fear and ask the family members whether, indeed, they have experienced similar feelings. She will be able to liken the process to the family poised over a precipice, and she can ask the others if they, too, are afraid of the danger that may occur from taking the next step. As soon as the counselor is free from the survival struggle in which the family believes itself to be engaged, she can become more flexible. Instead of two choices—to resist or to continue—a great many other solutions may occur to both family and counselor as they explore what is happening. Some families do break up in counseling. If counseling is effective, however, they will not break up as a disastrous consequence to an intolerable situation. They will break up because they felt strong enough to make a choice hitherto forbidden to them. The counselor who knows that her own family is not at stake will be able to help the family in treatment to approach dreaded situations at a pace that will allow gradual mastery.

Another aspect of counselor resistance—one that may impede his attempts to reduce the family resistance—is his desire to be liked by them. Family counseling has all the earmarks of a social get-together. There is a meeting of strangers. The room is usually on the informal, cheerful side, and coffee or tea frequently are available. The counseling situation requires a certain amount of acceptability of the counselor. If he remains an aloof, unfriendly outsider, it is not likely that the family will warm up to their work, except in the rare cases where the counselor is comfortable with his own peculiarities. Both the context and the role stir the counselor's feelings about being liked and accepted. When the family becomes resistant and he has to proceed in a way that may threaten someone's self-esteem temporarily, or cause discomfort, he becomes very cautious. In many ways, the process of family counseling proceeds along the lines of parenting: The counselor who cannot take a chance on losing the family's love and/or admiration quickly finds himself in the same bind as the parents who cannot set limits. He teaches the family to act without taking him into account.

Supervision frequently is used to help the counselor who is paralyzed by his feelings of inadequacy and rejection when confronted by a hostile, dissatisfied family. He may need to explore his conflicted feelings. On the one end, he wants to throw the family out of treatment, on the other, he wants to beg them to stay. In supervision and conversations with other staff members, the counselor can develop an understanding of the family's need to express their differences. If the counselor's need to be accepted by the family is so strong that he cannot tolerate their disagreements with him, he will become ineffective. Like a genuinely loving parent, he will need to take the chance of being disliked.

Finally, a counselor may have difficulty working with the family's resistance because she is uncomfortable taking charge of a situation. Many forms of counseling allow the counselor a passive role. She can sit back, ask her client or group members leading questions, and expect them to take the responsibility for moving the work along. Families are different. As a functioning unit, they are a group of people who have developed effective techniques to keep each other in line and to keep outsiders from impinging on their system. If a counselor is to have any chance of helping to change the homeostasis in a family, she must be able to step in, take charge, and interrupt the usual routines. The problem of taking charge is a problem in our society that extends from classroom teachers and scoutmasters to politicians and judges. It is difficult to find a model for a man or women willing to lead anyone in any direction. Here, also, the counselor can benefit from supervision, where she can explore her feelings about taking charge and call to mind those people in her own experience who can serve as models for the required behavior.

The Consultation Group

In most youth service settings, a consultation group is available to the student of family counseling, in addition to direct supervision. The consultation group, made up of staff members and volunteers concerned with family counseling and a leader with expertise in the field, can be the counselor's greatest source of support in facing family resistance. Here, he describes his problem families, explores his own reactions, and learns from others who are experiencing similar problems. When the work concerns resistance, the consultation group is faced with a recurring dilemma: The counselor seems as resistant as the family he is presenting. At such times, the counselor's wife may start complaining about his seeming obsession with his work or his stubbornness in dealing with the children. It seems as though the counselor has "caught" his clients' resistance and is acting it out everywhere. In the consultation group, it seems as though the counselor is playing "Yes, but. . . ." No matter what suggestion is made by the group members or consultant, he finds a way the family would defeat it. When discussion leads to this kind of impasse, role-playing techniques often give new life to a discouraged group. Role-playing difficult families has long been a mainstay of consultation groups. The "round robin" is a role-playing technique that greatly enhances the group's effectiveness when confronted with family resistance.

Round Robin: Resistance—One Family; Many Counselors

Marcia came to the consultation group in a mood typical of the beginning family counselor faced with a tough family resistance. She was frustrated, a little angry, exasperated, and filled with blame for herself, the family, and the consultation group for not helping her avoid this situation. She felt that the family banded together and kept her from making any progress with them. Instead of leading the family, she felt lead by them. She felt that she was just as ineffective as they were in getting at what was really bothering them.

In order to diffuse the negative group effect that was already beginning to spread as Marcia talked, and also to help her to find a way of helping the family, the group leader suggested the round robin technique.

CONSULTANT: Let's do a round robin on this family, Marcia. Could you ask others to role-play the one or two members of the family who give you the most trouble, and cue them a little bit about their background?

MARCIA: Okay. Jack, you play Dad. You remember, he's the lawyer. Real smart and totally in his head. Marlene, you be Mom. Real glamorous. Gorgeous clothes. Sort of vague, you know? She has this real high-pitched voice and she just sort of stares a lot. Franny, their daughter, is 16. She told both of them she knew they'd been having a lot of trouble and fighting and stuff about three weeks ago, and I thought, "Wow! Now we're really going to get going!" But nothing! They just sort of chit-chat in the session—mostly Mom—and I feel like I'm pulling teeth.

CONSULTANT: Okay, that sounds real clear. Why don't we start this way: Let's start with Dad and Mom, and Ned can role-play the therapist. [*The three actors go into the center of the room.*] But this is going to be different from other times we've done role-playing. This time I want everyone in the group to have a chance to be therapist. I'll give you a chance to show us something about your approach to this family, and when that becomes clearly defined, I'll ask the next person to take over as counselor. We'll continue until everyone has had a chance. [*Jack, Marlene, and Ned start to role-play.*]

DAD: Hi.

MOM: Hi there, how have you been this week?

NED: Okay. How about you folks?

MOM: Okay, too. I have something to talk about. I was reading the paper today and they gave some very nice coverage to a place that's a lot like this one, do you know about it? It's called Family Youth Agency? Have you ever heard of them?

NED: Yeah, they're in San Rafael.

MOM: I think it's wonderful that so many people are concerned about young people. Concerned enough to do something, you know?

NED: [*Turns around and looks helplessly at consultation group.*] They've got me. [*Laughs.*] I can't even think of any approach.

CONSULTANT: Jane, you role-play the therapist, now.

JANE: Let's not do this. Let's see, I seem to have been ending

	up talking about all sorts of interesting subjects with you guys lately, but I've been missing out on hearing about you, you know?
DAD:	Well, there just isn't that much going on, huh, Nancy?
JANE:	Well, I still feel unfinished about something we talked about three weeks ago . . .
CONSULTANT:	Good, Jane; you're on your way. Next! John, Okay?

As the consultant watched and took notes on the counselors' various approaches, it became clear that the successful counselors were able to take charge of the situation and define the context, setting limits for the parents' behavior. Taking charge of two such good-looking, sophisticated, smooth talkers was difficult for the counselors, who often were younger than the couple. Marcia got a lot of sympathy for her problems while at the same time, she learned alternative ways of coping.

Round Robin: Defensive Styles—Playing Both Client and Counselor

Paul came to consultation with a different problem. The family as a whole did not impede his functioning. He felt at ease with all the members except one, the father. He could not get him to stop intellectualizing. Paul described the father as having a lecture for all occasions and being ready to give it relentlessly as others in the room became increasingly bored, frustrated, and helpless.

Intellectualization is a defense used by many verbal family members. Beginning counselors often are disappointed that a family member, who seemed so bright and promising in terms of his initial grasp of matters, becomes so difficult to reach when the intellectual barricades are raised. One way the whole consultation group can profit by Paul's dilemma is for each person in it to play both the person using the defense and the counselor faced with it.

CONSULTANT:	Let's see if we can try a different kind of round robin to help us with this one, Paul. I want everyone of you to get a chance to be both client and counselor, so, Paul, why don't you start out as Mr. X. You know him. Role-play him and show us what he is like, and Jack will play the counselor.

PAUL
(AS MR. X):   I read somewhere that just recently Synanon published a statement about the need for more authority in the parental home, and you know that when we're talking about teenagers, we're talking about drug problems, so . . .

CONSULTANT: Okay, I'm afraid he's got you. Jack, now you be Mr. X. Start with what he just said and Kindra will be the counselor.

JACK
(AS MR. X):   . . . and you know that when we're talking about teenagers we're talking about drug problems, so . . . so, probably the same logic would apply, wouldn't you think?

KINDRA: I don't know. I do know I'm curious about all this though. Is it something to do with Jim? Have you been worrying about him?

JACK
(AS MR. X):   Well, you might say that's always a safe guess, with me and Jim. Yeah. But before we get into that, where do you stand on this? I think it's a legitimate question. I mean kids in general. We could all be completely on the wrong track, you know.

KINDRA: Well, I'll tell you. . . . I don't know just how to answer you because I don't want to get into a long discussion with you about . . .

JACK
(AS MR. X):   [*Very authoritatively.*] Oh, I don't think a long discussion will be necessary. I just want to know what your opinion is about permissiveness being a good thing in raising children, especially teenagers.

KINDRA: I agree. It's really hard to know what's right and what's wrong. I'm not solidly in either camp. But, what worried you about Jim?

JACK
(AS MR. X):   Well, his eyes looked dilated to me almost every day last week.

KINDRA: Well, that's important.

CONSULTANT: Good. Next? Kindra, you're Mr. X now. And David, since you're sitting next to Kindra, continue as counselor.

KINDRA: You mean each of us, in turn, first plays counselor and then Mr. X?

CONSULTANT: Exactly, until we've gone all the way around the circle. OK, David, why don't you go ahead?

The round robin continued until Paul had a chance to counsel the last student playing Mr. X. Paul's frustration was replaced by optimism and confidence in the many alternatives the group had provided. The zest with which the group members had portrayed Mr. X informed him of their problems with similar clients.

The round robin techniques provide insurance against the depression that often settles over a group listening to a counselor's frustration about his work. The technique is useful both in providing an emotional, active outlet for the group members' feelings and as a format for finding alternative solutions.

The Need to Change Counselors

Some relationships between family and counselor just don't work out. When a family complains about their treatment in family counseling, resistance to change is often the only interpretation considered by the counselor. It must be stated emphatically that the family may not be resisting change. In fact, they may be attempting to leave a situation that keeps them from making progress. Personality differences cannot always be bridged. Counselors sometimes make mistakes that keep trust from developing. The same snags affect counseling relationships that affect other human relationships. It is very important for counselor and supervisor to keep in mind the possibility that the family that requests another counselor actually does need to see someone else in order to work more effectively. Otherwise, the counselor may find himself in a coercive, dictatorial role. The questions that determine the answer to this dilemma are the following:

1. How motivated does the family seem to be? Have they come to appointments? Do all members come? Do they attempt to raise issues important to them? Can they be expected to come in to see someone else?
2. What is the counselor's assessment of the relationship? Does he feel close or distant from the family? Does he like the family? Is he in a coalition with any one member against

the others? Is he at ease with the family? Does he feel in control? Has he made errors?

3. How do the styles of family and counselor mesh? Do they talk the same language? Are they worlds apart?

4. Has the relationship between counselor and clients changed? Did the counselor feel comfortable with the family until recent problems arose? Or has the relationship progressed with an unchanging degree of discomfort from the beginning?

If the counselor and supervisor or consultation group determine that the family deserves another chance with a new counselor, a referral often can be made in such a way that both family and counselor profit from their frustrating relationship.

Summary

Resistance takes many forms. We have covered only a few, hoping to talk about those that the family counselor encounters frequently. The resistant family tests the counselor's sense of security in his work. Sensitive family members often will express their dissatisfactions in just such a way as to make the counselor feel that it is all his fault, that he has bungled it. In consultation with his supervisor, the counselor must explore his own feelings and reactions so that he cannot be manipulated by his resistant clients. Most of the time, if he agrees with them, both he and the family lose. Clearly, it cannot be *all* his fault, whatever "it" is. The family came in because there were problems before they ever met him. The counselor must develop enough security in his work to withstand the family's anxieties about change. He must not forget the family's ambivalence: They're coming to the sessions because they want to change; at the same time, they're wanting to stop working because change is imminent.

Resistance occurs at all stages of treatment. Because of the pervasiveness of family resistance, there are no specific techniques addressed to handling them; rather, all of the techniques the counselor has at her command are addressed to overcoming resistance and producing change. The counselor's art, that is, her style, sensitivity, sense of timing, and experience, will guide her in making decisions with any particular family.

Suggested Readings

Abroms, G. Supervision as meta-therapy. In F. Kaslow (Ed.), *Supervision Consultation and Staff-Training in the Helping Professions*. San Francisco: Jossey-Bass, 1978.

Anderson, Carol. *Mastering Resistance: A Practical Guide to Family Therapy*. New York : Guilford Press, 1983.

Boszormeny-Nagy, I., and Framo, J. *Intensive Family Therapy*. New York: Harper & Row, 1965.

Bowen, M. *Family Therapy in Clinical Practice*. New York: Jason Aronson, 1978.

Evans, J. *Adolescent and Pre-Adolescent Psychiatry*. New York: Grune and Stratton, 1983.

Framo, J. L. *Explorations in Marriage and Family Therapy, Collected Papers*. New York: Springer, 1982.

Gehrke, S., and Kirschenbaum, M. Survival patterns in conjoint family therapy. *Family Process, 6,* 67–80, March 1967.

Guerin, P. J. (Ed.). *Family Therapy: Theory and Practice*. New York: Gardner Press, 1978.

Haley, J. *Changing Families*. New York: Grune and Stratton, 1971.

Haley, J. *Uncommon Therapy: The Psychiatric Techniques of Milton Erickson, M.D.* New York: Norton, 1973.

Haley, J. *Problem-Solving Therapy*. New York: Harper & Row, 1976.

Hoffman, L. *Foundations of Family Therapy*. New York: Basic Books, 1981.

Jackson, Don (Ed.). *Therapy, Communication, and Change*. Vols. 1 and 2. Palo Alto: Science and Behavior Books, 1982.

Kramer, Charles H. *Becoming a Family Therapist: Devising an Integrated Approach to Working with Families*. New York: Human Sciences Press, 1980.

Langs, Robert J. *Resistances and Interventions: The Nature of Therapeutic Work*. New York: Jason Aronson, 1981.

Leveton, Alan. The art of shamesmanship. *British Journal of Medical Psychology, 35:*101–111, 1962.

Leveton, Alan. Time, death and the ego chill. *Journal of Existentialism, 6:*21, 69–80, 1965.

Leveton, Alan. Elizabeth is frightened. *Voices, 8,* 4–13, Spring 1972.

Leveton, Alan. Family therapy as play: The contribution of Milton H. Erickson, M.D. In Jeffrey K. Zeig (Ed.), *Ericksonian Approaches to Hypnosis and Psychotherapy*. New York: Brunner-Mazel, 1982.

Leveton, Eva. *Psychodrama for the Timid Clinician*. New York: Springer, 1977.

Leveton, Alan, and Leveton, Eva. Children in trouble, family in crisis. A series of 5 training films demonstrating a family counseling alternative. University of California at Davis, Administration of Criminal Justice, 1975.

Luthman, S., and Kirschenbaum, M. *The Dynamic Family*. Palo Alto: Science and Behavior Books, 1974.

Montalvo, B. Aspects of live supervision. *Family Process, 12,* 343–359, 1973.

Nagy, I., and Spark, E. *Invisible Loyalties*. New York: Harper & Row, 1973.

Papp, Peggy, and Aponte, H. J. The anatomy of a therapist: Clinical strategies and counter-transference. *American Journal of Psychotherapy, 7*, 11–12, 1979.

Perls, Fritz. *The Gestalt Approach: An Eyewitness to Therapy.* Palo Alto: Science and Behavior Books, 1965.

Rabichow, Helen G., and Sklansky, Morris A. *Effective Counseling for Adolescents.* Chicago: Follett, 1980.

Searles, H. F. *Counter-Transference and Related Subjects, Selected Papers.* New York: International Universities Press, 1979.

Whiffen, Rosemary, and Byng-Hall, John. *Family Therapy Supervision: Recent Developments in Practice.* New York: Grune and Stratton, 1982.

Whitacker, C., and Keith, D. Symbolic-experiential family therapy. In A. Gurnan & D. Kniskern (Eds.), *Handbook of Family Therapy.* New York: Brunner-Mazel, 1981.

III

Don't Enter a Power Struggle You Can't Win: A Casebook

10

Power Struggles and Trust

The title of Part III could serve as a guideline for the stormy course of counseling adolescents. I recommend it to oppose another one often implicitly present in the halls of youth services: "Justice for all."

My presence in the Youth Advocates System, for example, acted as a conservative force in relation to the frustrated idealism of both the counselor and his client. I knew that idealism was necessary for the growth and commitment of both, and, as a long-time closet idealist, I admired it. At the same time, I found that attitudes such as, "My client, right or wrong," or, "We'll do a better job than any of this kid's parents or teachers ever did," or, "We'll help each kid work out his own rules," frequently got both counselor and client in trouble.

I came to admire the motto, "Don't enter any power struggle you can't win," because it seemed to me that it opposed cleanly what I saw as endless, wasted conversations between teanagers and their parents or counselors, conversations in which one side knew for sure that the other didn't have a leg to stand on:

PARENT: You can't do this. We won't stand for your doing this.

TEENAGER: I'll do what I want to do. I don't have to listen to you.

Each side insists. The tone gets louder and louder. The challenged authority figure gives every appearance of having right on his side and acts as though he has the power and control to enforce it, but inside he experiences impotence and uncertainty.

Working with adolescents means working with people engaged in a struggle for freedom and independence. Friction in the families of adolescents frequently arises when the teenager demands a freedom that his parents, realistically or unrealistically, are unwilling to give him. Some teenagers become openly rebellious, while some passively protect their struggling parents. A teenager usually functions in a way that highlights the conflicts already existing in his family. The family that cannot solve these continuing struggles eventually arrives at an impasse, which often is broken by the teenager's developing symptoms and/or running away.

The struggles are so repetitive in the major areas of adolescent development that, to illustrate them better, we will be presenting the reader with a series of case examples in the rest of this section. Before we do that, however, two issues of relevance to the entire family must be discussed: the type of power struggles that revolve around authority, and the evolution of power struggles around trust.

Youth, Autonomy, and Authority

Adolescents in trouble are most often veterans of ill-fated struggles with their parents. When a counselor invites the youth's family in for the first counseling session, he often has the feeling that the session is running away from him. After some initial shyness, the family proceeds as though he weren't there, arguing, each side repeating lines the other knows by heart, and making no apparent progress. Counseling adolescents and their families means learning to understand as much as possible about the nature of their power struggles with parents and other authorities in order to become a helpful participant in the process, rather than a helpless victim.

We all remember our teenage years. Even if it has been quite some time, sometimes it seems like yesterday. For some of us, it wasn't very long ago, but we all can recall these feelings:

TEENAGER: *They're wrong and I'm right. They can't tell me what to do. I'm not a child anymore. . . . Sure, I take chances. I want to find out about things. How can you learn to drive without getting in a car? . . . I know what I'm doing. I feel I can do it. I really feel powerful sometimes. Really strong. I know I can do it. They're trying to cramp my style. Things were different when they were my age. . . . They don't know what I'm talking* about. I have a right to live the way I want to live. I have a right to be trusted. They want to run my life. Hah! I'll show 'em. I can run my own life. I don't need to be told when to be home or who I can have as a friend or what I can do and can't do. Trust me, that's all I ask.

And we all remember the other side. Many of us, by now, have been in the parent's position:

> PARENT: How can I trust you when you've let me down again and again? You can't even be relied on to do little things, like the dishes after dinner. How can I rely on you to do the big things like drive our car without getting into trouble? You've had one accident already. . . . Sure, I've had my share of fender benders, but I don't necessarily want you to be like me. I want you to have a better life. I've made my mistakes; I want to help you not make the same ones, don't you see? . . . How can I trust you when I know that all you care about in the whole world is what those friends of yours think of you? You'd do anything for them. Get into drugs, get pregnant—die, as far as I know—I wish you'd realize that I'm the best friend you'll ever have. I love you and I want what's best for you. I wish I could trust you. Lord knows, I'd like to. But you won't cooperate. I have to make rules to get any decent behavior out of you. The rules are clear. All you have to do is follow them.

A large proportion of those working with teenagers—counselors, teachers, doctors, ministers, probation officers—chose their work on the basis of sympathy with young people and an ability to get along with them. Most often, my own students were people in their twenties, not exactly teenagers any more, but not yet old enough to be parents of teenagers, either. Their main interest in joining the organization was to help kids who they felt, in some way, weren't getting a fair shake. If helping their client meant talking with his parents, that was all right, but the client—or youth or adolescent or teenager or person—was the focus of most counselors' goals. This commitment to helping a special group of people in trouble provided the impetus for founding youth services of considerable variety in many U.S. cities.

Such a commitment has its inherent problems, however. When parents and children are involved in a power struggle, the counselor may take a side, and, as soon as he does, he joins the war. His voice will be ignored, just as the client's voice was ignored by the parents before they came in. The parents will have difficulty trusting the counselor. Joining the war means that the counselor gives up the power he would have had as someone outside the family drama.

Let us suppose that the counselor is a good candidate for playing on the youth's team. Chances are that there will come a time when he will be alone with his client. The client will use his chance to prevail upon the counselor to "help" him, saying things like, "When I get with my parents, I can't say anything like we've been talking about. They won't let me talk. Why can't you talk to them for me?" It is hard to resist such talk. It could be true. The counselor may have experienced similar feelings. Let's assume it *is* true. The kid seems to mean what he says. Even then, playing along with him will do more harm than good. The counselor would be placing himself in a position of accepting his client's assumptions that

1. The parents are the kind of authoritative, unilateral, repressive people who make sensible conversation impossible.
2. The client is powerless to speak for himself.
3. The counselor has the power the client lacks and will use it to convince the parents of the client's essential rightness.

With these assumptions, can the counselor win? It is more likely he will lose the whole family in the first few minutes. The parents will sense his prejudice against them and become defensive. The client will resent the counselor's patronizing him because, even though he asked for the help he is getting, he really wants to assert himself against his parents directly. Later, when the battle is lost, the client will blame the counselor for representing him poorly.

It is more sensible for the counselor to answer his client's initial request by saying something like, "It sounds tough. I'd like to help, and I will try, but I have to do it my way. That means trying to get you and the folks talking together more successfully. I will try to help you make room for yourself and say what you think. I'll try and get them to really listen. But I'll be doing the same for them: trying to get you to listen to their side, also. First I want us all to get a clear picture of what's going on. Then, later, we can talk more about what to do." Let's take a little more detailed look at what happens when a counselor takes sides.

George:

George. 15 years old, confided in his counselor, Ben, who felt good wnen George began to talk. George told the counselor of his concern about smoking too much dope, his worries about a little brother who was beginning to run around with the wrong gang, his lack of closeness to his father. So far, so good. Then he let the counselor know—not in so many words, but he let him know— that the bicycles stored in the basement at the Youth Center were "hot." The counselor and George talked a little more and George came right out and told him he was keeping the bikes for some kids who had stolen them. Throughout the conversation, the counselor felt uncomfortable and more and more tense. The pressure was on. Could he be a real pal? A real pal would keep his mouth shut and give George a chance to get the bikes out before anybody else found out. Or, was he going to be just another one of those square dudes that rats on kids after pretending to be their friend? Well?

The counselor was tempted. George had been opening up more and more. If he crossed him now, that might be the end of the relationship. George could end up with even less trust in authorities. It hadn't been that long since the counselor had felt like George. It had seemed that adults were always out to get him. And, to get back to George again, there were extenuating circumstances. After all, George hadn't stolen the bikes. And he had told the counselor.

Then the counselor became aware of the other side. What if he kept his mouth shut? A counselor just wouldn't do that. He'd feel like he was helping out George's friends and potentially helping George get into trouble. Could such a position be defended at a staff meeting? Not really.

Okay, if the relationship had to be put on the line, that's the way it would have to be. The counselor told George he was sorry, but he'd have to find some way to help him tell the rest of the staff what was going on. It helped to tell him that this was not easy to do. The information George had given him put the counselor in a tight spot. He cared about George and felt the talks had been good. He didn't want to lose his trust. On the other hand, George was asking him to keep information secret that could hurt George and the other kids, and the counselor, in his job. After the counselor told him, George was furious. He didn't talk at all for a couple of hours. After that, he reluctantly agreed to see the director with the counselor. He seemed reserved for some time; in fact, the old informality never returned to the relationship. Still, the counselor was clear that his position had been right. Joining George's side of the power struggle would have meant joining his hood friends in their struggle against society. Not joining him provided the comfort of knowing he hadn't made matters worse. Without playing the role assigned to him or compromising his position, he had stood by the values of the house. He hadn't been one of the many who helped George make poor choices by silent affirmation. George had valued the counselor's opinions earlier. Perhaps someday he could value his opinion here also.

We will be returning to the subject of power struggles again and again. It is important to become aware of the power struggles that occur among teenagers and their parents, teachers, and counselors; between parents and counselors; and between counselors and others in authority. There are naturally attractive coalitions between counselors and their clients. It is important to learn to back off in order to get the perspective needed to comment on what is going on without taking sides. Peace talks must replace a continuing, fruitless war.

Trust

A large percentage of power struggles with teenagers center on trust. Few families discuss trust as often and with as much passion as those with adolescent children. Yet the children in these families have been growing more and more independent and trustworthy since they were small. The increase has been gradual, at times imperceptible. Why do events take such a radical turn during adolescence? If trust is such an old issue, why does it seem so new?

Adolescence is different from earlier childhood in many ways. During adolescence, less and less direct parental involvement is required for the child's learning at a time when the context of growth in our society provides him with a barrage of new events. These inner and outer challenges appear at least as difficult and dangerous as learning how to walk and talk once were. The teenager needs to learn skills involving greater and greater risk. From the use of the family car to demands for late hours, from experimentation with drugs or alcohol to sexual experience, the teenager demands more and more freedom to explore areas that the parent perceives as dangerous, or at least risky. The parent separated from his child by long school and/or work hours and the perennial "generation gap" has less information than ever about his child's ability to cope with these new situations. He has not been his child's major teacher for a good many years. Often, the parents of the teenager also are entering a new phase in their lives. Now in their mid thirties or early forties, they are facing the dilemmas that cause them to question their own lives. Individuals often reevaluate both marriage and career as the children need them less. While children get ready to leave the nest, parents may consider the same move. Children often are said to keep families together. Grown children often leave a gap in the parent's lives that leads to questions about career and important relationships, questions that make it difficult to pay adequate attention to the growth problems of the teenage child.

The major power struggles of adolescents and their parents occur around the teenager's demand for greater freedom and responsibility. Feelings run high, as these often are regarded as life-or-death issues. The teenager must achieve the freedom of movement and action that allows him to grow up. The parent must insure that his child does not endanger his life or that of others. Parents often become increasingly anxious. They feel pushed beyond endurance by teenagers who seem to disregard caution and safety. Teenagers feel stifled and enraged, protected against experiences vital to their growth. Adolescence is one of the great tests of the parent–child relationship, and mutual trust—if it is genuine—can be regarded rightfully as a measure of success.

The adolescent must learn to master the social skills necessary for his further development, for making friends, learning to cope in the work world, getting along socially. Failure may mean lack of acceptance by his peers, an inability to achieve independence by graduating from school or home, and a potential dependence on protective services or on an institution.

Ironically, the struggles around trust between parent and child gain their power because both want so much to succeed: The parent wants to trust as much as the child wants to be trusted. The parent both fears and hopes for his child's emancipation. He wants to avoid the fears that lead him to anticipate disaster all too easily. He is eager to trust blindly. The parent wants the freedom ensuing from his child's greater responsibility as much as the child does. If the parent were not so eager to trust, he would not jump so readily into the trap that opens up for him when he is challenged by his child. The trap, however, keeps growth at a standstill, because it is an endlessly repeated power struggle: "You can't do that!" "Why can't I; don't you trust me?" "I trust you. . . ." "Then why can't I?" "We can't let you!" "You guys just don't understand anything; everyone else is letting their kids do this! Why can't I?" Once caught in this cycle, both parents and teenagers want nothing more than to escape, and, because escape is impossible without changing a position to which each is committed, runaways are not infrequent among both parents and children. At home, the conflicts continue. The teenager, wanting freedom, builds himself a jail by ignoring restrictions. The parent, wanting freedom, imprisons himself in his role as guard. Both often fantasize running away.

The word "trust" alone comes to act as a red flag between parents and teenagers; it triggers strong emotions, like other red-flag words such as "love" or "responsibility." Here are some typical examples of how trust is used to challenge the parent who is attempting to set limits:

MARY
(AGE 14):   You want to talk to Joe's folks just because we're going to stay at their place on an overnight? Gosh, it's like we were still in grammar school. Don't you *trust* Joe and me? What do you have to talk to them for?

JOHN
(AGE 17):   You don't even *trust* me enough to let me drive your car? I can't believe it!

BILL (AGE 15):   Your idea of making me sit down to do my homework at the same time every day is ridiculous. I *said* I was going to improve my grades. You have to *trust* me enough to let me figure out myself how to do it.

Although Mary, John, and Bill differ from each other in many respects, each uses the word "trust" in the same way: It is said reproachfully, with slight overtones of disgust, intended to shame the parent into submission.

Let us assume that the context for each of these comments is a conversation in which the parent has set limits because her recent past experience with her child leads her to believe more controls are necessary. (The last time Mary stayed at Joe's place, his parents didn't know about it; when they came home, the liquor cabinet was empty and the house a mess. John has put some dents in his father's car. Bill is a bright kid who consistently neglects his schoolwork.) When the adolescent redefines the conversation in terms of trust, he is hoping to derail his parent's attempt to control him by telling her that she is doing a bad job of parenting. She's treating her child like a criminal. She's a suspicious, untrusting parent. Hearing these accusations, the parent, who wants to be good, kind, and just, is often hooked into a discussion of trust:

> PARENT: [*To Mary.*] I do trust you kids. It's just that I'd feel better if I could talk to Joe's parents.
>
> PARENT: [*To John.*] You know I trust you. I just need my own car; and anyway, it isn't that I don't trust you. It's just that I'm afraid it'll get wrecked.
>
> PARENT: [*To Bill.*] I trust you. And I am trying to help you. I am just simply trying to help you do better in school. Don't you understand that?

The parent is in a spot. She has lost sight of her goal. Instead of talking about her dissatisfaction with her son (or daughter), she's reassuring him. She finds herself agreeing with him; trust is one of his basic human rights. Her attempt to set limits has been undermined.

There is one main reason why the trust trap is so inviting: No one wants to be regarded as distrustful or suspicious. Each parent wants to see himself as a trusting person. The words "love" and "trust" often are used synonymously. Trustworthiness often is assumed to be a quality that is earned by virtue of intimacy, not action. In the mainstream of our culture, parental love is usually guaranteed "no matter what." The parent may disapprove or punish his child's actions, but her love remains. The teenager often argues that he must be regarded as innocent (trusted) until proven guilty—that's the law of the land. And a dented fender on the family car, a messed-up living room, and the depletion of a liquor cabinet after a teenage party are hardly proof of guilt, except in a minor, circumstantial way. Therefore, to the teenager, a person who has broken a house or family rule may have to be punished, but he still should be trusted. Trust should not be questioned until every other way of settling problems has been tried. It's the last bastion. When trust is gone, care is gone and the relationship is over.

The problem here is that this argument leaves learning out of the development of trustworthiness. It is as though trust springs forth, fully developed, when the teenager demands more responsibility, as preposterous a notion as expecting a newborn to be able to read. Learning, of course, does play a major role in the development of trustworthiness. An adult can be expected to be trustworthy in the areas the teenager is testing. He has had the benefit of experience. He has learned. The youth is still learning.

When a child is learning responsibility, having a parent who simply gives him the message, "I trust you," can result in a state of confusion that leads the child to make a test case out of every new situation. "You trust me," he reasons, "but I don't know what is expected of me. So I'll find out by trying different things." If the parent remains trusting and does not present her child with the negative consequences of negative actions, her child will not learn responsibility; he will remain at the stage of experimentation. He will use trial and error to determine the consequence of each situation that tempts him to act irresponsibly. The role of the teacher, be she parent, teacher, counselor, or friend, is to show the teenager that being responsible or trustworthy is a desirable quality, by giving praise and validation to him for responsible acts. She can reward such acts with positive consequences, such as material rewards or promotions to more responsible (and independent) positions; by giving permission for greater freedom of action; or by granting greater power to make independent decisions. The teacher must show her student that failing to be responsible or trustworthy also has consequences—negative ones. She will disapprove of irresponsibility, withdraw privileges, lessen freedom, and, finally, if all else fails, involve outside authorities.

The role of the student is usually to test the adult. That is his way of learning responsibility and trust. He wants to be respected by his teachers, and he wants to be free of them to make his own decisions. He also wants to experiment with forbidden areas. He doesn't want to follow an adult's blueprint for learning about sex or alcohol or drugs. He wants to find himself, not bump into his father, every time he tries something new. Furthermore, the adolescent wants to avoid the less exciting, more arduous parts of being responsible. When he is driving, he wants to be free to play a little, either with other cars or passengers in his own car; when he is baby-sitting, he wants company, and maybe he and his friends want to explore the house they find themselves in. He needs to learn that such activities, pleasurable and harmless as they may be on each individual occasion, carry the risk of negative consequences. The more he indulges his irresponsible tendencies, the less trustworthy he will be in the eyes of his teachers.

A parent, counselor, teacher, or friend who takes the view that trust is a quality that grows and diminishes as a relationship develops, and that responsibility must be taught, will not fall into the trust trap. The accusation that she is suspicious and untrusting will not upset her because she will know that she is doing her job: teaching responsibility. Her conversation with her teenager may go like this:

MARY: You want to talk to Joe's folks just because we're going to stay at their place on an overnight? Gosh, it's like we were still in grammar school. Don't you trust Joe and me? What do you have to talk to them for?

PARENT: The last time you and Joe stayed there, we thought his parents knew all about it and they'd be there also. That was a mistake. I don't want to go into all that; we've been over it already. But I'm not going to make that mistake again. That is why this time I'm not assuming anything. I'm going to call his folks and find out what the deal is, that's all.

MARY: Why can't you just trust us?

PARENT: I have no reason to trust you. I like Joe and I love you, but the last time we tried this, both of you got into trouble. We'll have to work up to trust in that situation slowly until I feel I really can trust you. And that can only be when I don't have any question in my mind about your ability to handle the situation. I do trust you to do a lot of other things by yourself and very responsibly, you know that.

MARY: Then why can't you trust me in this one?

PARENT: I just explained it to you. I don't want to say any more about it. If you keep pushing me, I'll just have to say, either I talk to Joe's parents, or you don't go on the overnight.

In this conversation, a parent discusses trust explicitly. She makes principles clear and disengages from the trust trap. (She points out that there is trust between them in many ways, but, in this case, she needs more information). Finally, she states her alternatives clearly and definitely. Her primary objective is not to be seen as a gentle, loving, wonderful parent, but rather to be a clear, consistent teacher of responsibility. In many such conversations, the basic process remains the same and there is no need to go into such detail. The situation becomes clearer sooner. The child doesn't push; the parent doesn't explain:

JOE: You don't even trust me enough to let me drive the car Saturday night. I can't believe it!

PARENT: Well, here's how I feel. It's my car and I need to be absolutely sure you can take responsibility for it. I'll let you continue to drive it to school for the next month. If that works out all right, you can have it every once in awhile to go out on a weekend night.

JOE: I don't think it's fair. [*Mumbles other complaining language as he leaves.*]

Here is an example where the child continues to push but the parent avoids the issue without much explanation. (The problem with explanations is that parents tend to lose ground once they start!)

BILL: Your idea of making me sit down to do my homework every day at the same time is ridiculous. I said I was going to improve my grades. You have to trust me enough to let me figure out how to do it myself.

PARENT: We already tried that. You know it didn't work.

BILL: Yeah, but that was because I didn't get any of the classes I wanted and I was late registering and . . .

PARENT: [*Breaking in.*] Let's not go over it. It just didn't work. I want to try another way of bringing your grades up. I don't want to use up more time trying a way that didn't work.

BILL: Well, you can't make me do it.

PARENT: It's true. I can't make you do it. But I'm telling you that for every day that you're not doing you homework right after dinner, your allowance gets decreased by $1.00.

In the last three examples, the parent is firm, clear, and consistent. She has demonstrated her firmness and consistency in enough other situations for the teenager to know that there is no point in arguing any further. This is perhaps the most important part of the power struggle we are considering: that the parent means what she says. She not only has to make a clear statement, she has to be able to back it up with equally clear actions. (No talk with Joe's parents, then no overnight. No car, except for transportation to school. A dollar less allowance for every infraction of the homework rule.) These struggles offer little opportunity for the parent to show herself in her kindest, most appealing light. They do offer an opportunity for her to earn the respect of her adolescent child by showing him that she means what she says, that she can't be conned or talked out of a position she considers serious, that she is prepared to risk her child's dislike in order to teach him responsibility.

So far, our examples have dealt with parent–child conflicts about trust and responsibility. The counselor or house manager at a youth service frequently encounters identical struggles. The teenager often assumes that a house parent at a youth facility or a counselor will be different from his parents. He's a youth counselor; naturally, he'll be on his side. The counselor or house manager may experience some pressure from within himself, as well, to be different from the way the teenager describes his parents. After all, something has gone pretty wrong between the teenager and his parents, or he wouldn't be there. The counselor may think he is still young enough to be different, better for the kid, not so uptight. He knows what's happening. He can give the teenager the understanding he never got from his parents.

That may be true, and yet, these thoughts will lead the counselor straight into the trust trap. The teenager will be experimenting with discipline in the counseling setting, just as he did at home. Frequently, he will say things like: "What? I have to be back at the house at 10:00? That's ridiculous. I thought this place was different. You guys don't trust us at all, do you? This is just another juvie. Guess I'll just have to go back to the streets, that's all."

He is shaming the counselor. The counselor is in the same spot as a parent. He wants to be the good guy, but if he wants to be effective, he needs to be firm and consistent, in a friendly way, if possible; if not, he may have to sound distant, even cold. He has to be a person who sets limits, knowing that he may not be liked for it.

Frequently, the counselor is afraid that a teenager may run away. He reasons that it may be better to let the teenager break a small rule than to expose him to the street culture again. It's a hard decision to make. The counselor's position is, once more, analogous to that of the parent who has to make his stand without guarantees that the immediate results will be what he wants them to be. The counselor must be able to demonstrate that he cannot be conned.

Our discussion leads to one emphatic conclusion: Nice guys finish last. As we develop our techniques for dealing with the thorny issues that accompany the adolescent's growth to responsible adulthood, we must risk being disliked, even hated for a time, if we are to be effective. The paradox is that the villain is really the hero of our process, whereas the parent or teacher who "can't say no" obviously fails to help his experimenting teenager learn responsible behavior.

Suggested Readings

Conger, John. *Adolescence: Generation Under Pressure.* Life-Cycle Series. New York: Harper & Row, 1980.

Erikson, Erik. *Childhood and Society.* New York: W. W. Norton, 1963.

Haley, J. *Strategies of Psychotherapy.* New York: Grune and Stratton, 1963.

Haley, J. *Uncommon Therapy: The Technique of Milton Erickson, M.D.* New York: W. W. Norton, 1973.

Haley, J., and Madanes, Cloe. *Leaving Home: Therapy with Disturbed Young People.* New York: McGraw-Hill, 1980.

Leveton, Alan. The art of shamesmanship. *British Journal of Medical Psychotherapy, 35,* 101–111, 1962.

Leveton, Alan. Family therapy as play: The contribution of Milton H. Erickson, M.D. In Jeffrey K. Zeig (Ed.), *Ericksonian Approaches to Hypnosis and Psychotherapy.* New York: Brunner-Mazel, 1982.

Leveton, A., and Leveton, E. Candy. In A. Leveton and E. Leveton (Eds.), Children in trouble, family in crisis. A series of 5 training films demonstrating a family counseling alternative. University of California at Davis, Administration of Criminal Justice, 1975.

Minuchin, Salvador. *Families and Family Therapy.* Cambridge, MA.: Harvard University Press, 1974.

Palazzoli, M. Selvini, Cecchin, G., Prata, G., and Boscola, L. *Paradox and Counter-Paradox.* New York: Jason Aronson, 1978.

Rabichow, Helen G., and Sklansky, Morris, A. *Effective Counseling of Adolescents.* Chicago: Follett, 1980.

Rabkin, R. *Strategic Psychotherapy.* New York: Basic Books, 1977.

Redl, F. *The Aggressive Child.* New York: The Free Press, 1957.

Winnicott, D. W. *Therapeutic Consultations in Child Psychiatry.* New York: Basic Books. 1971.

11

Power Struggles among Parents, Teachers, and School: Three Case Studies

In high school, the teacher or counselor often stands on the threshold that divides a youth from the beginnings of an independent life. The teenager who has not completed successfully his struggles to become independent often manifests his difficulties at school. As the family struggles to get him to attend school or find ways of helping him to succeed, other aspects of his problems in growing up usually emerge. Problems in school attendance often give the family a chance to retrace its steps and complete a stage of growth that has been neglected.

Let us begin by looking at three different families struggling with teenagers who are unwilling to attend school. Each family is at an impasse. The parents make threatening statements; the child shows his power by refusing to do what they ask. Counseling reveals some similarities in the process of these families; it also demonstrates their differences.

Kent: "We're going to make you go to school."

Kent and his parents have very little contact except for their fighting. When Steven, his counselor, asked for consultation, the entire third session with the family had been spent in repetitive and circular arguments about school. Kent wanted to return home. The parents were agreed that he could live at home only if he attended school. Kent said no. The real impasse occurred when the parents stated that they would force him to go to school and Kent answered that no one could force him to do anything. During consultation, the counselor asked, "*Can* parents force a kid to go to school?" His question raised several issues central to the struggles of teenagers and their families.

The consultation group discussed relevant facts about Kent's actual rights in the situation. He was 16 years old. California law requires a minor to attend school until he is 18 years old. The parents probably had some rights, but so did Kent. The group realized quickly, however, that the main difficulty was not legal in nature. The parents had not come to a probation department for help with a recalcitrant teenager. They, in fact, had not initiated any action, despite the fact that they knew the law was on their side. It was Kent who had run away from home and had gotten the family into counseling at Youth Service. Further, Kent's parents seemed to be hoping the counseling sessions would help them avoid the legal process. Clearly, there was something getting in the way of the family dealing with this problem that the law could not solve.

After hearing the counselor describe his last sessions with Kent's family, the consultation group first asked him to address himself to this basic question: "How did this struggle between Kent and his parents develop?" In order to answer this and make sense of Kent's case, the counselor must understand something about normal development, both for parents and for children of Kent's age. Let us, then, pause for a moment and review some of the normal growth processes that Kent and his parents can be expected to have completed by the time he is a teenager.

1. *The parents control through actions.* When Kent was still a little boy, his parents—like all parents of small children—knew that they had to make him do all kinds of things. And they could. They had to pull him out of the way of cars; they had to scream "hot" when he came near an iron or a stove; and, when he refused to leave his friends at the beach, they had to force him to come home by lifting him up off the ground and carrying him, kicking and yelling, back to the car. Like all parents, they got their first clear ideas about parenting from being responsible for a small, irresponsible child. Kent began to learn not only what things he could do and not do, but also who his parents were in terms of the

strength of their conviction, the firm touch of their arms holding him, the pain of a few early spankings, the ease of getting close and cuddly with them again. He learned to predict situations that would cause them to act in a restraining or punitive way, and he learned to avoid these situations.

2. *The parents control by talking (or yelling).* When Kent was small, his parents had to be alert, vigilant, ready to move in to support or protect their toddler who was learning to investigate and master the world. Initially, their words had little meaning and were used mostly to accompany parental action: "No!" "Come here!" "Don't touch that!" "Stop!" "Wait 'til mommy gets there!"

Slowly, Kent and his parents developed a vocabulary that allowed more and more freedom of action. The parents could talk things over with Kent when he was a toddler of three and four, before a disaster occurred, before action became necessary. "We're going to the drugstore. Don't touch anything. Just look, or we'll have to leave." "We're going to Johnny's house. You know his cat, Furry? Don't grab her; she might scratch; she's a little scared of children." "Don't touch, don't grab, don't eat the daisies," as Jean Kerr so aptly said. As Kent grew, he learned to understand what his parents and teachers expected of him. They needed to repeat less and less. Slowly, he developed into a person who made responsible choices. Slowly, his parents became aware that they no longer controlled this child in the way they once did. Kent had no difficulty understanding words. At this stage, his parents continued to be proud of him and of their own parenting skills.

3. *Parental guidance replaces parental control.* As Kent grew, his parents gave him more responsibility. He could play with the neighborhood kids, walk to school, take a paper route, and so on. When he was eight, his parents had some anxious moments after he had gone off to summer camp for the first time. He seemed to enjoy it, however, and his parents were proud of his excellent adjustment to this new situation. Kent was easy to raise. Before he reached his teens, most of the struggles between him and his parents were minor. He didn't talk much at home, but then, what was there to talk about? Things were going smoothly enough. Everything seemed to be okay. Here, Kent's parents were running into a little trouble without knowing it. They were missing out on a bit of insurance, just in case trouble might occur sometime along the way. They were not developing a foundation of verbal openness and trust. Further, they were lulling themselves into a mis-

taken belief. They didn't know that they no longer could control Kent. They believed that, if anything went wrong, they'd just go back to the ways they used when Kent was younger. They'd force him to do the right thing. It had always worked when he was younger.

By the time any child has reached adolescence, his parents need to have learned to relate to him almost entirely through words. Actions, even when explained by words, are experienced as belittling by the child who teeters on the edge of adulthood. It is no accident that the mother who tries to force galoshes on her teenage child on a rainy morning has been the subject of much satirical writing. Adolescence, and especially late adolescence, is a time during which the child's experience is intensely, sometimes overwhelmingly, affected by the processes of his physical growth. He is getting taller, stronger, more sexually attractive. He can feel his growth throughout his body. If he isn't growing as fast as his peers, physical growth also is likely to be his major concern. He isn't tall, strong, or attractive enough. Will he ever be? Both the rapidly growing and the slowly growing teenager are very sensitive to their status in the world of adults. They know that they are almost there, almost adults. They are sensitive to slights. They know that they are not yet fully adult but, at the same time, they are not children, and woe to the adult who treats them as such! The teenager is likely to resent almost any interference with his freedom of action. He resents verbal limit-setting. Attempts to influence him by taking action often result in rage. What can a parent do? Influencing the behavior of a teenage child is a subtle and delicate issue for all parents.

Kent's parents, even though they saw him become more and more responsible and independent, never quite relinquished the idea that they could "make him" do what needed to be done. They still were threatening him much the same way they had threatened when he was a toddler. "You can't do that. You don't know what's good for you. We do. We'll see to it that you do what *we* want." Knowing what they felt made Kent furious. They seemed not to realize that he was growing up. His thoughts were along these lines: They thought they could make him, did they? He knew they couldn't. He wasn't enjoying school at all. He didn't see why he should go. You didn't learn anything that mattered anyway. He knew he didn't want to go to school, and he knew something even more important, something his parents didn't know. No one could make him do anything he didn't want to do. He knew they could punish him. They could even kick him out. They could do whatever they could think of doing to make him go. But in the end, it would be up to him to decide. He was his own person, after all. So they thought they could make him go to school? Let them try.

Let's have a look at the family during one of their first counseling sessions. Kent was a tall, broad-shouldered 16-year-old who appeared older than his age. He had a quiet manner, said little unless asked a question directly, and sometimes betrayed stubbornness by thrusting out his chin and folding his arms over his chest while his parents challenged him. Father was a construction worker—burly, tanned, an older version of his son, and obviously out of place at the counseling center. His manner was a trifle embarrassed, sheepish; he often looked to his wife to answer a question for him. Mother was a former schoolteacher, a small, busy woman, neatly dressed, and, in contrast to her husband and son, quick to respond in an easy, social manner, in her attempt to provide a more pleasant framework for difficult conversations. Both parents were in their mid forties. Mother had not worked since Kent was born.

During the third counseling session, Kent began the conversation that, by now, had become so familiar. In the previous session, he had been asked to think of a school program he might enjoy, but he came up with nothing. Instead he repeated the old litany. He did not want to go to school, this one or any other. He would be his own man. He no longer needed school to plan his time for him. Couldn't his parents see that he was ready to be on his own? Hadn't he run away for as much as one week and proved that he would come to no harm? His parents, of course, stressed that he had returned, that he was unprepared for any career, that he was not old enough to take charge of himself, especially since they were still liable for him legally.

The game continued. The more Kent refused to go to school, the more the parents threatened to force him. Neither side listened to the other as argument after argument followed its predictably circular path. The counselor felt a sense of helplessness as he saw the family continue to repeat the same clichés. Kent should go to school for his own good. The parents were too old to understand. Kent would understand later. There was no point in talking.

Father wanted Kent to have more of a chance than he'd had himself. Mother wanted Kent to understand the meaning of sacrificing her life as a teacher. Kent could not see the relevance of his parents' life to his own. He remained intransigent. The parents, at the end of their rope, once more threatened to force him to attend school.

The counselor could empathize more readily with Kent than with his parents. They seemed to be listening only to each other without seeing their son's dilemma. The counselor also experienced a slight sense of embarrassment in relation to the father's awkwardness in this situation. It was impossible to find a way to put him at his ease, it seemed. Yet the counselor knew that, without becoming more comfortable, Dad could hardly be expected to participate in the counseling in any genuine way. Kent also seemed awkward. He avoided his parents' glances. In some ways, he seemed to have left home already. Didn't these parents know that they had to talk *with* their kid if they wanted to remain in any contact with him at all? How could any of them stand the dry, rote quality of their interaction?

The counselor asked the consultation group for help, and they explored several strategies. The counselor wanted to help the parents get a picture of the discrepancy between what they thought they could do and what actually was possible, but, before any meaningful conversation could take place, Steven had to get the family away from the present impasse. So, the first strategy was to lead them into a remembrance of another time—the time before Kent had been in trouble. This technique had the effect of making the family feel better—they had forgotten that they ever did anything right. Perhaps equally important, as they talked, the counselor found himself developing a liking for Kent's parents. For the first time, he really wanted to help these people.

COUNSELOR: We've been talking about where we're stuck for some time now, kind of going around in circles; school, home, no school. We don't seem to be getting anywhere. Let's try another way. Things haven't always been this hard for the three of you. Who can remember a good time? A time when the three of you could get together and enjoy each other?

MOM: Oh, I don't know. . . . I really hate to think that . . . but we have been having a really hard time for so long that . . .

COUNSELOR: That's what I was thinking, too. That's why I'm asking you. Take your time. I don't care how far back you have to go. I just know there's got to have been some time or other that was better than this.

MOM: Oh, well, of course, I enjoyed teaching school, but you mean with the family.

COUNSELOR: Yes. You really can all just think back for minute without talking. It's not all up to you, Mom. Give the others a chance. [*There is a short silence, during which Steven nods and smiles encouragingly to the family, indicating that it's all right to take their time.*]

DAD: You sure do come up with some hard questions. [*Another pause, during which the family members start to look tentatively at one another.*] Oh, wait a minute! How about the time when Kent was in the seventh-grade play?

KENT: No, come on; not that! [*Looking very pleased but a little embarrassed as well.*]

MOM: What are you talking about?

DAD: You know, when they did that Robin Hood and Kent and I ended up doing all that work to make the sound-track? We had all those animal noises in the forest and that?

MOM: Oh, yes, I seem to recall. Weren't you in the seventh grade, Kent?

KENT: Yeah. [*It's clear that he doesn't know how to relate to these two friendly people.*]

COUNSELOR: Do you remember that time, Kent? What do you remember?

KENT: Well, my dad and I recorded all this stuff off the TV. [*He smiles a shy smile.*] The animal noises, like Dad said, and some music, too.

COUNSELOR: How was that for you?

KENT: Different. I mean from now. I'd forgot we ever did that.

MOM: Well, I sure had!

The counselor needed to do very little. The magic of remembering did its work. As the family recalled the Robin Hood Pageant

Kent's seventh grade put on for the school, their behavior was transformed by their happy memories. They talked *with* each other. There was a unity of purpose about the conversation that had been lacking in the past counseling sessions. The counselor began to understand Kent's parents in a new way. He got a sense of the pleasure they had felt parenting a younger Kent, a child who needed them and naturally included them in his activities. Instead of helpless frustration, the parents clearly experienced a sense of satisfaction and success. No wonder they wanted to stay at this earlier stage of development.

The counselor knew, however, that exploring the past wasn't enough. He knew that, if he did not help the family make a bridge to the present, the experience would remain unintegrated, an isolated moment of reminiscence in a miserable life. These parents had been unable to accomplish a step in their growth as parents. Helping them to learn to parent their adolescent was one of the counselor's main objectives. The reminiscence had been the first step. Negative rigidity had been replaced by a shy, halting exploration of something new. Instead of speaking in rigid, monotonous dialogues in which the parents constantly vied for the one-up position with their son, there had been an exchange among equals, a regular conversation. To help consolidate these gains and aid the family in integrating the experience, the counselor explored the differences between the past and the present with the parents. Using this second strategy, he could point out the impossibility of physical control over Kent and lead the parents to see that their trump card was worthless. Having helped the family to explore pleasant memories, the counselor's second strategy was to use the mood that had been created as a bridge to the present:

COUNSELOR: What a good time that was for all of you! That's the first time I knew you were interested in tape recorders, Dad. It's really nice for me to get to know this part of you. Could we do one more thing with this? Remembering the mood in the family when Kent was in the seventh grade, could you each make some "then and now" statements? Like, "Then we could work on tape-recording together; now we don't seem to work on any common project." Does that fit, Kent?

KENT: Yes.

COUNSELOR: Why don't you start with that one or something like it, in your own words?

KENT: We used to do stuff then, and now we just argue. [*He looks sad.*]

COUNSELOR: And that makes me feel———?

KENT: Kind of sad, I guess.

COUNSELOR: Mom?

MOM: Then we felt like a family; now we don't. [*Cries.*]

DAD: If we could just get some cooperation from Kent, it would be different. [*He's getting harsh; apparently wants to keep Mom from crying by distracting her with an argument with Kent.*]

COUNSELOR: What did you see on your wife's face?

DAD: Sadness. I feel so darn bad when she cries.

COUNSELOR: Tell her.

DAD: I feel bad for you.

MOM: I know.

COUNSELOR: Wouldn't this be a true statement? "We used to be able to cooperate, and now we can't."

DAD: Yes. We used to be able to cooperate, and now we can't. But I can't see how any of these kids want to cooperate any more, anyway.

KENT: God, Dad, what do you want?

COUNSELOR: [*Realizing the family is heading back toward the old familiar ground of the hopeless impasse.*] Is there any part of you, Kent, that misses that time when you guys could do things together?

KENT: Yeah, but not all the time.

COUNSELOR: Of course, not all the time. You're growing up. Does it seem like if you admitted liking spending any time with them or enjoying doing things together, you'd have to do it all the time? Give an inch and they'll take a mile?

KENT: I guess. Yeah. Because we used to do so much together and that was okay then, but. . . . Anyway, I think she ought to go back to teaching.

COUNSELOR: [*This is a turn he had not expected.*] You've been thinking your mom should go back to teaching? How come? Why don't you talk to her about that?

KENT: Well, gee, you always talk about how great it was, and you really dig all that stuff . . .

COUNSELOR: [*Finishing his sentence.*] . . . and if I knew you were doing your own thing, it'd be easier to be around you?

KENT: It sure would.

MOM: I know you think that. Both of you. [*Now she looks a little sheepish.*] You don't say much, but I get the idea. And I've thought about it, but with all the trouble we're having, sometimes I think I can't leave. There's got to be something more I can do, and sometimes I'm so upset and exhausted I can't even think about working.

COUNSELOR: So, I can understand why that's hard for you, Kent. Seems like your mom is staying home because of you. I'm glad you brought that up; it's something we'll have to talk more about. For right now, I want to hear something from you, Dad. Mom said you want her to go back to teaching school also?

DAD: [*Slowly, looking at his wife with care and some apprehension.*] Yeah. Yeah, I think she'd be happier. But I don't want to pressure her.

COUNSELOR: Okay. I still want to finish the task we started on, but we'll come back to Mom's work later. Okay? So, now, let's go back to the "then and now" statements. Dad, could you say again, "Then we used to be able to cooperate, and now we can't"?

DAD: Okay. Then we used to be able to cooperate, and now we can't. You're still talking about us and that play, right?

COUNSELOR: Right. Anything to add to that?

KENT: I have something. Then isn't now.

COUNSELOR: Any particular way?

KENT: Well, it's not that I don't want to, but I have different friends now.

COUNSELOR: And that makes it harder to cooperate?

KENT: Yeah, well . . . I live differently; you know what I mean.

MOM: But how can we get along? I know something. Then we felt like a family, and now we feel like enemies with our son.

COUNSELOR: Maybe we can learn a new way to cooperate that fits for now.

The counselor had prepared the way for an important new strategy. He wanted the parents to comprehend that they no longer could control Kent in the way they once did. They were ready to do some work in this area. They were in touch with their difficulties with Kent, but they were not feeling defensive in the way they had. The family was experiencing sadness and a longing for a time when they functioned successfully as a family. They were ready to start developing realistic expectations.

COUNSELOR: [*Knowing the lesson he wants the parents to learn.*] Kent, is Mom right? You used to do what they told you?

KENT: Yeah, some. They can't tell me what to do anymore, I guess. They just can't. But . . . well, God, I was little, then. That was different.

MOM: It's just so hard to believe. I know it's true, but I don't want to believe it. I know I believe it more than he does. [*Looking at her husband.*]

DAD: That's a tough one all right. Seemed like my parents could make us do what they wanted.

COUNSELOR: Really? [*Smiling a skeptical smile.*]

DAD: [*After a short pause.*] Well, we got away with a few things, but not like these kids.

COUNSELOR: But you got away with some things?

DAD: Yeah.

COUNSELOR: Say it again, Kent.

KENT: Okay. You can't make me do anything I don't want to do.

COUNSELOR: [*Looking at parents.*] Is he right? [*The parents nod in reluctant agreement.*]

MOM: I'm just so afraid you'll botch it up for yourself.

COUNSELOR: [*Speaking for her.*] And I can't *make* you do it right.

MOM: [*Sighing.*] And I can't *make* you do it right.

COUNSELOR: Dad?

DAD: Oh, oh, that's a tough one, that is.

COUNSELOR: I *will* make you do what I think is right——?

DAD: Well, I'd sure like to. I'd sure like to.

COUNSELOR: *Can I?*
DAD: Well, I'm not scoring too high right now, I'll have to admit that.
COUNSELOR: Tell him again, Kent.
KENT: You can't make me, Dad.
DAD: I guess you're right, at that. [*Dad looks at the counselor, puzzled.*]

By using the strategies of remembrance of the past and comparison to the present, the family had found their way out of the impasse. The parents had begun to develop an awareness of the inappropriateness of their expectations. Kent felt closer to them. He recalled some of the better times, and he saw their good intentions. He could allow himself to feel more friendly toward his parents. Finally, the counselor had helped the parents to begin to be more realistic about their ability to control Kent's actions.

Awareness prepares the way for change, but it seldom provides the entire impetus for it. The parents remembered a better time, but the present remained tinged with helplessness and frustration for them. The family, as they talked, became more available to each other and to the counselor. The main feeling in the room, however, was one of discouragement. The counselor already knew that this discouragement was not entirely attributable to the difficulties with Kent. Mom apparently had missed her work and, at the same time, had been unable to return to it. The counselor set out to find out more about the parents' past.

In the next session, the counselor learned that Kent's father had had a miserable childhood dominated by a tyrannical father who expected complete obedience under threat of punishment. He had feared his father, and, in fact, got away with very few infractions of the rules. He remembered sneaking out of the house with some friends one night after hours and being so nervous that he had broken out in a rash. He had lied to his father about anything that he thought might upset him. He didn't want that kind of relationship with his own son. When he had succeeded in becoming his son's friend in his younger years, he had felt reassured. But, lacking a model for adult communication with a growing son, he could think of nothing except force—the same force that his father had used—to control Kent. Kent's mother had tried to placate both Kent and his father, explaining to each that the other meant well. She, too, felt her efforts were futile.

In order to help counteract the sense of sadness and futility experienced by Kent's parents, the counselor set out to help the family to plan a family strategy for coping with their difficulties.

The counselor knew that, if the relationship between Kent and his parents was to change in a positive direction, he would have to help the family recapture their capacity to relate in a warm, friendly manner. The parents had become so involved in fighting with Kent that, in his eyes, they had attained an undifferentiated image. They were "the enemy" instead of "Mom" with her good and bad characteristics and "Dad" with his. Kent had lost contact with the real people behind the angry parental masks that faced him each day. Similarly, the parents had lost sight of Kent, the person, part child, part adult, and replaced him with Kent, the bad boy, who needed control. The counselor used the information about Kent's and Dad's common interest in sound systems to build a bridge to the reestablishment of friendly relations between the two.

COUNSELOR: So, back to the two of you working on a soundtrack together. Wow, I'm still impressed with that. Are you still interested in sound, Kent?

KENT: Yeah, taping records and stuff like that.

COUNSELOR: [*To father.*] Did you know that?

FATHER: No. . . . Well, sort of, but I don't know much about any of that stuff.

COUNSELOR: Are you still interested in working with Kent in this area?

FATHER: I guess.

COUNSELOR: Kent, is that a possibility for you?

KENT: Sure, but I just don't think Dad's interested in the same kind of music I am.

COUNSELOR: OK. Here's what I want you to do. I want each of you to think of a simple project you could do together. Something you could use some help on. Think of it now, and when you've figured it out, I'll give you a piece of paper to write it on. Then give the piece of paper to me. Mom, we're going to leave you out of this one. Your turn will come later. Okay so far? [*Steven wants to strengthen the alliance between Kent and his father. In order to accomplish this, he attempts to keep Mom from interfering by commenting.*]

KENT: I guess.

FATHER: Yeah, I guess so.

MOM: [*A little worried.*] I sure hope it works out.

COUNSELOR: Well, you're the one person who doesn't have to worry about that. [*He realizes that his comment could be received by her as rejection and decides to give her something to do as well.*] As a matter of fact, let's give you something to think of also. Why don't you think of something to do for yourself, just for yourself, not with the family—and write it down. Something simple, but something you've wanted to do. Okay?

MOM: [*After a pause.*] Okay.

COUNSELOR: [*After allowing five minutes and collecting the slips of paper.*] Okay, now I want to see you follow through and get those things done before I see you next week. I want some action. Remember, you and Dad aren't to tell Mom what you're doing together. And Mom, yours is a secret also, okay?

With this move, the counselor broke up the parental coalition and sought to establish a friendship between Kent and Dad, while rewarding Mom for not interfering. The next week, the counselor found out that the technique was, in fact, successful. Kent had asked Dad to help him make tapes of some favorite records, using Dad's expensive equipment. Dad had agreed and supervised the project. Dad, who couldn't think of a "sound" project, asked Kent to help him with some carpentry, which he did. Mom went out for an evening at a good friend's house to play bridge. All reported their achievements with considerable pride.

The counselor had helped the family to learn to make new coalitions with each other. He had praised Dad for his interest in sound and given support to both him and Kent for working together. He had supported Mom by giving her the message that she was important, too, and suggesting that she do something for herself. When he collected the slips of paper on which each family member had written a task, he was making an unspoken bond between each of them and himself. His strategy paid off. The family was beginning to change. Through the next few months, he would assign further tasks to the family in an effort to build a backlog of positive experiences.

The counselor had done the groundwork that prepared the family for cooperation and success. He had taken charge of the sessions from the beginning. The family had learned to accept his authoritative guidance as a stimulus for doing their own work. He had won the first power struggle without difficulty; he had not joined the family in their fruitless battle about Kent's school attendance. Before assigning any tasks, the counselor had helped the family members to rebuild the necessary confidence to try again.

The counselor had succeeded because he chose tasks that the family knew how to do and because he knew they were ready to do them, or at least believed they were. Success, of course, was not guaranteed, and he was prepared for that. Had the family failed to accomplish the task, they would have needed to explore further their fears, their feelings of helplessness, and their reluctance to begin to hope again. The counselor was ready to coach the family in some father–son activities in the office, if necessary, to prepare for the next project. Once the family accepts an assigned task, a major goal has been accomplished. Little doubt remains about each person's wish to work on change. Failure to accomplish an assigned task spells a delay, rather than failure of the strategy. The counselor's ability to cope with such a failure will provide modeling for the easily discouraged parent.

The family had become more at ease. They talked more easily. Dad no longer was awkward; his slow and thoughtful manner had become relaxed. Each family member was experiencing hope. The parents had relinquished their hopes of controlling Kent's behavior and replaced them with prospects of disciplining him. The counselor knew that he would have to teach the parents new methods that transformed the power struggle between them and their son from an unrealistic, fruitless battle to one in which the stakes were real and neither side was without power. Disciplining meant parental action designed to teach Kent that negative behavior would be followed by negative consequences. The parents would have to come to an agreement about what they considered negative behavior—not a difficult task—and also decide on what the negative consequences would be, as well as how far they were prepared to go to enforce them. The parents had no guarantee of success, but, even if they failed, their message would be clear: They did not want to help Kent act in a way they believed to be harmful, by standing by helplessly. Earlier in the session, the counselor had been concerned about the parents' united front. It seemed that they had formed an unsuccessful but unbreakable coalition against Kent, who felt that no one was on his side. Since the family had done well when an activity for Kent and his father was assigned, the counselor decided that he would continue to help the family to plan more activities that would involve Kent with one of his parents, hoping to continue to break up the parental coalition that had been so unsuccessful.

The counselor already had noted that, together, the parents were getting nowhere in their attempts to discipline Kent. He therefore decided that his next strategy would be to encourage them to split up the job of parenting Kent, each negotiating with him separately at different times.

COUNSELOR: Two against one hasn't seemed fair a lot of times; isn't that what you were saying earlier, Kent?

KENT: Right on!

COUNSELOR: [*To parents.*] How would it be if you split the job of parenting? You would each take a different area, or you could alternate. Dad one week, Mom one week, something like that. What do you think?

DAD: I don't know; it might be a good idea.

MOM: I wouldn't know where to begin.

COUNSELOR: Well, what areas are there?

MOM: There's school—no, let me say school first, that's the hard one, then chores. Sometimes Kent wants more freedom socially, but that hasn't been such a big deal.

COUNSELOR: Ask Dad if he agrees.

MOM: Do you?

DAD: Yeah, I'd put it the same way.

COUNSELOR: What would you prefer, dividing the areas or alternating times, or both?

DAD: I think I'd rather do areas; how about you?

MOM: Me too. I'd like you to do school. I'm up to here with that myself.

DAD: Well, I don't know. It's worth a try, I guess. Would you do the other two, then? Chores and social, I think you said?

MOM: I could try.

COUNSELOR: Terrific! Okay, now let's talk in more detail about how to go about this.

Kent's parents had negotiated a contract that would change radically the way they parented him. Kent no longer would deal with a united front. To the extent that each parent's messages were clear and consistent, there would be less tension in the conversations about discipline. Kent would be able to complete a transaction with one parent, rather than hovering somewhere between two rather frustrated, helpless individuals. Each parent would be able to talk to Kent without experiencing the burden of the other's pain, a problem they had raised often before. "It's hard enough between me and Kent," Mom had said, "but when I see you get so upset, something just cracks inside me."

In order to promote the productiveness of this phase, the counselor asked the parents to commit themselves to one other requirement: noninterference. If disturbed by what Dad did about Kent's schooling, for example, Mom was not to interfere. That meant not talking to Kent about it at all, nor challenging or undermining Dad's methods in any way. If her disagreement persisted throughout the week, she was to raise it at the next counseling session. The parents agreed. Kent commented that he liked the last part of the plan best. He'd always hated it when his parents fought with each other on his account.

In the following session, the parents brought up some of their problems with the new strategy. By and large, they had been able to accomplish their goals, but, when things got tough, it seemed that it was hard to stay out of each other's way. Kent said that he and Dad got to fighting about school and Mom had tried to break it up. Dad wore his sheepish expression again. He had not been able to tell his wife to stay out of his new territory. The counselor worked with Mom's need to help when she saw anyone in pain. Could she imagine Dad handling Kent without her help? She answered that what was really bothering her was the counselor's lack of trust in her. For the first time, she lost her pleasant, social manner and burst out in a flood of words against the counselor, saying that she felt she was just a third wheel, unnecessary to family life as far as he was concerned. The counselor remembered that he had wondered whether she'd felt rejected by him earlier and wished he'd cleared the matter up at that time. He told the mother that he could understand her feelings and that he could see that his enthusiasm for promoting the father–son interaction probably was excessive, and related to his own life as a son who wanted more closeness to his father. The frank interchange cleared the air. The counselor worked on some activities for Kent and his mother, and the family worked further on developing adequate discipline for Kent.

When the counselor saw that the parents had been giving unclear messages, he knew that he wanted to teach them how to be more successful. Kent's parents needed to learn that their actions had consequences, just as Kent's did. Each of them needed to learn what he had been doing and why these attempts had negative consequences. Steven pointed out two typical sequences of their interaction with Kent, around the issue of school. The first is called, "Kent promises not to skip school again," and goes as follows:

1. Kent promises not to skip school again.
2. Mom feels hopeful and says so.
3. Dad feels skeptical but says nothing, fearing that he will upset Mom who will blame his negative attitude for ruining the moment *and* for Kent's skipping school when he does it again.
4. Kent cuts school.
5. Both parents confront Kent in a talk that quickly ends with Mom's tears, Dad's yelling that he will make Kent go to school, and Kent's walking out, slamming the door.
6. Kent comes home late at night, sees Mom's drawn face, and promises not to skip school again.

The second sequence is called, "I won't go back to school," and goes like this:

1. Kent says he's not going back to school.
2. Both parents argue and plead with him; he counters all their arguments.
3. The parents go out to a prearranged dinner, both feeling that they are losing the battle, but not wishing to say anything for fear of making a bad evening worse.
4. When they return, Kent is not at home. He has run away.

The counselor taught the parents that, in both sequences, there was a discrepancy between feeling and doing that resulted in ignoring something important. In both instances, the major process was avoidance of parental control. In both sequences, the parents failed to make a consistent statement about their demands and the consequences that would ensue if these demands weren't met. In both sequences, the parents lose, but Kent doesn't win, either.

The counselor's last step as "coach" was to teach the parents to give clear messages in times of stress, messages that both let Kent know what was expected and what the consequences would be if he failed to meet his parent's expectations. The counselor showed the parents and Kent a more productive sequence:

1. Kent promises not to skip school again, after cutting.
2. Dad, who is in charge of the school area, tells Kent he doesn't want any promises. He wants Kent in school regularly and he will contact Kent's principal to make sure he's kept informed of any cutting. Meanwhile, Kent is grounded for a week because of today's cut.
   a. If Kent goes a week without cutting, Dad will permit him to go out on weekend nights again.
   b. If Kent cuts during the week, he will lose his allowance for a month.
   c. Further cuts will cost further privileges. Further attendance will restore privileges or gain rewards. Evaluation will be weekly.
   d. Kent goes to school the whole week.

Slowly, as the counselor worked with the family, the parents learned to state punishments without backing down. Not surprisingly, Kent reacted strongly. His parents were changing! At times, he had thought he wanted them to be stricter, but this was too much. He tested them hard, forcing them to do what they had said they would do. With the counselor's help, the parents prepared for the worst. If Kent kept testing them, they knew they would have to let him take the consequences all the way to juvenile hall, if need be. They learned that the battle was harder because they had neglected to fight it for so long. They stuck to their plan, and Kent came around. The positive experiences had reestablished some good times in the family. Kent was not ready to leave for good. Eventually, Kent decided against juvenile hall. The problem that had brought the family for counseling was resolved.

This is the ending we all hope for, but Kent's parents, Kent, and, especially, the counselor all had to be ready for a negative ending as well. Much depends on the length of time the family has spent in the downward spiral. If positive contact cannot be reestablished, the situation may not resolve happily. Parents may learn to be more and more firm, but, even though they change their pattern, their son may not be ready to change. He could continue to test their limits by escalating his antisocial behavior, ending up in juvenile hall. He might not stop at just cutting school; for example, he and his friends may get caught one day for stealing.

The counselor must be prepared for this possibility so he can help the parents to be ready for it. If the parents want to give in, or if the counselor finds himself investigating ways to help Kent avoid the consequences of his actions, chances are the whole cycle will begin again. If, with the counselor's help, the parents can express their feelings of frustration and disappointment and, at the same time, stay firm in their resolve to let Kent take the consequences of his actions, the family process will have changed. For awhile, that may not be very comforting. Kent may still get into trouble; in fact, he may get into worse trouble. Yet there is some comfort in the parents' stance: At this point, they no longer are helping Kent get into trouble. Of course, they did not think of themselves as helping their son to get in trouble before. No parent does. Their motivation, like that of most parents, was to help their boy avoid problems, not create them. Through counseling, however, they have learned that they were involved in a process that accomplished the opposite of what they wanted. They wanted to use threats to discourage Kent from skipping school, but, since Kent had learned that they would not make good on their threats, he reacted first by testing the limits set by his parents, and then by disregarding them. They learned that they had played a part in Kent's skipping school, a part they no longer wanted to play. Now they were clear about what they wanted. Perhaps he would continue to act out for a while longer, as proof that they could not make him change. That was the lesson Kent's parents needed to learn—they cannot *make* him change. All they can do is what they have learned to do: Give clear messages, enforce them with consistent behavior, and hope for the best. The rest is up to Kent.

Now let's take up the same basic issue—a child who refuses to stop skipping school and eventually runs away—and see how it takes its course in a different family with a different counselor.

Scott: "We're going to make you go to school."

Scott was well known at Grove Lane, a residential housing facility for youths, before he came to live there. He had visited some of the other kids and frequently had gotten into trouble by breaking house rules. The staff members all were in agreement that Scott seemed to do things just to get the adults mad at him. Once, when the kids had been fairly quiet, watching TV and talking, he had started throwing water balloons in the living room. Another time, he had lit a cigarette and thrown the lighted match in the wastepaper basket, starting a fire. Two weeks before the consultation, Scott had run away from home. His counselor, Terry, had seen him and his parents for two interviews.

The counselor smiled helplessly when she talked about Scott's parents and how much they sounded like the staff at Grove Lane when they talked about Scott. They just could not understand. Things seemed to be going perfectly, and then, suddenly, Scott would be in trouble: smoking in school, truanting to help a friend plant a marijuana garden, truanting and stealing some magazines. Scott's mother repeated her discouragement because Scott simply didn't seem to care; she thought he was defiant just to be defiant. Scott's father, a man of few words, talked about Scott's downward path—from breaking the rules at home, to defying the school authorities, to breaking the law. Both parents saw Scott's poor school attendance as a symbol of his failure in society. They threatened to *make* him attend school, but Scott truanted quite frequently.

Terry, a counselor with a good deal of experience in seeing families, noticed that the parents seemed to talk of little else except Scott and his misbehavior. They were rather quiet, discouraged-looking people, when they were not speaking of Scott; but, when they recounted his exploits, they became animated and energetic. Family therapists often see family interaction quite differently from how it is seen by the family members themselves. Kent's parents thought they were helping Kent to go back to school; in family counseling, they learned that they were helping him to avoid it. In Scott's family, the parents seemed to feel that their lives would be all right if it weren't for Scott. The counselor soon began to suspect that the opposite was the case, that Scott was one of the many teenagers who react to parental discouragement and depression by what seems to be a rescue operation for himself and his parents. He thinks up wild, rebellious adventures that serve a double purpose. They assure him that he is not a sad sack who has given up on life like his mother and father. At the same time, Mom and Dad are helped out in two ways: Their dull, depressed lives become dramatic and exciting, and their low self-esteem is helped by the accomplishment of coping in a crisis. Scott knows his parents verbally object to what he is doing, but he can't fail to notice what the counselor observed: When they talk about him, his parents become different people. He has found a way to transform their depressed, passive stance into an active, lively one.

The first strategy that the counselor used to help Scott's family was to separate the problems between his parents from problems each had with him. In family therapy, this sometimes is called relabeling the problems in the family, so that the identified patient, Scott, no longer is seen as the only problem.

COUNSELOR: You know, I've had a terrible time trying to get you two to talk about anything besides Scott. He's been doing a little better, thank goodness, so that gives me a chance to ask something I've really been curious about. What else is there for the two of you? What else is exciting besides that awful stuff of wondering what Scott's been up to?

MOM:	Well, I have my garden club. [*A concerned look at Dad.*]
COUNSELOR:	Is that exciting?
MOM:	Well, you might not think it, but I do. It's a lot of fun.
COUNSELOR:	How about you, Dad?
MOM:	He doesn't believe in garden clubs.
DAD:	No, I don't.
COUNSELOR:	Do you do anything like that for yourself?
MOM:	He doesn't.
DAD:	I don't. I never was the type of person with hobbies or anything like that.
COUNSELOR:	Well, I bet there's *something* that's really been exciting for you and possibly could be again, be we can get into that later. Right now, I want to know about the two of you. What do you do together besides worry about Scott?
MOM:	Well, we used to go out to dinner every once in a while.
DAD:	Not much, I guess.
COUNSELOR:	[*To Mom.*] Have you missed that—going to dinner together?
MOM:	Oh, yes!
COUNSELOR:	When's the last time you asked him for a date?
MOM:	Me, ask him?
COUNSELOR:	Why not? [*Dad is smiling. He hadn't expected this turn of the conversation. He had expected to be blamed for not having taken his wife out to dinner.*]
MOM:	Well? Would you go?
DAD:	I think it might be arranged.
COUNSELOR:	I think it's going to be arranged right now, because I'm going to assign a dinner date for the two of you as homework for next week's session.

It often is difficult for family counselors to shift the focus of attention from the teenager, who, after all, is the family's stated reason for coming for counseling, to the parents, who have not asked for help. The family counselor has to take an authoritative position in order to work on a problem the family has not mentioned. To the degree that he is inexperienced, as well as perhaps younger than the parents, he feels insecure as he makes his first move. Chances are the parents will resist him. In our culture, people seldom confess their marital discouragements to total strangers. The counselor expects to be rejected by parents who see him as rude and intrusive. Although coming for "help" is becoming more and more acceptable, it is the rare counselor or client who begins with the expectation that anything truly pleasurable should occur during, or even as an immediate result of, counseling.

The counselor's intervention is an illustration of how a counselor can address what appears to him to be serious marital difficulties in a gentle, nonthreatening way. Both parents feel supported by her manner.

Some counselors are reluctant to assign homework because the couple may not follow through. The counselor was ready for that possibility. She knew that, even if the couple reported failure, the topic of conversation would have to be their relationship, and that was her primary target. As it turned out, the parents went out to dinner and had a very good time, causing Mother to remember similar times earlier in the marriage. Then, slowly, she began to talk about an issue everyone had avoided, namely, Dad's depression.

Although both parents seemed quiet and discouraged, the counselor had suspected that it was Dad who most concerned the family. In contrast to his wife and son, his eyes never lit up. He walked slowly, with a stoop that made him look older than his age of 41. He had an air of having given up. He had said little during the sessions. The counselor had the impression that he was a proud man. She knew it was important that he talk, but was afraid to scare him away by asking too many questions.

Now the mother talked about Dad as he had been eight years before, when they had lived in a small town in the Midwest where Dad had been one of the big fish. Since they had moved to San Francisco (a move initially regarded as an honor, coming as a promotion in Dad's company), nothing had seemed to go right. He could not get along with the other people in his job. He felt smaller and smaller. His wife didn't know how to help him.

During their fourth session, the counselor listened without much comment. She wanted to assure Dad that she would not shame or pressure him. It became very clear to the counselor that the mother had felt increasingly helpless and resentful as her husband failed to accomplish the goals they both had hoped for. She was visibly relieved as she told her story, especially when, as the counselor noticed, she saw that her husband was not upset by her talk. The counselor guessed that this was a marriage founded on the myth that husbands are strong and wives weak. When the husband foundered, there had been no way for the wife to show her strength without further undermining his picture of himself. That, and her doubts about her own true capabilities, had kept her in a passive, resigned position. As his wife talked, the husband listened quietly, orchestrating her narrative with deep sighs.

In the fifth interview, the counselor was determined to have Scott's parents address what seemed to her to be the deeper, more disturbing issues in the family. She was a little apprehensive about the father. Had he felt that there had been too much talk about him, or that he was exposed in an unfavorable light? To the counselor's relief, he arrived for the fifth session a little early. She resolved that she would continue in the way she had started, proceeding slowly and continuing to give Dad and Mom as much support as possible.

The counselor was aware that Scott had been listening intently to what his mother had been saying in the previous interview. She had been watching him, partially because she knew that he was keeping an eye on his father and would let her know if something was going wrong by putting on one of his usual shows. He did not. The counselor suspected that, with a little help, Scott would be able to express his positive feelings for his parents and decided that this would be the most productive strategy for making sure that the family continued with the previous week's material and, at the same time, began to change Scott's role in the family. Thus, her second strategy was to transform Scott from villain to hero, from identified patient to rescuer.

COUNSELOR: Well, that as an important session last time. I never got a chance to ask you to comment, Scott. I could see you were really involved in what Dad and Mom were saying. Is that true?

SCOTT: Yeah. Well, you know, Dad—I mean, Mom—I mean, I *have said* that before, that I don't know why you can't be more like Joe's parents. Seems like they have all the fun.

COUNSELOR: Have you been worried about the folks, Scott?

SCOTT: It's true; they *never* have any more fun. Dad used to go out and play poker, but he doesn't even do that any more. They never go to the movies.

COUNSELOR: [*To parents.*] Did you know Scott thought about you in that way?

MOM: No. Well, yes, come to think of it, he does make suggestions that we do this or that. He does!

COUNSELOR: So that's another side of Scott. The side that's concerned about the two of you.

MOM: I guess so.

COUNSELOR: [*To Dad.*] What makes it hard to follow his advice?

DAD: Well, you know how it is, you get too busy and too tired.

The counselor's strategy paid off. Scott as rescuer appeared quite different from Scott as provocateur, troublemaker, and general nuisance. He showed how sensitive he was to his parents' problems, how eager to help. The counselor's success may seem surprising to the inexperienced family counselor, yet this particular strategy often works quickly and easily, as it did with Scott and his parents.

Most children develop an exquisite sensitivity to the problems of their parents. They know when a parent is upset, angry, or depressed. After all, children depend on parents for support and sustenance of all kinds. It is only logical that they should be on the lookout for signs that would deprive them of such support. At the same time, any child who has developed even a small degree of trust in his parents' love, in their continuing care and recognition, will respond sympathetically to their pain. His father and mother show their feelings of sympathy when he needs it. The child will experience sympathy and empathy for his parents as well. How does the child express these feelings? In a normal, well-functioning family where symptoms are few or nonexistent, the child expresses his sympathy for a suffering parent simply and clearly. The toddler brings his diaper for Mom to wipe away her tears. The eight-year-old girl sits on her mother's lap and gives her a hug. The adolescent boy asks his dad if he could go out and toss a ball with him.

Dysfunctional families make it hard for children to express their feelings for a parent in pain. Most of the time, an adult in our culture who is experiencing pain feels inadequate as well. Whatever is wrong, it shouldn't be. When life becomes painful, our view is seldom that fate has played us a dirty trick, or that we have acquired a new burden to shoulder, or that "this too will pass." Rather, we are ready to assume personal responsibility. Many of us believe that we each control our own destiny to the point that we experience every blow life deals us as a personal defeat. Success, well-being, and material wealth are important goals in our culture. When we fail to achieve these, severe feelings of inadequacy are often unavoidable. At that point, pride enters in, and a family often develops rules that, although intended to prevent pain from becoming intolerable, indirectly increase it. Scott's family is a good example. His father felt himself a failure. He gave a message that his pain was unbearable, that no one was to mention it. His family lovingly avoided him and thereby unknowingly deprived him of comfort and advice. At the same time, his son found out that both of his parents seemed less depressed when he got in trouble with the authorities. Since he also harbored a good deal of anger against these parents, whom he loved and whose existence proved more and more depressing, it was easy to develop a pattern that served both to express his hostility and divert his parents from their pain.

Even the normal teenager sometimes finds himself unable to express sympathetic feelings for his parents. The development of a parent–child relationship often is so concentrated in the obvious need for the parent to care for the child, that the parent forgets to teach the child how to take care of his parent. The rule seems to be: Parents help children; children don't help parents; parents take care of themselves.

The family counselor can make the assumption safely that a teenage child will have a great deal of concern about a suffering parent. The teenager usually has given a lot of thought to his parent's problems; he may even have discussed them at length with a sibling or friend. He is eager to share his concern about his parents, but he is at a loss to do so without upsetting them. Unless the counselor's intervention is very ill timed, helping a child to make explicit his care for his parents can hardly fail as a strategy of family counseling.

After this session, in which the family talked more about their concern with Scott, who still was not attending school regularly, the counselor felt that the family was ready to work more deeply. Dad seemed to be feeling more at ease. He still spoke few words but he joined into the conversation more spontaneously. The family appeared more relaxed. The counselor felt reasonably certain that she could address Dad's depression directly without losing the family. Her third strategy, then, was to bring the deeper problems into awareness.

COUNSELOR: What's made it hard to accept Scott's advice, Dad?

DAD: Oh, I don't know; you get into a kind of a rut, I guess.

COUNSELOR: Mom?

MOM: [*Cries quietly.*]

COUNSELOR: What do you see in your wife's face?

DAD: Oh, she just gets easily upset with Scott and all that.

COUNSELOR: Is that it? [*Unbelieving, wanting to avoid Dad's attempt to put the blame on Scott and go back to the old pattern of not talking about himself and his wife.*]

MOM: No, hon, I *do* think we're in a rut. I'd like to do more with you, I really would.

SCOTT: Why don't you go to that club you guys used to go to?

COUNSELOR: [*Realizing that Scott has been praised for his concern for his parents, and yet, that he cannot continue to help them without taking on an insoluble problem; they must help themselves.*] I know how much you care about these folks, Scott, and it's neat. This time though, do you think you could just let them try and work it out themselves?

SCOTT: I still think that would be a good idea.

COUNSELOR: Dad? Did you hear your wife ask you out?

DAD: No. Well, yeah . . . [*Smiles.*] I hate to spend the money, I guess.

COUNSELOR: The money? [*Unbelieving again.*] Are you worried about the money, really? Or is it more than that?

Doesn't this have something to do with what we were talking about last week? [*Terry is taking a big risk here, breaking the family rule that Dad's pain is not to be confronted.*]

DAD: Well, it *is* the money. Partly. [*Long pause.*] And, well, I just don't seem to feel like going out anywhere these days.

COUNSELOR: What's keeping you home?

DAD: It's worrying about the job. It just gets me down. . . . I don't want to keep burdening her with talking about it—I've told you. [*Sighing and averting his eyes.*]

COUNSELOR: [*Relieved that Dad's going along with her.*] What's been hard at work?

DAD: Well, I guess you might as well know now as never, but I don't know if they are going to keep me on.

COUNSELOR: [*Feeling that the cat is out of the bag and ready to support the family.*] Well [*looking at each family member*], that must have been hard to say. And hard to hold back, too. What are you feeling now, Mom?

MOM: Well, I really didn't know. . . . I feel so bad for you. . . . Is this recent? Did somebody talk to you?

DAD: Yes. About two weeks ago. I really didn't want you guys to know . . . but you would have found out anyways . . . hell . . . [*He has tears welling up in his eyes.*]

MOM: [*Looking over at Terry, who nods encouragement, then taking her husband's hand.*] We'll work something out. This is just really tough but, you know . . .

The rest of the session was spent exploring the couple's communication, including Dad's conflicts about showing weakness and Mom's difficulty in approaching him without hurting his feelings. Mom talked about how lonely she had been feeling. Scott sat quietly, apparently touched by his parents' pain and, at the same time, relieved not to be occupying center stage. The counselor ended the session by planning to have the next meeting with the parents only, and recommending that Scott think about joining a teenage counseling group. The counselor's main goal had been accomplished. Scott's problems still existed, but they no longer served as a cover for his mother's and father's unspoken sadness and defeat. The family used a few more sessions to work out plans for Dad's job and Scott's schooling. Altogether, the family accomplished changes in the space of three months that led each of them in a more rewarding direction.

So ends our second case on this issue. Our third and final case for this chapter explores yet another angle on counseling a family in which a child has problems attending school.

Joan: "We're going to make you go to school."

Joan was waging war against her school. A quiet girl, who had seldom gotten into any kind of trouble, she had been surprising her parents by truanting over and over again. In the past year, she'd been suspended twice. Her parents were at a loss to understand her. How could the daughter whom they had known and loved for 15 years suddenly turn out so different? There were many quarrels, which consisted mostly of the parents' reiterated threats to turn her over to probation, threats which they didn't fulfill, basically because they like having Joan at home. She helped Mom with her two smallest brothers, liked doing housework (although her mother jokingly complained that Joan charged the family too much), and got along with her family except when it came to school. Father and Mother were at a loss to explain it. They always had stressed academic success; with their older boy, it had worked. Joan seemed bright enough. She just didn't seem to care about learning.

A contact with the Mobile Unit—a van sent out to visit local high schools, loaded with counselors and information for teenagers—brought Joan in for a counseling session with Marcia. The counselor described Joan as an unemotional but pretty 15-year-old girl who talked in a halting, low voice and expressed herself with a simple vocabulary. She seldom looked at the counselor at first, but, as she talked, her manner became warmer and more spontaneous. Joan talked about how much she had enjoyed school at first. As a doting younger sister, she had been eager to follow in her brother's footsteps. She told the counselor that others had said maybe her problem was that everyone, her teachers, her parents, and she herself, compared her to her successful brother, and she usually fared badly in the comparison. She did not think her brother was the problem. She thought it was her own problem. She had really tried to like school, but she couldn't seem to. She didn't know why she couldn't get interested, she told the counselor, but finally figured she was just "dumb" and there was nothing to be done about it. By the third grade, she had started to lie awake nights trying to find a way to avoid going to school. She was sure that many of her frequent bouts of childhood flu were just a way to get out of going to school. Her best classes were Physical Education and Cooking. She was a poor speller, didn't like reading, and math frightened her. Throughout school and in any crowd of people, she had a lot of trouble talking. She couldn't seem to find words to say what she wanted to say.

Marcia praised her for the good job she was doing in the interview. Joan went on to say that her teachers had suggested over and over again that she lacked motivation, but Joan knew better: She reiterated that she was just too stupid and no one would tell her the truth for fear of hurting her feelings. She had come to the point where she couldn't pretend any longer. All she wanted was never to go to school again.

When the counselor questioned Joan about her family, Joan cried. She felt terrible about disappointing them all. She felt she was the only bad apple—all the others were bright and happy. She felt closest to her mother, but even her mother didn't seem to understand that she no longer wanted to go to school. She often thought the family would be better off without her.

As the counselor thought about this initial interview, she was struck by the fact that, in fact, Joan had expressed herself in strikingly simple language. She did not really believe Joan was not bright enough for school, but she knew that there was a category of learning problems that were not related directly to intelligence. She decided to take Joan's complaint seriously. For her first strategy, the counselor arranged to have Joan tested by a psychologist. The counselor found out, by checking with the family and Joan's school, that Joan had never been evaluated with tests. Like so many youngsters, she had been assumed to have normal capacities.

The psychologist's report confirmed the counselor's hunch. Like many youngsters who appear bright enough but develop a strong dislike of school, Joan had a specific learning disability. Her general intelligence was well within normal limits, but her school achievement was very low indeed for a sophomore in high school.

The tests showed that Joan had hardly attained third-grade spelling levels and was reading at the fourth-grade level. No wonder she felt stupid! But how could that happen? Was it really that she simply was not interested? The tests suggested that that was not the case; rather, they showed a picture often seen in children of Joan's age. She showed an excellent ability to solve problems and to arrive at solutions to highly abstract puzzles on the nonverbal tests. On any test depending on verbal ability, Joan lagged behind. Thus, her own assessment of her difficulties proved to be correct, to the degree that she was aware of her learning problems. "Dumb" she was not.

Discussing these test results with Joan and her parents proved helpful. Here was an explanation of Joan's difficulty in school that all of them could accept: Joan was neither stupid nor lazy. After the counselor had explained the test findings to the family, all of them were eager to add more information.

JOAN: It still seems like the main thing is . . . I'm just not smart enough.

COUNSELOR: That's true in one way and not true in others. It's true that the other kids have been ahead of you as far as using words is concerned. But do you remember how well you did when you were working with those blocks?

JOAN: They were easy.

COUNSELOR: They're one of the hardest tests they give. You did them above average.

JOAN: I did?

COUNSELOR: Yes. Why don't you ask your folks if they ever noticed that you were a lot smarter when it came to other things than words? Like sewing or cooking or repairing toys?

JOAN: [*Shyly.*] Was I?

MOM: Oh, yes; that's why we always knew you were smart, because you were better than your brother, even with some mechanical things.

DAD: [*Overlapping, eager to explain.*] That's why we always thought you were lazy! You seemed so smart in everything but school!

MOM: You always said you couldn't say things right. I thought it was just an excuse.

COUNSELOR: So it looks like you've had some trouble expressing yourself in words for a long time. That could prove pretty discouraging. Was it?

JOAN: Yes, I guess. It seems right. I always felt the others could say things better than me.

MOM: You know, you were a little slower at learning to talk than the other kids, but I didn't think it meant anything.

DAD: Weren't you the one we used to tease about having a mouth full of mush? I guess that didn't help much. Is there anything we can do to help?

COUNSELOR: Joan doesn't really have the kind of problem that benefits by a specific kind of therapy. Here's what happened. When Joan was five and six years old, she had some problems with expressing herself in words. That really handicapped her when she was learning to read and spell. Reading and spelling are taught mostly through language skills. Joan needed a special program that could teach her reading and spelling, using other areas, such as kinesthetics and visual memory. Such programs are now readiy available. But when Joan was in the first grade, problems like hers were only beginning to come to the attention of primary-school teachers. As it was, Joan learned the essentials anyway, but at great expense. She had to work especially hard, you see, and no one knew it, so no one could give her any praise for it. And so she grew up thinking she was lazy and stupid. Does that come anywhere near it, Joan?

JOAN: Well, I don't know. I don't think I'm exactly very bright. Especially when I think of Dick. God . . .

MOM: Well, what she's saying is that maybe you're just different. Isn't that what you're saying?

COUNSELOR: That *is* what I'm saying. I'm saying that there are other ways to judge how smart you are and what you can do, besides comparing yourself to your brother. [*Turning to parents.*] All of you can work together to help Joan see where she *is* bright. It's not going to be school, because language isn't her thing. But it could be working with kids, or using her hands to make things, for example.

JOAN: "It's true I was always good at that stuff, but isn't everyone?"

The counselor was well on her way to acquainting Joan and her parents with the facts. Slowly, over a period of three or four weeks, she coached the family (Dick was included in the later sessions) in how to validate each other's skills, thus helping Joan to feel more confident.

COUNSELOR: Have either of you ever experienced feelings of inadequacy?

DAD: Not me; I always think I'm pretty darn good at what I do—but *she* sure does! [*Looking at wife; at the same time, Dick is nodding his head in agreement.*]

COUNSELOR: Is he right? Is this a family where the men feel bright and the women dumb?

MOM: [*Nodding.*] Oh, I never seem to do anything right, at least on some days.

COUNSELOR: Joan, did you know Mom felt that way?

JOAN: No.

MOM: When I cook the dinner? Or how about when Dad hollers at me about the budget?

JOAN: Well, I don't know how you feel . . . okay, yeah, I guess you feel bad then.

COUNSELOR: Maybe you're not the only one in the family who feels dumb. Ask Mom what helps at times like that.

JOAN: [*Looks at Mom questioningly.*]

MOM: I don't know. That's why I don't know how to help you, I guess. Nothing seems to help me. I know what makes it worse.

COUNSELOR: What?

MOM: When he rubs it in.

COUNSELOR: Tell him.

MOM: You know. "I told you so." Or, "How could you do anything so dumb?" That really makes me feel low.

JOAN: Oh, yeah.

COUNSELOR:	[*To Dad.*] Did you know that?
DAD:	Well, I just can't believe any grown woman would act the way she does!
COUNSELOR:	Are you aware of how she feels?
DAD:	I guess.
COUNSELOR:	Do you want to ask her what might help?
DAD:	Okay. [*Looks questioningly at Mother.*]
MOM:	Don't rub it in, okay? Just ignore me. [*To Marcia.*] I don't think he can, though.
DAD:	I could. At least some of the time.
COUNSELOR:	And Joan could use some of that, too.
JOAN:	Yeah, from both of them.
COUNSELOR:	How about you, Dick? Do you know that the folks are proud of you?
DICK:	No, not really. I mean . . . well, I know they are, but they don't have to say it.
COUNSELOR:	Do other people tell you? At school?
DICK:	Well, I get my grades and stuff. Yeah, some tell me.
COUNSELOR:	I guess this is a family that feels kind of embarrassed to pay compliments; is that right?
DAD:	You got it.
COUNSELOR:	Yeah, I can understand that, and it would be okay, I guess, but it looks like everybody—maybe everybody but Dad, I don't know—is missing out on really knowing that the others appreciate them in some way. I'd sure like it if that would change a little. Let's try it. I know it feels awkward, but how about each of you thinking about one thing you like about the three others and telling it to them? Dad, could you start? [*She knows he is the most confident one and can take the lead most easily.*]
DAD:	Okay, you got me. I'll try. Let me see here. First you, Joan. I like how you are with your younger brother and sister. Seems like you know just how to handle them. Sometimes you know even when Mom and I don't. And you make great apple pie. [*Joan and he are smiling.*] Now, Dick. Okay, that's easy. You do great at school. You don't get in trouble. [*Turning to his wife.*] And you, well, you're no darn good! [*Laughing.*] Ex-

<table>
<tr><td></td><td>cept you're a very understanding person. And you're pretty, too!</td></tr>
<tr><td>COUNSELOR:</td><td>[*Noticing that he seemed to be having a hard time and covering up with humor, but happy he complied.*] Thanks a lot. Who's next?</td></tr>
<tr><td>MOM:</td><td>Okay. [*To husband.*] You're a good provider and you're real smart, but [*looking at Marcia*]—no, I won't go into that. And you, Dick, well, I guess you're smart like your Dad and you really know how to get things done. And Joan, well [*her eyes well up with tears*], you're just the most helpful one, that's all, and I just can't bear to think you don't know it . . .</td></tr>
<tr><td>COUNSELOR:</td><td>Looks like you feel really strongly about that.</td></tr>
<tr><td>MOM:</td><td>[*Nods.*]</td></tr>
<tr><td>COUNSELOR:</td><td>[*To Joan.*] Did you know that Mom felt that way?</td></tr>
<tr><td>JOAN:</td><td>No.</td></tr>
<tr><td>COUNSELOR:</td><td>Do you believe her?</td></tr>
<tr><td>JOAN:</td><td>I guess . . . yeah . . . I guess I do. [*Joan and Dick repeat the task of complimenting the family.*]</td></tr>
<tr><td>COUNSELOR:</td><td>Terrific! How did that feel?</td></tr>
<tr><td>DAD:</td><td>A little peculiar, but okay, I guess.</td></tr>
<tr><td>MOM & JOAN:</td><td>I liked . . . that was neat . . .</td></tr>
<tr><td>COUNSELOR:</td><td>It was a really good start. I don't want to compliment you too much, because I know that would embarrass you. [*Everyone smiles at Marcia's humorous comment.*] We're going to have to practice some more, I hate to tell you.</td></tr>
</table>

In three further sessions, the counselor helped the family to learn to express positive feelings more spontaneously. She also set out to change Joan's image in the family, by helping other members to validate her strong points and avoid making comparisons with her brother. Joan became visibly more confident. As the last part of the treatment, the counselor set out to help the family to develop a more suitable program for Joan. She did this by arranging for a school meeting that included herself, Joan, Mom, Dad, Joan's counselor at school, and Joan's homeroom teacher. The counselor reviewed for the school personnel the results of the psychological tests and then recounted briefly some of the highlights of her work with the family.

COUNSELOR:	I wanted to acquaint you with as much material about Joan's situation as possible, because I'm hoping that you'll agree that she could use an alternative school program for her last two years here. I'm thinking of something less academic, more practical—I don't know what's available.
SCHOOL COUNSELOR:	There is a part-time work program that allows the student to have a smaller amount of academic requirements and fill up the rest of her program with an actual work placement. We had offered that program to Joan before, and I understood that her parents had objected.
DAD:	Well, it looks like that might have been a mistake. We just didn't want her to get further behind . . .
MOM:	Would she still get graduation credit?
JOAN:	Could I work with kids?
MOM:	How would she get enough school?
COUNSELOR:	[*Realizing that the family is still holding out for the miracle that would turn Joan into excellent academic material, and that this confrontation of real choices is very hard for them.*] I'm glad you're asking all these questions. It's really important that everyone is clear about what's involved here.
TEACHER:	I'm afraid that, if you didn't have to come here all the time, you wouldn't show up for the few classes you have to take, Joan.
JOAN:	I would if it were the right kind of job!
COUNSELOR:	[*To the teacher.*] I know Joan has truanted a lot and that you've had a hard time getting her to cooperate. Are you saying that it may be kind of late to work out a special, part-time work program?
TEACHER:	No. No, I wouldn't go that far. I just wanted to be sure Joan is interested, that's all. And, and . . . well, that we have the whole family's support.
MOM & DAD:	Oh, yes . . . well, we. . . . It was hard to understand before. This might be the answer. Let's try it.
SCHOOL COUNSELOR:	I'd suggest giving it another try.
TEACHER:	All right. Let's figure out what would be possible.

The rest of the meeting was spent working out an alternative school program for Joan that included

1. A part-time placement as assistant teacher in a nearby nursery school
2. Tutoring in civics, a required subject that Joan was failing
3. A plan to gain needed credit for some oral presentations in history and English, which Joan would tape-record instead of handing in written assignments
4. Tutoring in spelling
5. Another meeting in three months, to evaluate the plan at semester's end.

The meeting with the family to review plans and consolidate the gains made during the past sessions ended Joan's family counseling. Another power struggle had ended. Joan and her parents were on the way to solving problems that had been obscured partially by the impasse about Joan's truancy.

Joan's problem was picked up very late, partly because little was known about specific learning problems when she started school, and partly because she was so much better at covering up her troubles than at asking for help. Had she been younger, chances are that an "E.H. Program," a program in the regular school designed for educationally handicapped children, would have been both available and helpful to her. As it was, her counselor's decision to have her evaluated with psychological tests led to the resolution of the family's impasse.

Suggested Readings

Allmond, Bayard. *The Family Is the Patient*. St. Louis: Moseby, 1979.

Anthony, E. J. The significance of Jean Piaget for child psychiatry. *British Journal of Medical Psychiatry, 20*, 20–34, 1965.

Boyer, Pat, and Jeffrey, Ronn. *The Family, A Living Kaleidoscope: A Guide for the Beginning Family Counselor*. Cheyenne, WY., Pioneer Printing and Stationery Company, 1981.

Carter, Elizabeth A., and McGoldrick, Monica (Eds.). *The Family Life Cycle: A Framework for Family Therapy*. New York, Gardner Press, 1980.

Erikson, Erik. *Childhood and Society*. New York: W. W. Norton, 1956.

Erikson, Erik (Ed.). *The Challenge of Youth*. New York: Doubleday, 1965.

Evans, J. *Adolescent and Pre-Adolescent Psychiatry.* New York: Grune and Stratton, 1983.

Gehrke, S., and Kirschenbaum, M. Survival patterns in family conjoint therapy. *Family Process, 6,* 67–80, March 1967.

Gesell, A. *The First Five Years of Life.* New York: Harper & Row, 1940.

Haley, J. *Changing Families.* New York: Grune and Stratton, 1971.

Haley, J. *Uncommon Therapy: The Psychiatric Techniques of Milton J. Erickson, M.D.* New York: W. W. Norton, 1973.

Haley, J. *Problem-Solving Therapy.* New York: Harper & Row, 1976.

Haley, J., and Madanes, J. *Leaving Home: The Therapy of Disturbed Young People.* New York: McGraw-Hill, 1980.

Kephart, N. *The Slow Learner in the Classroom.* New York: Merril Books, 1960.

Leveton, Alan. The art of shamesmanship. *British Journal of Medical Psychology, 35,* 101–111, 1962.

Leveton, Alan, and Leveton, Eva. Children in trouble, family in crisis. A series of 5 training films demonstrating a family counseling alternative. University of California at Davis, Administration of Criminal Justice, 1975.

Luthman, S., and Kirschenbaum, M. *The Dynamic Family.* Palo Alto: Science and Behavior Books, 1974.

Papp, Peggy (Ed.). *Family Therapy: Full Length Case Studies.* New York: Gardner Press, 1978.

Rabichow, Helen G., and Sklansky, Morris, A. *Effect Counseling of Adolescents.* Chicago: Follett, 1980.

Rabkin, R. *Strategic Psychotherapy.* New York: Basic Books, 1977.

Redl, F. *The Aggressive Child.* New York: The Free Press, 1957.

Taichert, Louise. Specific learning disorders. *California Medicine, 4,* 109, October 1960.

12

Power Struggles between the Family and Society: Four Case Studies

Case 1

So far, we have talked mainly about the teenager's struggle for independence. This struggle is an inherent part of adolescent development in our culture. In a dysfunctional family, the problems and symptoms discussed in the last few case illustrations often ensue.

We now are going to talk about a struggle that may appear to be the same, but represents, in fact, the reverse process of the one we have described already. We are talking about the struggle to achieve *dependency*, the struggle that occurs in the life of a teenager who has lacked adequate parenting. He has experienced independence all of his life. Now that the normal adolescent experiences are bombarding him, he feels he cannot cope. He is looking for structure, for limits—in short, for parents. To achieve his goal, he often does the very same things the teenager struggling for independence does. He engages in antisocial behavior, takes drugs, steals a car, runs away. Even more than his counterpart, however, he wishes to be caught. His actions express his often unconscious wish to transform his faltering, wishy-washy parents into the strong, true figures of authority who could guide him through this difficult time.

Not all parents are cut out for the job. They are often helpless, immature persons who don't know who they are or what they want from moment to moment. They may be needy, drunk, sick, or incompetent. In other words, *they* need help. Often such parents give birth to children in the hope of gaining strength and status in the world, only to find out that the experience leaves them further depleted.

Our children quickly become attuned to parental pain. A toddler learns to comfort his mother by sitting on her lap or bringing her his bottle. Another learns to divert his parents' attention from their conflicts with each other by making mischief. He can see that, left to their own devices, his parents often look sad, angry, or helpless, but, when they are disciplining him, they look strong. When his parents fight, the toddler pulls a vase off a coffee table and breaks it. When they are calm, he plays quietly by himself.

Slowly the toddler learns that his parents depend on him in many ways. They seem to pay a great deal of attention to him; in fact, he may experience them as having no life separate from him. As the family grows older, the parents often ask the child's advice or consult him about problems with the other parent. Their decisions about where to live, whom to see, and how to spend time seem to depend solely on him. When he leaves home to see friends or go to school, they let him know he will be missed a lot.

While his parents clearly do not neglect him, they also seem incapable of giving him leadership or support. Their teaching is replete with messages to stay with them and warnings not to trust outsiders or new situations. Paradoxically, because he is taught so little, the child often becomes enormously skilled. Feeling his parents' inadequacy, he looks about and finds substitutes to teach him skills that help the whole family. Feeling imprisoned by their demands, he forges ahead and learns to cope in the world outside.

As this toddler–rescuer grows up, he becomes more and more the parent in the family. He dimly suspects something is wrong here—other families seem so different. He sees other kids break down and cry at home, even call their parents rude names. He would never do these things at home. He would be afraid his parents could not take it. His own family remains his norm throughout early childhood, however, because it is the only family he really knows.

When adolescence hits, with the changes of height and hormones that cause him to question and challenge almost everything, he takes a new look at his parents and himself. He feels more and more uneasy, alone in the task of exploring a world transformed by sexual impulses and physiological changes. He wants someone to look out for him. He develops symptoms. He doesn't want more freedom—the freedom he has already is scary enough—he wants parents who will set limits for him, take care of him, and show him that they love him in a strong, protective way.

The counselor's role in such a struggle for dependence requires him to assess the parents' capacities. If they show any inclination or ability to do what their child is asking, the counselor can help them in the same way he helps other parents who need to learn to set limits and show that they care for their child. If the counselor feels, on the other hand, that these parents are, indeed, incapable or unwilling to perform the usual parenting functions, then he must help the teenager to see his parents realistically and give up his frustrating struggle. Perhaps they really are unable to cope. They may be physically, intellectually, or psychologically handicapped. They may be debilitated by over-whelming circumstances that have had a temporary or permanent effect—such as repeated death in the family, illness, or financial ruin. Unable to parent the challenging teenager, they may need specific help in order to better their own situation. The counselor may have to help the teenager to work out the same dilemma he often clarifies for parents: how to let go of a person who appears to depend on him. Further, the counselor may be able to help such a teenager find other adults who can provide the care and limit-setting he needs—people he knows at school or from recreational activities, or in organizations such as Big Brothers, or in a foster home placement.

Carol: The Struggle for Dependency

Carol is typical of the "parental" child. Pretty, with dark, long hair, and large, bright, brown eyes, Carol is a 16-year-old girl who is obviously very capable. At the youth center, she talks easily, and with apparent confidence, about what had made her run away from home. Her life, she said, had gotten to be too dull and routine. She lived alone with her mother, with whom she did not get along very well. Before she ran away, she had been ex-perimenting with drugs to stop the boredom that began when her best friend moved away. Carol had left home looking for adven-ture. Now she seemed eager for counseling that would help her find a new situation.

Mary, her counselor, was struck by the fact that, although Carol had talked a lot, she felt no closer to her. Something was missing. Carol seemed so sure of herself, fully capable of handling any situation. Why couldn't she get along with her mother? The coun-selor pressed Carol with questions about the relationship. Carol was evasive at first. "Just the normal struggles of mothers and teenage daughters." "I don't know why; we just don't see the world the same way." But she soon ran out of light conversation. She sighed, gave the counselor a long, searching look and said, "Okay, so you're going to find out—my Mom's a drunk. She . . ." Carol began to cry as she described her mother's increasing drinking. There had been a divorce five years before; since then, it had gotten worse and worse. For the past two months her mother had stopped leaving the house and had stayed home drinking every day. She was practically a zombie. The counselor tried to comfort Carol with sympathetic comments, but she could not seem to reach her. Carol seemed to need a certain amount of distance. When the counselor finally asked her what she thought she might need, Carol was resolute. She wanted a placement in another home. She wanted it immediately, before the family meeting that had been scheduled later in the week.

The counselor felt touched by Carol's lonely struggle. For so many years, there seemed to have been no one to talk to, or at least to help with her mother's increasing problems. Carol had mentioned being close to her sister, who had left home recently to move to San Francisco, where she worked in an office. So Carol had lost her best friend and her sister, and her mother had let her down. No wonder she ran away. The counselor felt very empathetic toward her. She told her supervisor that she wanted to find a placement for Carol. As she talked with her supervisor, she became aware of how little she knew of the rest of the family. She did not really want to make a decision until she could form her own view of what the mother's condition was and also learn something about how ready Carol actually was to leave the family. She had never run away before.

During the interview, Carol, her 19-year-old sister, Marilyn, and their mother were present. Marilyn was a slightly older, more fashionable version of her pretty sister. The mother looked pale and thin. She was obviously sober, but seemed shaky and unsure of herself. Although the tension in the room grew, everyone smiled a good deal in the beginning of the interview, as though this were a social occasion. The counselor realized that her first strategy would be to try to break the ice.

COUNSELOR: Well, Carol has been here for three days now. How

	about the three of you deciding how you want to use this hour.
MOTHER:	I'm really interested in your facility. How long have you been open?
COUNSELOR:	[*Realizing that Mom is feeling defensive and wants to take control of the interview; Mary wants not to oppose her if possible.*] About eight months now.
MOTHER:	How has the community responded? I read there was a lot of objection from the neighbors.
COUNSELOR:	Well, we had a few open houses, and things seem to have calmed down quite a bit. Did you want to ask Carol anything about what it's been like for her to be here?
MOTHER:	Yes, as a matter of fact. I don't know whether this has been the place you thought it would be, dear; have you liked it?
CAROL:	Yes, it's okay.
MOTHER:	Do you have a roommate?
CAROL:	Yeah; I'll introduce you to her later. She ought to be back by then.
MARILYN:	Will you give us a free tour as part of the session? [*Turning to Mary and maintaining a light tone, although her face looks tense and strained.*]
COUNSELOR:	No, Carol will show you around afterwards. It's nice that you're so interested in the place. Is this your first acquaintance with this kind of setting? [*Hoping to get to a more substantial part of the conversation soon.*]
MARILYN:	Well, no; I had a friend who ran away about—what is it?—six years ago, in the Haight, and I visited her at that place. It wasn't this nice, though.
COUNSELOR:	So you're an old hand at this.
MARILYN:	Yes, I must say. I can't believe Carol did it, though. Wow! I mean, it's just not like her to hurt Mom's feelings that way. I just totally can't believe it, even yet.
MOTHER:	[*With bitterness in her tone of voice.*] Well, it certainly was a surprise to me!
COUNSELOR:	How about talking directly with Carol about that?

At the end of this sequence, the family was beginning to talk about the real issues. The counselor had felt a little shaky while both mother and sister joined in an attempt to use up the hour with small talk about the agency. She had found it difficult to remain friendly and open, and had been tempted to counter with a sharp remark about the information being available in a pamphlet they'd mailed to the whole community. But she had succeeded in waiting for the right time to intervene, and now the family was beginning to engage. The next step was to put a stop to the moralizing, shaming tone that Marilyn and her mother were using with Carol.

MARILYN: [*Looking at Carol as though she'd committed a crime.*] Mom was worried sick about you. The least you could have done is left her a note, or told me. Why didn't you tell me? We always got along pretty well, didn't we?

COUNSELOR: Did you? [*Looking at Carol.*]

CAROL: Yeah. We got along okay—for sisters.

COUNSELOR: What do you mean?

CAROL: Well, like, we weren't like other sisters, you know what I mean? I mean, we didn't fight over clothes or friends or anything like that. We usually got along really good, really.

COUNSELOR: [*Looking at Mother.*] Boy, you sure must know something a lot of other mothers would like to know. That's really nice. [*Smiling, glad to have found a way to give some support to everybody.*]

MOTHER: No, they just were always those kinds of people. I never really had that much to do with it. [*Looking at Marilyn.*] But I think Carol's missed you very much since you left the house.

COUNSELOR: Is that right?

CAROL: Yeah, I guess so. . . . Well, I just kept hoping I'd get used to it, but it's been really hard, sort of.

COUNSELOR: Tell her that's why you didn't want to get her involved. [*Mary is playing a strong hunch here.*]

CAROL: Well, it's true. I thought of calling you or something, but when I thought you had just left and you didn't or you wouldn't want me tagging along . . . [*Carol was crying; Mother was fighting back tears.*]

The counselor was moved by the amount of feeling the two sisters showed as they talked about how difficult Marilyn's move had been for Carol. Mom also seemed accepting and warm toward both her daughters. Still, the counselor knew that the most important part of her job had not begun yet. Neither Marilyn nor Carol had mentioned Mom's drinking. Both had joined in what was apparently one of the main functions of the family system: protecting Mom. And yet, this was the part of family life that had become intolerable to Carol, now that her older sister had left. The counselor's next strategy was to bring this problem into the open and help the sisters to see that protecting Mom had cost them too much.

It took courage for the counselor to persist in her plan to encourage the girls to talk to their mother about her drinking. Finding an opening seemed impossible. If she simply put her cards on the table and told the mother what Carol had said, the counselor felt she would land right in the middle of the family power struggle. Carol certainly would have felt betrayed. Mother would have felt insulted, shamed, and caught without a way of saving face—good excuses to get drunk again. The counselor knew that the mother, like all alcoholics, experienced such guilt about her drinking that talking about it seemed like a punishment. Yet, talking about it was necessary. The counselor decided to go on a fishing expedition. She had her fish clearly in mind; she hoped she could land it.

COUNSELOR: [*Looking at Mother.*] Let's see, Marilyn left about— what?—three months ago? I wonder, was your leaving the family, Marilyn, difficult for someone else besides Carol? How about you, Mom? How's it been for you since Marilyn left?

MOTHER: Well, of course, I encouraged Marilyn to leave. I felt it was important for her to strike out on her own at this time.

COUNSELOR: I don't doubt that you supported her. But how did it—does it—feel? Is the house different without her?

MOTHER: [*Pauses for a moment.*] Yes, oh my, yes. [*Her eyes are tearing up again.*] Can't we talk about something else? I don't seem to do this too well. [*Breathing rapidly and tensing her brows.*]

CAROL: That's it, Mom. That's just it. You never . . . [*Mary notices that now Carol's tone is just as blaming as the others were earlier.*]

COUNSELOR: [*Interrupting Carol, who she thinks is trying to rescue Mom by fighting.*] No, this is the important part. Your feelings. [*Looking at Mom.*] Can you tell Marilyn?

MOTHER: I . . . I . . . it's just that I've been so lonely. . . . Well, you girls don't know this . . . [*Knowing glances exchanged by the two girls.*] But I do feel lonely very easily. Oh, I know what you're going to say, so I might as well say it. I shouldn't drink. I know. But I . . . [*beginning to sob*] have a very hard time with this . . .

COUNSELOR: That took a lot of guts. [*She knows this is an important moment and wants to proceed slowly.*] Have you girls been aware of Mom's loneliness?

CAROL: Sure. I've tried all these things but she won't do any of them—P.T.A., going back to school and becoming a lawyer like she used to want to, taking art classes . . .

MARILYN: [*Interrupts, smiling.*] Me too. I used to tell her, too, but . . .

COUNSELOR: [*Thinking how hard children work to raise their parents.*] Sounds like you girls care a lot. Have you been worried about Mom's drinking?

CAROL: [*Crying.*] It's so terrible. But Mom, I know you don't want to talk about it . . .

MOM: Oh, we might as well do it, now that we've started.

In the discussion that followed, it became clear that Mother's pride had kept her from sharing any of her difficulties with her friends or her daughters after her husband left, so she had become more and more walled off from the rest of the world. The counselor felt relieved that a beginning had been made in discussing the real pain in the family. Before closing the interview, however, she felt that one more aspect of the process needed to be addressed: the role reversal in this family, that is, Carol's feeling of total responsibility for her mother.

COUNSELOR: You know, one of the things we know about families is that when any one family member is in pain, all of the other members share in it to some degree. You said earlier [*addressing Mom*] that the girls didn't know how lonely you felt. I believe that you haven't talked much to them about your feelings. You seem like the kind of person who hates to complain. Is that right? [*Mom nods, smiling.*] But I imagine the girls knew something about it anyway. Let's find out, okay? What have you girls thought about Mom's social life? Have you thought about it? Tell your Mom what you have thought, if anything.

MARILYN: Well, I haven't really thought too much about it. I used to ask you why you weren't dating, I do remember that. Right after the divorce, I made a real pest of myself, remember?

MOTHER: Do I remember? How about the time you asked the grocery clerk to come over for your lunch to keep me company?

COUNSELOR: You're both laughing, and it sounds like your loneliness hasn't been much of a secret, doesn't it? Did it work, Marilyn? Did she date the grocery clerk?

MARILYN: No way! She hasn't dated yet, as far as I know, and it's been five years!

COUNSELOR: [*To Carol.*] Has Marilyn been the only one that was concerned about Mom's social life?

CAROL: No, I've tried, too. Mom, why don't you go to Parents without Partners? I left you the stuff on the kitchen table again last week because you said you didn't know where they met or anything.

COUNSELOR: How does it feel, Mom, to have these two working so hard to get you out of the house to have some fun?

MOTHER: Well, you know how kids are. They think it's all so simple.

MARILYN: I know it's hard to start, Mom, but . . . well, I know you might not want to hear this from me, but even AA might be a good place to start. I mean, I could drive you to meetings and . . .

MOTHER: Marilyn, when you get on one of these kicks . . . [*Falls silent, looking uncomfortable.*]

COUNSELOR: [*To daughters.*] Has Mom been a hard or an easy person to raise?

MARILYN: Real hard. I finally gave up. [*Starts out smiling, but ends with a sigh.*]

COUNSELOR: Carol?

CAROL: I just keep thinking it would be so simple to just *do* something. I know you could do it, Mom, I . . .

MOM: I know you think it would be easy, but it's not.

CAROL: I just get so mad at you [*her voice rising in pitch and volume*], because you won't even start!

MOM: [*Sits, staring ahead, looking upset and withdrawn.*]

COUNSELOR: [*To Mom.*] Could you say to Carol, "You can't do it for me. I have to solve my problems in my own way."

MOM: That's certainly true. Carol, we just get into hassles when you try to do it for me. I have to do it my own way. [*Heaves a sigh of relief.*]

CAROL: [*Looks sad.*] I just don't see you doing it, Mom.

COUNSELOR: Is that what's hard?

CAROL: Oh yes. I just keep thinking . . .

COUNSELOR: Do you think you could let your Mom grow up on her own? Or do you have to keep helping her, even if she doesn't want it?

CAROL: Well, it's real hard to be at home when she seems to not have anything, really, and then she drinks and . . .

COUNSELOR: Hard to be at home, huh? Say, I have an idea! Did you run away partly because it's one of the few ways you can think of not to get into these arguments with your mom?

CAROL: That's one way to put it, I guess.

COUNSELOR: So that would be something to work on here. Could there be any way of the two of you living together with you, Mom, making some attempt to solve your own problems? If Carol, here, promises not to help you unless you ask for it? How would that be?

It was easy to elicit Mom's cooperation in this scheme. She would be willing to come in for further interviews to work on developing more effective ways of relating to Carol. She was silent on the topic of finding better ways to take care of herself. The counselor had expected that. Alcoholics are often difficult to engage in therapy. Mother's desire to continue the interviews was enough for the beginning.

At the end of the interview, the counselor realized that the topic of placement for Carol hadn't even come up. Clearly this was no time to place Carol in another home. All the negative things she had said about her own home were true, yet she was not ready to leave it. Had she been placed in a foster home, her strong emotional commitment to her own mother would have interfered with her ability to become a part of her new home. Carol felt responsible for her mother. Frequently, that responsibility overwhelmed her and she wanted to leave, but, when she went, she carried her mother with her. She thought about her, called her on the telephone, worried about her physical condition; in short, she was attached in the same way that a mother is attached to a helpless child.

While she was reasonably sure that Carol would not do well in a placement, however, the counselor also was concerned about sending her back home. Would these interviews be sufficiently successful to ease the situation that had caused Carol to run away? She decided to attempt to provide one more support for Carol before sending the family home. This strategy involved making some practical plans for what the family was going to do.

COUNSELOR: I want to come back to something that you said way back in the beginning of the interview, Marilyn. You said you were surprised that Carol hadn't talked with you or come to see you instead of running away. Is that something you still want Carol to know? That you'd be there for her if she needed help?

MARILYN: Sure. Really, Carol, I know I was real upset with you for getting Mom so upset with running away and everything, but I *do* want you to, well, come over and talk and stuff. I really do.

CAROL: But you're so busy and your new roommates don't even know me, and . . .

MARILYN: Look, that just isn't true. It was true right during the first week, but now I'm all moved in and I have my own room if you want to be private, and I'd really like you to come over more. Just for no reason. Just to come over.

COUNSELOR: That's nice. Would you do it, Carol?

CAROL: Yeah, I could just go over.

COUNSELOR: Neat! That would be a good way to start, because, the thing is, I'd like you to have something else to do besides lecture Mom when you get upset, you know?

CAROL: Okay, okay, you made your point.

The next few interviews were spent working on the relationship between Carol and her mother. The counselor knew that, unless Mother asked, she could not focus on helping the mother stop drinking. Even if the mother had asked for help, the short-term counseling available through the counselor would not have sufficed. Instead, her goal was to help clarify the family process in order to help Carol feel less responsible for her mother, more genuinely independent. She helped Carol see that, in fact, she couldn't make her mother stop drinking. More important, she helped Carol understand that there were many complex reasons for her mother's drinking, that it was not, as Carol had always thought, simply a rejection, proof that her mother didn't love her. Carol and her mother discovered that things went better when Carol did not attempt to "parent" her mother. Like the parents of rebellious teenagers, she had to learn to turn her mother loose, to show her that she was on her own. It became clear to Carol and her mother that their best times together were spent on outside activities, such as shopping trips or going to the movies. With the counselor's help, Carol learned to disengage from her mother when she was drinking and to use her sister and school friends as supports in order to avoid a home situation that depressed her.

The plan worked well. The mother's drinking decreased but remained a problem. Carol became a more genuinely independent person by learning to *use* help, rather than attempt to give it in an unrewarding situation. At the end of six sessions, the mother had begun to attend meetings for Parents without Partners, an organization that provided both help and social contact for single parents. The counselor planned to have one more interview with the family in a month's time, where, if everything continued to go well, she planned to encourage the mother to join Alcoholics Anonymous.

Case 2

Perhaps the most common battlefields for power struggles and arguments are topics of drugs and sex. While the first arouses the parent's fear for his child's survival, the latter engages the family in a struggle that contains strong moral and ethical values and, at the same time, usually presents a problem in articulation for both parents and children. The following case presentation typifies these struggles and presents some ways the counselor can deal with them in an initial interview.

Cathy: O.D.'d on Reds

A long-haired teenager, Cathy looked different from her parents as they walked in. Her extreme mini-skirt and high boots—very much in style at the time of the interview—provided a strong contrast to their quiet, plain way of dressing. She was pale and obviously tired. She trailed her parents, apparently reluctant to come in, casting her eyes skyward now and then, in a gesture of disgust. Her parents appeared serious, eager to tell their story, somewhat deferential to the counselor, but personally shy and skeptical. Cathy's father, a tall, relaxed-looking man with sandy hair and casual plain clothes, seemed most accessible, most eager to talk. His wife was more somber in dress as well as manner; she seemed tense and was deliberate in her comments. Cathy spent the first few moments of the interview looking visibly embarrassed and apparently determined not to talk. The family had come in because Cathy had taken an overdose of barbituates the night before. The counselor, Helen, decided that her first approach would be to get the feelings behind the story.

DAD: Well, she came home on drugs last night and we want to know what to do about it.

COUNSELOR: And I'm here to see if I can help you guys talk things out a little bit. [*To Cathy:*] I notice you kind of looking over at Dad. Have you two had some chance to talk since yesterday?

DAD: Yeah, we talked last night and today.

COUNSELOR: How did that conversation go?

DAD: At first I was very emotional, and it was quite loud, and so forth.

COUNSELOR: What emotion was on top of you?

DAD: I don't know how to describe it. You know, I was shaking, excited, and so forth, when I saw her out on the lawn stumbling around. I never saw this before. I

	never saw anybody like that, and for my own kid . . . coming home from school.
COUNSELOR:	Were you pretty scared?
DAD:	In a way, right. There's probably a lot of emotions there that my mind was going through.

These were the first words exchanged in the interview. The counselor's goal, in the beginning of the interview, was to acquaint the family with the way she worked. Cathy's symptom, an overdose of drugs, led her to expect that Dad and Mom would launch into a detailed account of Cathy's drug ingestion, her behavior, and especially her betrayal of the family's rules and standards. The counselor let the family know immediately that her primary interest was in the way they interacted, in their emotions, their way of talking to one another. Next, she needed to know what had kept the family from helping Cathy earlier and what were the rules of communication.

MOM:	I have suspected for awhile that there was a problem. I know that there is a problem.
COUNSELOR:	Is this something that you've talked about as mother and father?
MOM:	Yeah, we've talked about drugs all the time for the past 10 years.
COUNSELOR:	Well, ask your husband how it was a surprise to him. Would you ask him that?
MOM:	Yeah. Why was it a surprise to you?
DAD:	Because my own daughter was on them. We discussed them with somebody else's daughter on them.
MOM:	I know one time when she took something about four years ago and she was sick from it. She came home sick from school and it was a drug that she took, a pill that somebody gave her.
COUNSELOR:	[*To Dad.*] Could you ask how it is that they kept it from you?
DAD:	Did you tell me that?
MOM:	I think I told you that Karen gave it to her and that's why she doesn't see Karen any more. I didn't want Karen around. Karen's parents knew about it, and they did nothing also. That's been about three or

four . . . I don't know . . . what grade were you in? Seventh? That was four years ago.

COUNSELOR: Was Mom supposed to tell Dad, or not supposed to tell Dad?

CATHY: No.

COUNSELOR: [*To Mom.*] Cathy says that you are not supposed to tell Dad. So what's that all about?

MOM: And it's not that I didn't want to share it with him. It's just that I didn't want to get him upset about something that wasn't important.

DAD: No. They want to keep it from me, and I guess that's the way it is. There is nothing that I can do about it, actually.

The counselor has clarified one of the dysfunctional rules in the family: Keep Dad in the dark. Like anyone caught in the stable rules of a dysfunctional system, he feels there's something vaguely wrong but immediately asserts his helplessness to change the rule, thereby reinforcing it. The counselor's next strategy is to find ways for Dad to be included in family communication. Her assumption is that more open communication in this family will reduce the likelihood of Cathy's hidden and destructive use of drugs.

COUNSELOR: You could say how it makes you feel. That would be one thing.

DAD: Well, I would like to know what's going on, right?

COUNSELOR: Could you say that to your wife?

DAD: I would like to know what's going on.

COUNSELOR: See if she believes you. Could you ask her if she believes you?

DAD: Do you believe that I want to know what's going on?

MOM: Sometimes.

DAD: I don't want to know what's going on?

MOM: No, not if it's going to rock the boat. You'd rather have things go smoothly and nobody bother you. . . .

On the basis of what the counselor knew at this point, she decided on two goals for further work: (1) to challenge the family system by bringing Dad and Cathy closer and (2) to free up Cathy's communication in the family so that she would be able to use words rather than symptoms to relate her troubles. Next, the counselor attempted to help Cathy make a beginning in bridging the gap that had caused her to isolate herself as the identified patient. Her strategy was to talk about the absent siblings, to find out why Cathy became the drug user in the family.

COUNSELOR: What's it like to be the youngest member of the family? Anything different about that? Different from you're sister and brother?

CATHY: Well, I don't know. It just seems like they got . . . they have more than I did. Maybe it's because Penny and Bruce are so perfect.

COUNSELOR: [*To Mom.*] Could you ask her where she got that idea?

MOM: Yeah, where did you get that idea that they are . . .

DAD: Well, it's just because Penny never did anything wrong; she cleaned up the house and did everything.

COUNSELOR: Your dad is agreeing with you.

CATHY: It's true . . . she did. But now she's not there any more, and I have to do it all. And I'm not like her. I try to be, but I'm not.

MOM: I never expected you to be like Penny. I told you that time and again, also.

COUNSELOR: It would help me to get a picture of the family. I wonder if you could think of three words that could describe Penny. Her personality—what three words would you use—like outgoing or friendly, or whatever words they would be—conscientious—what words would you pick to describe her?

MOM: She's sweet.

COUNSELOR: Sweet . . . let's hear two more.

MOM: She's kind.

COUNSELOR: Kind—let's hear one more.

MOM: She's understanding.

COUNSELOR: Understanding. Anybody want to add anything to that list?

DAD: She's thoughtful, and she's made of all the good things.

COUNSELOR: It's just like Cathy says; she is perfect, so she's got all the good things in the family.

DAD: Pretty close to it.

COUNSELOR: The boy's name is Bruce. What would be some words that would describe him, so I can get a mental picture of this family's constellation?

MOM: Quiet.

CATHY: Not married. Single.

DAD: Well, he's home-loving; what I mean is, he likes to . . . he's 21 years old and he isn't going out with girls. He's staying with his parents is what he's doing.

COUNSELOR: [*To Cathy.*] How about the three words you would use to describe yourself?

CATHY: Rotten.

DAD: Well, I said she had a good heart. Her mother was telling me a couple of years ago that something was wrong with her, and I said no, she'll be all right.

COUNSELOR: Do you think she's generous; is that one word?

DAD: No. I'm saying that, if ever we were in trouble, she would be there. [*Cries.*]

COUNSELOR: [*Relieved that, finally, there is an expression of emotion for Cathy.*] You've got a lot of feeling about that. Did you know that, Cathy? Did you know that your father felt so strongly about you being a really dependable person?

CATHY: No.

DAD: I'm saying, if we're ever desperately in trouble, she'll be there.

COUNSELOR: 'Cause she's a kind person that you can rely on? And rotten isn't exactly the word that you'd choose?

DAD: I wouldn't. No. At times I believe she's self-centered and she thinks about herself only. Sometimes I think she doesn't love her mother and father. There's no love there whatsoever.

COUNSELOR: Sometimes you feel pretty far away from her. Is that true?

DAD: Right.

Cathy's isolated, guilt-ridden stance suggested that she—like the identified patients in many familes—had developed a picture of herself as the bad one, the child who disappoints everyone, the child who is different. Had Cathy's siblings been present, they would have been important sources for drawing a comparison. The counselor's request to the family to supply three adjectives for each of the children served as an exercise to supply some of the missing information. In fact, the parents agreed with Cathy's descriptions of her sister, Penny, using definitions like "sweet," "understanding," and "she's made of all the good things." Cathy's own description of Penny was "perfect."

The most important result of this exercise was the first spontaneous, emotional interchange between two family members, which occurred in response to Cathy's denigrating herself as "rotten." Her deep conviction seemed to touch something in her father, causing him to describe her as the person the family could rely on if ever they were in trouble. His tears and his quick return to a negative definition of Cathy as "self-centered and unloving" demonstrate the usual attachment to the homeostatic process, attempting to return Cathy to the role of identified patient. In order to begin to cement the relationship between Cathy and her father, the counselor intervened to let him express his positive emotion more fully and to reframe his negative comments as expressing his emotional distance from his daughter.

Cathy seemed genuinely surprised by this turn of events. She had not counted on having any ally, even one so short lived, in this discussion, and she cooperated fully with the counselor's suggestions to question him further. This helped the counselor to obtain more of the family's developmental history.

COUNSELOR: I've been kind of getting the picture that there is a lot of distance between you and your dad some of the time. Is that true?

CATHY: Yeah. When I was little, I used to be so close to him, and now I'm not. [*Bursting into tears.*]

COUNSELOR: Why don't you say that to him?

CATHY: I used to to be so close to you, and now I'm not. I don't know why. [*Still tearful.*]

COUNSELOR: Maybe you two could figure that out. Ask your dad why.

CATHY: Do you know why?

DAD: Mmmm, uh . . . yeah. All you kids were close when you were small.

COUNSELOR: [*Aware of a chance to clarify an aspect of normal development.*] Let's have a few ideas about that. They are close to you when they are little. Then they grow up, and they don't seem so close to you any more. That's true for you with all of the kids?

DAD: Probably.

COUNSELOR: Well, you must have figured that it was your fault for some reason or another, Cathy. Ask him if he thinks you're judging him badly.

CATHY: Am I judging you badly?

DAD: Yes.

CATHY: Why?

DAD: 'Cause we have a generation gap—you keep telling me. Which I don't believe in—generation gaps.

COUNSELOR: About when were you two feeling closest? If you look back on the history of this family, when did things start to change . . . would you guess . . . the two of you? Junior high? Somewhere around there?

MOM: Yeah, when boys came into the picture. When boys came in the picture she didn't need her father any more. She didn't go with him, she didn't want to go anyplace. She had her boyfriend.

COUNSELOR: Are you saying that your husband is kind of a jealous type?

MOM: Yeah, I would say. He didn't like the boyfriends taking his little girl away.

COUNSELOR: So it seems like everybody understood that you are kind of a jealous guy—and a lot of fathers are. And Cathy, you came up with a bunch of boyfriends there and that didn't go so well and you two kind of split. But now it's gone further than that. It seems like you think she's just kind of ruled you out as the person to talk to because of this "generation gap."

At this point, the counselor had brought the family back to a gap in Cathy's development. Apparently, in this family, the normal distancing that occurs between father and daughter around adolescence had gotten out of hand. Instead of distance, there had been estrangement and an erosion of the affection and communication between father and daughter. Thus, the isolation in which a teenager is able to develop a drug habit was created. The counselor suspected that it was not only her use of drugs that Cathy failed to talk about with her parents. The estrangement seemed directed at her relationship with boyfriends. Sex, also, would be hard to talk about in this family. Here, the counselor had an opportunity to pursue a point that usually would have been lost in argument.

COUNSELOR: How are differences handled in this family?

DAD: Usually I get loud. And I told her this last night also, after the policemen left. I went into her bedroom, and I told her the only reason I get loud is because I care about you. If I stop getting loud, then I don't even care about you any more.

MOM: Possibly you listen to me, but not to the kids.

DAD: I don't listen to them? Well, they can't convince me if they are talking about something immoral, or some dope or something. I just can't believe it. That's the truth.

COUNSELOR: [*To Mom.*] And then, you are in the spot of keeping peace. Is that how it goes?

MOM: No. I don't keep peace. I just stay out of it.

DAD: Well, I can't see how anybody could be so wrong, is why I start yelling.

MOM: Well, it's a matter of opinion on whatever it happens to be. If I say anything, or side with anybody, well, then there is an argument.

COUNSELOR: What we're talking about is kind of the kids . . . when they are little . . . you being able to be pretty close to them. Then, as they grow up and talk about more argumentative stuff, it seems like it's harder to share with you. It sounds like to me that you are talking about things that you feel a lot about and that you've thought about, but that you don't make the difference between something that you have a strong opinion on and something that you're definitely right on.

DAD: Well, that's the way I gotta think to keep my own sanity, that I am right. Because she says the other day, a week ago, that she . . .

CATHY: We were talking about one of my girlfriends being on the pill. Would you rather have them on the pill or get pregnant?

DAD: You say that you could . . . you sleep with anybody and I get loud on that. Because you are going completely against my moral standards. So I have become very emotional. And I was trying to explain to you that you don't sleep with everybody. Yeaaaah!

CATHY: Get pregnant!

DAD: I'd have them on nothing.

CATHY: Well, you had a choice there because they are going to do it anyway.

DAD: Yeah, well, that's where I go all emotional. With statements like that I can't get it in my head that that's the right thing to do—go on the pill, and then go all over the place hopping.

COUNSELOR: [*Doubling.*] So, to me there is a wrong and a right. And if things are different now than when I grew up, it's very hard for me to talk about the shades of difference. So I miss out a lot on my kids trusting me and telling me what they are really concerned about.

DAD: Well, I guess that's probably true.

COUNSELOR: There is some sadness in that.

DAD: Well, I'm only doing this for her.

COUNSELOR: I *believe* you, but how is it working?

DAD: It ain't working too good.

The argument had been typical. Cathy had watched her father become more and more upset, his voice growing louder and louder, his face red, as the discussion progressed. She, on the other hand, had become more and more rational. Having provoked her father and set the process in motion, Cathy and her father seemed to reverse roles. She became the quiet, sensible parent, while the father spluttered helplessly. Mother, as predicted, remained quiet. Further work with the family would mean continuing to approach these difficult subjects until they could be tolerated and discussions could be completed.

The counselor knew that the drug issue was not settled yet. It was important to raise the seriousness of Cathy's symptom with the family in this first interview. Cathy had been under so much stress that she had attempted suicide. The counselor's next strategy, then, was to talk about the unthinkable.

COUNSELOR: [*To Cathy.*] I have a sentence for you to say. I'd like you to see if you could say to the folks, "I really feel different from the rest of the family."

CATHY: I really feel different from the rest of the family.

COUNSELOR: Is that true?

CATHY: Well, I do. I hardly ever agree with anything they say.

COUNSELOR: Do you ever have real bad depressions where you think the family would be better off without you?

CATHY: Yes; all of the time.

COUNSELOR: Do you ever think of hurting yourself?

CATHY: Yes.

COUNSELOR: Do they know that?

CATHY: No.

COUNSELOR: It would sure be good to get that one out in the open before we get into real trouble here.

DAD: Of course she told us yesterday that she wanted to kill herself when she took seven reds. She took a lot of them. Five is an O.D.

COUNSELOR: How did that make you feel to hear that?

MOM: Well, . . . terrible. [*Cries.*]

COUNSELOR: Could you let her know that? Because it would be an awful way to get this family together, through the death of somebody.

Often, the symptom bearer is not the only identified patient in the family. To complete the picture, the counselor investigated the subject of depression in the rest of the family. The result was surprising.

COUNSELOR: [*To Mother.*] Have there been times in your life when you've been pretty down in the dumps, too?

MOM: Yeah.

COUNSELOR: Other than this time, I mean?

MOM: Yeah. Isn't there for everybody? [*She sounds defensive.*]

COUNSELOR: What's gotten you down in years past? [*Though the question is addressed to Mom, Dad answers it.*]

DAD: My drinking.

COUNSELOR: Sort of a family secret, huh?

DAD: No.

COUNSELOR: It's not a family secret?

DAD: No. When I get drunk everybody knows it.

COUNSELOR: You are so willing to be the villain.

DAD: No. It's the truth. You're asking her what gets her down, I might as well get it out there before she does. Just get it right out in the open. That's the worst thing I do. . . . I don't cheat on her, I don't gamble, I don't run at night, so I have a few drinks.

COUNSELOR: Is that what you were going to say?

MOM: I don't know whether I was going to say it or not.

COUNSELOR: No, because you are a protector. Don't rock the boat, because when you get out of here, who knows what's going to be said.

The interview concluded with the counselor arranging for an appointment for the entire family—including Cathy, her parents, her sister, Penny, and her brother, Bruce—with one of the probation officers trained in family counseling.

Counseling with this family continued for five further sessions, conducted over a period of two months, during which various groups of family members attended. These sessions continued the work the family had begun in the first interview. Dad and Cathy continued to develop their communication. Their arguments, which previously had ended with one of them walking out, began to last and provide challenge and stimulation to both of them. Mother and Father worked on ways of addressing some of the problems that they previously had handled with a mutual agreement to be silent. Bruce talked about some of the disadvantages of his living at home. Cathy became visibly more confident and joyous. Eighteen months later, she had not had any recurrences of her symptoms. Her parents, however, were not interested in pursuing any further work.

Case 3

Sometimes power struggles take place with the wrong person. Parents whose lives have been affected by some severe trauma during their own youth often spend a great deal of time actively trying to prevent their children from suffering equal pain. The war victim who attempts to teach his child to be prepared for sudden disaster, the orphan who wants to raise a child that depends on no one, the Depression survivor who instills a religious reverence for work in her children—we all have met such families. Our next case study concerns Tina, whose mother's life had been sadly affected by the early death of the mother's own brother.

Tina: A Stand-In for the Dead

When Tina first came to the youth service, she had run away from home. Her story sounded the same as many others. She felt like a prisoner in her own home. "She won't let me have any freedom. I have to be home at this exact time every day. My mom wants to know every detail of what I'm doing when I'm gone. She even reads my diaries! I feel like I'm being watched by the secret police."

In the first family session, Tina's mother countered, predictably, with, "If I don't check on her, she cuts school, runs around with really bad characters, and gets into all kinds of trouble. She pays no attention to dinner time. She stays out 'til all hours of the night. I try my best, but she just doesn't listen. She simply does what she pleases."

After the first interview, Barbara, one of the older counselors at the youth service, sought help in our consultation group. Although she found herself liking to work with both Tina and her mother, she had not been able to get them to stop blaming one another. Tina, a tall, good-looking 15-year-old girl with a dramatic appearance, flamboyant clothes, strikingly light blonde hair and blue eyes, glowered at her mother between bursts of accusations. The mother, also a good-looking woman, but with a quiet, understated demeanor, looked frustrated, helpless, and very worried. She was a single parent—the counselor noticed that she mentioned it several times, to underline her sense of responsibility in this time of crisis—and was working as a full-time accountant in order to support herself and Tina. Life appeared to be very exhausting. The counselor related her feelings of hopelessness to the consultation group as she described the mother and daughter struggling, like two countries at war, to paint a propaganda picture of the other side as bad, sinful, immoral, and destructive.

The counselor often gets caught up in the family's feeling of hopelessness. "They're really at it," she thinks. "How can I stop such a well-oiled machine? How can I say anything while they're all screaming at each other? The mother sounds impossible. Nobody can be expected to put up with Gestapo techniques. But maybe the girl does get into a lot of trouble. She seems to be playing into this somehow. They're going on and on. I feel swamped and confused. What can I do?"

The counselor found several strategies useful in finding a way out of the impasse. We have presented them without much further reference to the consultation group in order not to impede the natural flow of the material. The first was to find out what really was going on—to investigate the actual circumstances of Tina's life.

COUNSELOR: Tell me about a typical day in your life, Tina, okay? A school day. I want to know everything from when you wake up to when you go to sleep. And Mom, I know you're going to want to hear Tina's version. You'll get your chance later; I promise.

TINA: Well, okay, I guess . . . [*She is smiling and begins to talk in a sing-song voice, like a little girl doing a rote task.*] Well, I get up in the morning and eat my breakfast . . .

MOTHER: [*Interrupting.*] Don't I wish? [*Turning to Barbara.*] The most I can get her to have is orange juice . . .

COUNSELOR: [*Cutting Mother short and turning to Tina.*] And then?

TINA: I go to school.

COUNSELOR: Are you usually on time, a little late, or what?

TINA: No. Honest. I just get there at the regular time.

MOTHER: Well, she's no truant, that's true, but she . . . well, she doesn't seem to take it really serious, you know?

COUNSELOR: Okay, I'll give you a chance in a little bit, I really will, but for now I want to continue through the rest of Tina's day . . .

MOTHER: Ask about her friends!

TINA: Oh, f—— you, Mom.

MOTHER: [*Another pointed look at Barbara.*]

As the counselor continued her exploration of Tina's day, no material emerged suggesting that Tina was in any kind of serious trouble. The counselor saw Tina's rebellious manner. Tina disagreed verbally with her mother on many points and started yelling whenever her mother attempted to set limits. She used language that upset her mother. She was given to exaggeration, saying for example, that her mother was a Nazi and she, Tina, refused to live in a concentration camp. The more the counselor checked the facts, however, the more she found the mother's concern exaggerated. Tina went to school regularly. Her grades were good in some areas, average in the rest. She had never been in trouble with the police. She had experimented with drugs but was not doing so now. The counselor could understand the mother's frustration—her daughter was difficult to live with—but she could not understand why she failed in her attempts to control Tina's behavior. Nor did there seem to be any symptom that justified her anxious concern for Tina's safety.

What other reason could there be behind the mother's anxiety? The consultation group urged the counselor to explore the mother's personal history with the hope of finding a clue about her fears for her daughter.

When Tina and her mother came in for their third counseling session, they immediately started one of their well-known battles.

MOTHER: Well, maybe now that you're here you'll start talking about who called you up last night. I don't . . .

TINA: Mother! I just won't let you question me like that! It's none of your business! Geez; you want me to type up a resumé every time I get a phone call?

MOTHER: Well, you sure sounded different than you do talking to your regular friends! You sounded funny, sort of, well . . . I know you *say* you haven't been taking anything but [*turning to Barbara*], I wish you could have heard her; she always seems so normal here . . .

COUNSELOR: You know, it's hard for me not to follow this up, but I've really learned that I can't seem to help you two fight more successfully. I wonder if you could help me with something that I've been wanting to know more about.

MOTHER: [*Interrupting.*] Well, sure; but can we get back to this? I really am seriously concerned about these strange phone calls, and . . .

TINA: [*Glowers at her mother, then rolls her eyes upward.*]

COUNSELOR: If it still seems important, we can talk about it later, but here's what I've been thinking. I've been thinking that I know very little about your family, Mom. We seem to concentrate so much on you and Tina that I don't know you that well. Could you tell me something about how you grew up? What kind of family, and . . .

MOTHER: Oh, just the usual family, I guess. Kind of quiet. I grew up in Fresno, in the country. My dad worked hard. He wasn't there that much, but my mother wasn't a single parent like I am, either. Well [*looking at Tina*], well, you knew this would come out, *you* told me—there was something really terrible that maybe has something to do with how I am right now . . . [*Her eyes tear up.*] It's my brother. Tina reminds me a whole lot of him. He was in trouble all the time. And he . . . committed suicide, or . . . well . . . maybe he just O.D.'d; I don't really know, but he died in his teens.

COUNSELOR: That really is important. [*Speaking very quietly to give Mom support.*] So you really have known someone who got into a lot of trouble? That helps me understand.

The counselor pursued this important clue to the mother's behavior. As the mother went on to describe the loss of her younger brother, her protective behavior with Tina began to make sense. She had experienced a terrible loss, one that left her helpless, bereft, and probably angry as well. Like many of us in similar circumstances, she had vowed that she would never undergo such an experience again. Her attempt to control Tina's life was performed with the dual intentions of saving Tina's life and saving herself the repetition of nameless grief and anxiety.

The paradox was that the longer the mother attempted to protect herself against the repetition she dreaded—her daughter's following the same self-destructive path that had killed her brother—the more she was forced to live in full awareness of the scene she feared. In wanting to avoid pain, she caused it. Wanting to live without the brother whom she recalled with so much anguish, she re-created him every day. The counselor thought that it was a testimonial to Tina's will to survive that she was not following her mother's unconscious suggestions to get into trouble.

In keeping her brother's memory so vividly present, the mother was not only attempting to avoid her daughter's following in his footsteps, she also was keeping herself from completing the grieving process and actually facing his death. The mother was not ready to express her grief. First, she would have to learn to differentiate between her brother and her daughter. Together, neither was quite dead or quite alive. Once she could separate the two, perhaps she could let her brother die so that she could begin to see Tina as the resilient, responsible rebel she really was, freeing her from the shadow of death.

COUNSELOR: Well, that's really something. You've had this terrible thing happen in your family, and now Tina reminds you of it. Is she a lot like your brother? I can see how that might be hard. Could you tell me some ways in which Tina and your brother were alike?

MOM: Oh yes! They're so much alike I sometimes think I'm talking to Tom when I'm talking to Tina. He was a real, well, a rebellious kid, just like she is. I was the quiet one . . . you know. He had to be in on all the latest stuff. If the other kids were smoking dope, well, he had to do it too. Just like Tina. [*Tina looks away.*] My mother tried so hard to tell him what trouble he was getting into, but she just couldn't reach him, and I can't reach Tina either. [*Tina is still avoiding her mother's glance.*]

COUNSELOR: So that's how they're alike. They're both rebellious, and they want to be in with the rest of the gang, and they don't listen to their mother. Is that right?

MOM: [*She nods yes.*]

COUNSELOR: [*To Tina.*] Did your mother give a fair description of you? Do you think you're like her brother in those ways, too? Or don't you agree?

TINA: Yeah, well, I can see where she gets it in some ways. Like she says about not listening to her and mouthing off a lot and all that, I guess. . . . But I don't think I have to be doing what the other kids do all the time. That's not why I smoked dope when I did. And I stopped, too, and he didn't.

COUNSELOR: [*Looks at Mom questioningly.*]

MOM: Yeah, well, I'll have to give you credit there. That is true. In that way you didn't act like he would have.

COUNSELOR: Are there any other ways you can think of in which Tina is different from your brother?

MOM: Gee. I never gave it much thought. Well, what she said. She uses her head some of the time. [*Grins at Tina.*] He never did. I guess she takes better care of herself in some ways. I worry about her so much, being a single mother, I sometimes forget that. I can't think of any other ways she's different . . . no . . .

COUNSELOR: [*Says nothing; waits.*]

MOM: Different, huh? [*Pause.*] Oh, I know something. She gets better grades than Tom did. And she takes things more seriously. With Tom, he had a better sense of humor. You could always laugh things off with Tom. Tina's more of a real fighter. [*Tina is now looking at her mother.*]

COUNSELOR: So they're really different in some ways. Could you say that to Tina? Tell her, "You really are different from Tom in some ways, but I've been treating you like you're just like him."

The point was made. Mom began to perceive her daughter as different from her brother. The counselor could work on helping her elaborate those differences. What were the consequences of Tom's ability to laugh things off? Did he feel badly about his poor grades? Were Tina's good grades reassuring? Was Mom saying that Tina's judgment was better than Tom's? Once Mom could see clearly that Tina was not Tom, Barbara could move to the next step in counseling Tina and her mother, namely, to help Mom to realize that she could not save Tina from her own mistakes.

The counselor knew that the seeds for Mom's attempts to control

Tina were imbedded in the relationship with her dead brother. Like many survivors of seemingly unjust deaths, she could not rid herself of the notion that her brother's death could have been prevented. Probably she thought that she herself, had she only been older, wiser, or more conscientious, could have kept him alive.

COUNSELOR: Let's try something a little different. Here's what I want you to do. [*Pulling up an extra chair and placing it directly in front of Mom, facing her.*] I want you to put your brother in that chair.

MOM: But . . .

COUNSELOR: [*Interrupting her.*] I know it seems a little weird, but it's worth it. What did he look like? If Tom were sitting there, whom would I see?

MOM: Well, he was good looking. Brown curly hair. Deep brown eyes. Freckles! He wasn't real big. Sort of on the short side. He didn't like us to mention that. [*Smiling, Mom clearly shows her fondness for her brother.*]

COUNSELOR: Thanks. Now could you go back to what we were talking about, only speak directly to him. I get the idea that you were telling us if you only had been able to talk to him, you could have kept him from doing such a terrible thing. Say that to him. "If only I could have talked to you, I would have kept you from doing such a terrible thing."

MOM: Well, it's true. I could have talked you out of it. You always listened to me. [*Turning to the therapist.*] Is that what you want me to do?

COUNSELOR: That's fine. Keep talking to him.

MOM: Why didn't you talk to me about what was troubling you?

COUNSELOR: Now you've asked him a question. Go sit in his chair and answer as Tom.

MOM: [*Switching chairs.*] You know we didn't talk about that kind of stuff. We kept it in.

COUNSELOR: Switch back and answer yourself. Keep up the conversation. Write a script between yourself and your brother.

MOM: [*Switching back to herself.*] I know what you mean.

But . . . but . . . there must have been something so terrible . . . [*tears are coming to her eyes*] . . . something so terrible . . . [*She starts to cry a lot.*]

COUNSELOR: Let yourself cry. It's okay.

MOM: [*Through her sobs.*] I just can't bear to think of you all alone with that. [*Cries more.*]

COUNSELOR: Ask him if he wanted anything from you.

MOM: Did you want anything more from me? [*Switching chairs again and speaking for Tom.*] No. [*Switching to herself.*] Didn't you know I cared about you? [*Switching to Tom.*] I don't know. I was mostly thinking about myself, I guess.

COUNSELOR: Tom, could you say to your sister, "You couldn't keep me alive."

MOM: [*Still as Tom.*] You couldn't keep me alive.

COUNSELOR: Switch chairs and be yourself again.

MOM: [*Switching back to herself; crying.*] I know I couldn't, but I really wanted to. I really did.

COUNSELOR: What are you experiencing right now?

MOM: I know that's true. [*Sighs deeply.*] I couldn't live his life for him. [*She has stopped crying and speaks in a quiet voice.*]

COUNSELOR: Could you say that to Tina? "I can't live your life for you."

MOM: Sure. I can't live your life for you, Tina.

TINA: [*Very relieved.*] That's true, Mom.

MOM: I just wish I didn't worry so much. [*She is no longer crying and is projecting a softer, thoughtful mood.*]

This is what the counselor wanted Mom to understand. She loved her brother. She loves Tina. She couldn't keep her brother alive, and she can't keep Tina from suffering, either. She has to live with her own worries. She can communicate her worries, but she has to give up the illusion that she is in charge of Tina's life. Tina is in charge of her own life. She may want to listen to advice—especially when she asks for it—she may even use it, but she no longer can be controlled by her mother.

While the mother's pain touched her deeply, the counselor felt relieved when the mother used her help to start grieving. Mom had recalled her brother easily, with a mixture of pleasure and sadness. During the empty chair exercise, Mom's tears began to flow whenever the memory of her brother's death became real for her. The counselor thought that she would need to do quite a bit more crying to really say good-by to her brother—at least enough to allow Tina a life of her own.

COUNSELOR: Look at Tom again. He's still right here. [*Pointing to the empty chair across from Mom.*] Could you start by saying to him, "You know, I never felt I had a chance to say good-by"?

MOM: Tom . . . [*She begins to cry, but keeps up the rest of the dialogue through her tears.*] Tom, you know, you never gave me a chance to say good-bye. [*Sobbing.*] And you know, there is a whole lot I wanted to say to you.

COUNSELOR: Tell him now.

MOM: Well, I didn't want you to go. You shouldn't have left us like that. We all loved you. How could you do a thing like that? How could you do it to Mom?

COUNSELOR: Go over and answer.

MOM: [*Switching to Tom.*] Oh, don't you remember? I was always in trouble. Mom didn't care about me. Nobody really did. [*Switching back to herself.*] But *I* did! I really did. Tom! I feel so bad that you didn't know it. [*Crying hard again.*]

COUNSELOR: Tell him something about your caring for him.

MOM: Oh, you know I liked you. I . . . I . . . I really loved you, Tom. [*Crying very hard.*] I thought you were lively and fun, and, well . . . I know I ratted on you a lot, but that didn't mean I didn't love you.

COUNSELOR: Do you want to tell him that you feel really bad about that?

MOM: Yes, I do. I'm so sorry you took all that stuff so seriously. I really cared for you. I really did.

At the end of this dialogue, Mom looked softer. She had expressed grief. She had talked about her guilt, and she had had a chance to tell Tom how much she cared about him, a chance that life in her family of origin failed to create. The counselor guessed that she would continue to grieve in a more normal manner now. Her brother would recede gradually in her memory and let her devote her energy to the living.

The empty chair technique quickly projects the client into deep intrapsychic work. It is a technique that can be used in an individual, group, or family setting (see Chapter 6). On completing a segment of this kind of work, the counselor is faced with the problem of making a transition back to interpersonal work. Here the counselor attempted to accomplish this transition simply by asking Tina to tell her mother about her reactions.

COUNSELOR: That was good work, Mom. Let's see, Tina, there seemed to be a lot going on with you while Mom was working. It would be good if Mom could hear some of that. Tina, could you tell your mother what you were feeling when she was talking to her brother?

TINA: Wow, that was heavy! It was real heavy to cry and all that.

COUNSELOR: I can see that would be hard. Were you feeling anything else?

TINA: I feel real sad.

COUNSELOR: Tell her directly.

TINA: I feel real sad, Mom. I could see you really cared for him. [*Cries.*]

MOM: I did. I really did. [*She gives another sigh and stares straight ahead. Tina stirs to call attention to herself. Mom turns to her.*]

COUNSELOR: There's a lot of caring in this family. It just gets lost in all the complaining.

The exploration was helpful to Tina as well as her mother. The counselor believed that Tina had never heard her mother compare her with her brother except in a fearful and punitive way. Now that she could see how much her mother had cared for her brother, how helpless she had felt, she could empathize with her. At the same time, the work of differentiating Tina from her dead brother enabled Mom to make a new beginning with Tina. Telling her that she cared for her, the mother began to express loving feelings that had long been inhibited because they were invested in the past.

Tina's case illustrates how a child can be the recipient of intense parental feelings that belong elsewhere. Once the mother's feelings were expressed appropriately, the family could begin to relate to the real Tina, uncontaminated by the premature death of her uncle. As Mom learned to deal more appropriately with Tina's provocative behavior and give her praise and recognition for her many successes and responsible actions, Tina's feelings of betrayal at the hands of her unjust mother abated and she had less difficulty accommodating the family rules.

Case 4

The separation or divorce of parents is a crisis in the life of any child. The adolescent already is experiencing major changes in her physical and psychological world, many of them mystifying and confusing. She differs from children of other stages of development in her greater sense of drama, her greater sense of her own power, and her greater experience in the world. She feels deeply and acutely. She has a sense of justice, which she applies when her parents enlist her to take sides in their disagreements. Few teenagers feel both their parents are strong enough to take care of themselves in a divorce. Many stay involved in parental quarrels because they themselves feel threatened by the potential loss of a parent.

Every once in awhile, however, a teenager is able to keep from taking sides in parental quarrels. She may go elsewhere physically or psychologically, temporarily or permanently. But even if she is able to withdraw, the teenager usually does not escape the parental conflict altogether. She still has an interest in preserving her parents as a couple, the most important symbol of her once-stable home life. In fact, she may behave like the more apparently enmeshed teenager and develop symptoms in order to bring her parents back together again. She may run away, for example, so that her parents can catch her.

I chose the following case study because it illustrates the problems of divided loyalties and challenges the counselor to confront another difficult issue: helping his client face realistic limitations in an area where the client held cherished illusions.

Paul: Hard Reality versus Cherished Illusions

In many marriages, one parent is seen as "stronger" than the other. Paul came from a family where Mom always was seen as strong. She seemed to have a better time in life than Dad. She had friends; he didn't. When she went back to school after Paul entered high school, she was very successful. After finishing a law degree, she immediately got a job in a well-known San Francisco law firm. Paul's father didn't talk much about his business, but Paul knew that he struggled to make ends meet. Dad seemed to be more vulnerable than his wife. He frequently had his feelings hurt by other members of the family or people he worked with. When someone upset him, he often reacted with stunned silence. His silences dominated the household.

Paul's parents separated after Paul's mother found someone else. His father became very depressed. Paul and his mother agreed that Paul should live with his father. Their decision apparently served to assuage Mom's guilt, and Paul agreed because he was afraid that his dad couldn't make it alone.

For the first few months, the plan seemed to be working. Paul and his father moved to another small town in the area. Their life seemed to run along smoothly enough. On weekends, Paul visited his mother, who still lived in the former family residence. They often talked about Dad. Both were genuinely concerned about how he was doing. His deep depression seemed to be lifting, but one could never be sure.

Then Paul, who always had been a relatively quiet child, started to get in trouble at school. First he was truant. He had wanted to see some of the kids from his old school, about 15 miles away, and had simply got on the bus one morning to do so. He began to miss school frequently. When his teachers confronted him, he either accused them of lying or argued that he didn't see why he had to go to school in the first place; he hated it. When a counselor from a nearby youth clinic visited the school, Paul began to talk. After a few more talks, the counselor, Ben, suggested that Paul and his father come in for a family session. Paul said that he would like his mom there also, and family counseling began.

It wasn't long before the counselor saw that both Mom and Paul were protecting Dad, who did his part by describing his disappointments, first in his wife, and now in Paul. Both Mom and Paul countered Dad's shaming with attempts to cheer him up. Both were experts at changing the subject with a joke, a smile, or a bit of conversational hocus pocus.

At school, Paul's behavior worsened. He was suspended for truancy. Then he missed a family session. The counselor called him up and set up an individual appointment, which Paul seemed eager to keep. During this session, Paul began to talk about the underlying cause of his pain. He didn't quite come out and say it, but his nostalgia for his old hometown and for his friends, and his talks about his mother's exciting life, clearly suggested that he wanted to live with his mother but didn't have the courage to say so. He was certain his mom wanted him with her also. The counselor guessed that Paul could not take a direct stand with Dad. Instead, he was getting in as much trouble as possible, hoping someone would see the light and send him back to Mom, or, at least, that his father would react in a stronger, more manly way to his behavior and kick him out, so he could live with his mother.

Paul's counselor was glad that the private meeting had taken place, but he felt in a dilemma as to how to deal with the new information. He came to the consultation group at his youth clinic worried that, since Paul had not given him permission to talk about the interview, he would not be able to use any of his new information at the next family meeting. Moreover, he was worried about Paul. There was a pathetic quality about him. He seemed too certain that his mother was ready to have him live with her. The counselor had a hunch the path wouldn't be so smooth. Paul's mother was in a new stage of her life. She was busy. She was living alone for the first time in years. Those were the very reasons that Paul wanted to live with her, in fact. How should he proceed? If his hunch were correct, should he try to convince Mom to take Paul? But what about Dad? He clearly was depressed, enough to require therapy. How would he handle Paul's rejection? Would he take a referral? A consultant suggested considering the following aspects of the problems:

1. First, since he got a different picture of Paul's situation in the individual session than he had earlier, he needed to explore this discrepancy with Paul and encourage him to raise these important issues in a family session.
2. In the family session, Paul would require support for going slowly enough to voice his concern about Dad's depression and his fear of hurting him, in order to express his desire to live with his mother without being cruel or rejecting.

3. The toughest and most important part of the family session would center on helping Paul to test his assumption that his mother wanted him to live with her. Paul was counting on his mother. Could he? Was there room in her life for Paul? Perhaps Mom was enjoying her newly found freedom. Perhaps there were parts of her new life that she didn't want to share with her son. She had always been busy. Would her present schedule allow time for Paul? The counselor's job was to clarify this situation.

The various possibilities inherent in Paul's dilemma merit further discussion. Since Paul, like so many other children in his spot, built up an illusion about life with his mother as a cure-all for his problems, he had a clear plan for the interview: The father was to accept his plan in good spirits and without recriminations, and the mother was to welcome the change.

There were, however, a number of other ways the interview might develop. Let us consider these hypothetically. Mom, for example, already caught feeling guilty about leaving her depressed husband, could give a mixed message. Paul would have to draw his own conclusions about the meaning of Mom's ambivalence.

PAUL: So, okay, Mom, I know it isn't the way we planned it, but Dad doesn't mind, and could I go live with you, like we said?

MOM: Sure, that seems like a good idea, sometime soon.

PAUL: [*Brightening.*] Next month! It wouldn't matter about going to another school, because I haven't been going anyway.

MOM: No . . . well, I think that would be too soon, don't you? [*Looking at the counselor.*]

PAUL: But Mom! Why?

MOM: I've told you before that you may not think it's such a big deal about changing schools midterm, but I do, and I think your counselor agrees with me.

COUNSELOR: [*Feeling on the spot; not wanting to side with Mom against Paul.*] I don't know. I do know I want to explore something else before we talk about school. Talking about school seems to be a way of talking about so many other things in this family, remember? I want to

	know more about how Paul would fit into your life right now, Mom.
MOM:	Oh, that would be all right. [*Her tone is unenthusiastic.*]
PAUL:	Sure, I practically take care of myself, anyway.
COUNSELOR:	[*To mother.*] Would it be all right?
MOM:	But I also think he ought to stay with his dad a little longer; they haven't really had a chance to get used to each other yet, without me.
DAD:	Well, I'd sure prefer that.
COUNSELOR:	[*Seeing Mother use Dad in an attempt to avoid rejecting her son.*] Well, we have done a lot of talking about whether or not Dad's ready to live by himself. I thought we'd all agreed that he is.
MOM:	Oh, that's not it.
DAD:	No; I know what she means.
COUNSELOR:	[*Seeing that he cannot seem to get Mom to talk about her own life situation in relation to Paul, and resolved to end the interview on a note of unambiguous realism.*] Well, Paul, what do you think? Do you think you'll be moving in with your mom next month?
PAUL:	[*Carefully.*] I still want to, Mom.
COUNSELOR:	Yes or no, Mom?
MOM:	It has to be no, for now.
COUNSELOR:	What did Mom say, Paul?
PAUL:	She said, "no, for now," but, Mom, can I next semester?
MOM:	Maybe; I'm just not sure.
COUNSELOR:	That's important, because, remember, Paul, you told me it was all settled, Mom was sure.
PAUL:	That is what I thought. [*Tears welling up in his eyes.*]
COUNSELOR:	It sounds like it'll be quite a while before the move, if that ever happens. Do you folks agree that Paul will have to accept the no for now? [*The whole family looks sad as they nod agreement with the counselor.*]

With this strategy, the counselor has helped Paul to accept the negative consequences of his mother's ambivalence. It was not easy for the counselor to work toward a conclusion that ultimately caused his client so much pain; however, he knew that, if he didn't, Paul would continue to be neither here nor there, neither accepting his real situation nor able to change to a more satisfactory one. It wasn't easy to sort out the negative aspects of Mom's doubletalk or to prevail on Paul to accept a view of things that he had long attempted to ignore. The counselor identified with Paul sufficiently to want the situation to have a happy ending. The advantage of his approach, however, was that now the work could proceed to help Paul to adjust in his relationship to his father, his new school, and his peers, without running into the wall of his denial. He could help him grieve his unfulfilled dream and begin to move forward. This work with Paul's grief and disappointment would become even more important if Mom's eventual decision should be out and out rejection.

COUNSELOR: Well, Paul, this is the time to get it clear with your mom and dad as to which one you're going to live with.

PAUL: Well . . . Dad . . . you probably know this but it's kind of hard to say, but I really want to go back to the old house and live with Mom.

DAD: Well, I got the drift of where all this running back there was going to end up. [*Sighs deeply.*] Heck, I just wish you'd give it more of a chance; it's just . . .

COUNSELOR: We haven't heard Mom's response to Paul's plan yet. He's kind of assumed you are open to his living with you, Mom. Is he right?

MOM: Gee, Paul, I . . . well, I . . . [*Obviously taken by surprise.*] We didn't say you were just coming over and moving in, did we?

PAUL: I thought we did!

MOM: When? I just don't understand, I . . . I mean, you're always welcome to visit, but . . .

COUNSELOR: [*Seeing the stunned look on Paul's face.*] Wow, this is kind of a tough one for you, isn't it, Paul? Could you tell us what's going through your mind?

PAUL: No.

COUNSELOR: Well, if it were me, I'd sure be upset. [*Beginning to double.*] I just don't know where I'm at any more; I'm really confused—I'm trying to be another part of you, Paul—and I'm mad at Mom! Wow, I never thought she'd . . .

PAUL: I sure didn't think she'd just fink out on me just like that. I'm sure she wanted me there.

COUNSELOR: Could I ask her if anything changed?

PAUL: Did anything change?

MOM: No, dear, no. It really didn't. I mean, I'm always glad to see you and all that, and that isn't any different now, but I am just really, really busy, and I just don't have room to live with anybody right now—it's not against you.

COUNSELOR: Well, she *is* busy. But why didn't she tell me?

PAUL: She's not that busy! She's . . . she's just selfish, that's all! [*Begins to cry.*]

COUNSELOR: I was really counting on this.

PAUL: I was. I . . . [*Still tearing up.*] Look, do I have to stay here; couldn't you talk to them for awhile?

COUNSELOR: Okay, I'm not a part of you any more. [*He is no longer doubling.*] Sure, but I'd like you to stay. Maybe you could just stay on the sidelines for awhile, while I work with Mom and Dad.

With this outcome, Paul's bubble was burst. Mother clearly felt badly, but she showed no signs of changing her mind. Paul had to face the fact that he'd be living with Dad. With the counselor's help, Paul could begin to work through his pain.

The counselor often is faced with the task of helping the adolescent to confront reality. Rescue fantasies abound in adolescence. The fantasy of being an adopted child and ultimately finding understanding and validation through meeting the true parents is a familiar one among children who are the natural offspring of their parents. Adopted children also often fantasize a nearly perfect existence if and when their true parents are found. Sometimes rescuers appear in the form of teachers or other helping adults who seem to offer a perfect alternative to a life situation filled with problems. Because emotions and fantasies run so high in adolescence and are invested with such fervent hopes, it is important that the counselor help the adolescent check out his dreams by comparing them with a picture of the reality in which he is most likely to find himself. In order to accomplish this, the counselor first must join the adolescent and reassure him that, while some dreams must be given up, they can be replaced with others that enrich the adolescent's life.

Suggested Readings

Anthony, E. J. The significance of Jean Piaget for child psychiatry. *British Journal of Medical Psychiatry, 20,* 20–34, 1965.

Bank, Stephen, and Kuhn, Michael. *The Sibling Bond.* New York: Basic Books, 1983.

Bloom, Michael V. *Adolescent–Parental Separation.* New York: Halsted Press, 1980.

Brehnenfeld, Florence. *Child Custody Mediation.* Palo Alto: Science and Behavior Books, 1983.

Erikson, Erik. *Childhood and Society,* New York: W. W. Norton, 1956.

Glasscote, Wayne. *The Treatment of Alcoholism: The Study of Programs and Problems.* Washington, D.C.: The Joint Information Service of the American Psychiatric Association and the National Association for Mental Health, 1967.

Haley, J., and Madanes, J. *Leaving Home: The Therapy of Disturbed Young People.* New York: McGraw-Hill, 1980.

Keith, D., and Whitaker, C. The divorce labyrinth. In P. Papp (Ed.), *Family Therapy: Full Length Case Studies.* New York: Gardner Press, 1977.

Kübler-Ross, E. *On Death and Dying.* New York: Macmillan, 1970.

Leveton, Alan. The art of shamesmanship. *British Journal of Medical Psychology,* 35:101–111, 1962.

Leveton, Alan. Time, death and the ego chill. *Journal of Existentialism, 6:*21, 69–80, 1965.

Leveton, Alan. Elizabeth is frightened. *Voices, 8,* 4–13, Spring 1972.

Leveton, Alan, and Leveton, Eva. Children in trouble, family in crisis. A series of 5 training films demonstrating a family counseling alternative. University of California at Davis, Administration of Criminal Justice, 1975.

Leveton, Eva. *Psychodrama for the Timid Clinician.* New York: Springer, 1977.

Luthman, S., and Kirschenbaum, M. *The Dynamic Family.* Palo Alto: Science and Behavior Books, 1974.

Minuchin, Salvador. *Families and Family Therapy.* Cambridge, MA: Harvard University Press, 1974.

Nagy, I., and Spark, S. *Invisible Loyalties.* New York: Harper & Row, 1973.

Perls, Fritz. *The Gestalt Approach and Eyewitness to Therapy.* Palo Alto: Science and Behavior Books, 1965.

Satir, Virginia. *Peoplemaking.* New York: Basic Books, 1972.

Siggins, L. D. Mourning, a critical survey of the literature. *International Journal of Psychoanalysis*, 47, 14–25, 1966.

Tatelbaum, J. *The Courage to Grieve*. New York: Lippincott and Crowell, 1980.

Wallerstein, J., and Kelley, J. *Surviving the Breakup*. New York: Basic Books, 1980.

Willi, J. *Couples in Collusion*. New York: Jason Aronson, 1982.

Epilogue _____

During the time that I have worked in family therapy, the atmosphere has changed radically. When I began, family therapy was also in its beginning stages. For the clinician taught to see his patients in terms of the medical model, the notion of family systems required a complete change of perspective. Instead of working with one patient and relying chiefly on the information supplied by personal history and dreams, the family therapist saw the whole family and attempted to explain problems by looking at the way the family members behaved with one another. The symptom bearer, or identified patient, no longer was regarded as a sick individual, but rather as a messenger of family pain. If the family could change its way of functioning, it was argued, there would be no more need for any one person to be the symptom bearer. During that time, about 25 years ago, family therapists often were considered oddballs who stubbornly clung to a definition of problems different from that of most of the professional world around them. They were pioneers: enthusiastic, opinionated, and optimistic.

On the West Coast, the development of family therapy was paralleled closely by the development of many of the "new" therapies: Gestalt, body awareness, new versions of Psychodrama, and movement and art therapies, many of which were combined with group and family work. Most of the family therapists I knew at that time worked hard to develop clinical models that would use the theoretical approaches developed by Jackson, Bateson, and Satir and combined them with active, experiential methods that would help clarify and take charge of the complex variety of behavior presented by families.

New ways of looking at and working with families were developed. Instead of simply talking about what was happening with family members, we worked out ways of observing the family's behavior directly. We included our own personal reactions in the treatment process, modeling behavior, attempting both to comment on what was going on in the family and to let family members comment on what might be going on inside of us, working together with our patients to develop an awareness of the process. New to the clinical scene at that time was the degree of openness observed in the new therapists. They encouraged other professionals to watch them at their work. They developed the use of one-way mirrors and video- and audiotapes, and they interviewed families in classrooms surrounded by their observing students. Gradually, the more conservative members of the new group, feeling that, after all, systems theory did not explain *all* of each family member's behavior, developed ways of combining with family work what they had learned earlier as individual therapists. Thus, dreams, fantasies, and reveries reentered the treatment process. My own eclectic development in this context is described in the first chapter of this book.

Of course, the atmosphere of burgeoning growth had to change. Every bohemian neighborhood eventually becomes too staid and too expensive for the artists who developed it. It is said that Jung once stated, "I hope that I will have followers but that there will be no "Jungians." Revolutionary as our ideas had seemed to us, we were to see them become more and more accepted during the first 10 years. Our students learned their lessons well, and many became teachers of family therapy. The field itself entered the Establishment. One of the drawbacks of the earlier work had been a certain amount of confusion. Many new things were tried, many hypotheses ventured, and many dropped. It was hard to know where the truth lay. Now the tide has turned. Family therapy has become institutionalized. There are national and international organizations and several journals to report research and case material. Systems theory now is understood well by clinicians. We of the older generations view these developments with mixed feelings. We worked hard to propagate our work, and, much of the time, we are happy to see families getting help, as well as reassured that the next generations of clinicians will continue to develop our work. On the other hand, institutionalization brings with it a degree of rigidity. Family therapy has always been a house divided. Our theoretical differences have been pretty much geographically determined. Along with the West Coast school of family therapy, there were concurrent developments in the Midwest and on the East Coast. As long as these differences represented variously arrayed wayfarers along an unknown path, they were more educational than divisive. Now, alas, various groups have come to describe ways of working that suggest certainty is just around the corner. The student of family therapy now can learn ways to map the family structure, methods for learning and deciphering the language of metaphor, and strategies for intervening in either a direct or paradoxical manner. A review of the current literature would lead one to believe that the family therapist has been transformed from a sentimental seeker to a master manipulator. Instead of pursuing the path of discovery together with the families he is treating, he has once more stepped behind the scene, from where he makes detailed observations and a failsafe plan and comes up with a cure in a startlingly short period of time.

The reader knows that, while I welcome the new techniques, I continue to tolerate a certain amount of confusion; in fact, I have struggled hard—if sometimes unsuccessfully—to avoid what I call the delusion of certainty.

If clinicians can be divided into two categories, they might be (1) those who continue to search, convinced that the mystery of human behavior will continue to present new challenges, and (2) those who work to discover truth in scientifically predictable behavior and technique. I clearly belong to the former group. I have tried to clarify those techniques and processes that have been most useful in my work with adolescents and their families. This book is an attempt to review my work in progress. In ending the book, I want to present the reader with a caution in the form of a quote with which the great German writer Goethe is said to have signed his letters: "Respect the unexplainable."

Bibliography

Abroms, G. Supervision as meta-therapy. In F. Kaslow and associates (Eds.) *Supervision, Consultation and Staff-training in the Helping Professions.* San Francisco: Jossey-Bass, 1978.

Ackerman, N. *Treating the Troubled Family.* New York: Basic Books, 1966.

Allmond, Bayard. *The Family is the Patient.* St. Louis: Mosby, 1975.

Alport, Gordon, W. The fruits of eclecticism. In G. W. Alport (Ed.), *Selected Essays.* Boston: Beacon Press, 1968.

Anada, Gerald. *A Guide to Psychotherapy.* Washington, D.C.: American Universities Press, 1983.

Anderson, Carol. *Mastering Resistance: A Practical Guide to Family Therapy.* New York: Guilford Press, 1983.

Anthony, E. J. The significance of Jean Piaget for child psychiatry. *British Journal of Medical Psychiatry, 20,* 20–34, 1965.

Bank, Stephen, and Kuhn, Michael. *The Sibling Bond.* New York: Basic Books, 1983.

Berne, Eric. *Transactional Analysis in Psychotherapy.* New York: Grove Press, 1964.

Blatner, Howard. *Acting–In: Practical Applications of Psychodramatic Methods.* New York: Springer, 1973.

Bloom, Michael V. *Adolescent–Parental Separation.* New York: Halsted Press, 1980.

Boszormeny-Nagy, I., and Framo, J. *Intensive Family Therapy.* New York: Harper & Row, 1965.

Bowen, M. Toward a differentiation of a self from our own family. In J. L. Framo (Ed.), *Family Interaction: A Dialogue between Family Researchers and Family Therapists.* New York: Harper & Row, 1972.

Bowen, M. *Family Therapy in Clinical Practice.* New York: Jason Aronson, 1978.

Boyer, Pat, and Jeffrey, Ronn. *The Family: A Living Kaleidoscope. A Guide for the Beginning Family Counselor.* Cheyenne, WY: Pioneer Printing and Stationery Company, 1981.

Brehnenfeld, Florence. *Child Custody Mediation.* Palo Alto: Science and Behavior Books, 1983.

Brill, L. (Ed.). *The Basic Writings of Sigmund Freud.* New York: Modern Library, 1966, 1983.

Brown, Frank. *The Transition of Youth to Adulthood: A Bridge Too Long.* New York: Westview, 1980.

Brown, Frank, and d. Stent, Madelon. *Minorities in U.S. Institutions of Higher Education.* New York: Praeger, 1977.

Brown, Tom, Jr. *The Tracker.* New York: Berkley Books, 1979.

Carter, Elizabeth A., and McGoldrick, Monica (Eds.). *The Family Life Cycle: A Framework for Family Therapy.* New York: Gardner Press, 1980.

Chapman, A. H. *Harry Stack Sullivan: The Man and His Work.* New York: Putnam's, 1976.

Conger, John. *Adolescence: Generation under Pressure.* Life-Cycle Series. New York: Harper & Row, 1980.

Erikson, Erik. *Childhood and Society.* New York: W. W. Norton, 1956.

Erikson, Erik (Ed.). *The Challenge of Youth.* New York: Doubleday, 1965.

Evans, J. *Adolescent and Pre-Adolescent Psychiatry.* New York: Grune and Stratton, 1983.

Ewalt, P. (Ed.). *Mental Health Volunteers.* Springfield, IL: Charles C Thomas, 1967.

Ford, F. Rules—The invisible family. *Family Process,* 22:2, 135–145, June 1983.

Ford, F. R., and Herrick, J. Family rules/Family life styles. *American Journal of Orthopsychiatry,* 44, 62–69, 1974.

Ford, F. R., and Herrick, J. A typology of families: Five family systems. *Australian Journal of Family Therapy,* 3, 71–81, 1982.

Framo, J. L. *Explorations in Marriage and Family Therapy: Collected Papers.* New York: Springer, 1983.

Frostig, M. Teaching reading to children with perceptual disturbance. In R. M. Flower, H. F. Gofman, and L. Lawson (Eds.), *Reading Disorders: A Multidisciplinary Symposium.* San Francisco: F. A. Davis, 1965.

Gardiner, Muriel. *The Wolfman by the Wolfman.* New York: Basic Books, 1971.

Gehrke, S., and Kirschenbaum, M. Survival patterns in conjoint therapy, *Family Process,* 6, 67–80, March 1967.

Gesell, A. *The First Five Years of Life.* New York: Harper & Row, 1940.

Glasscote, R. M. *The Treatment of Alcoholism: The Study of Programs and Problems.* Washington, D.C.: The Joint Information Service of the American Psychiatric Association and the National Association for Mental Health, 1967.

Golan, Naomi. *Treatment in Crisis Situations.* New York: The Free Press, 1978.

Green, Hannah. *I Never Promised You a Rose Garden.* New York: New American Library, 1964; New York: Holt, Rinehart and Winston, 1964.

Group for the Advancement of Psychiatry. *Normal Adolescence: Its Dynamics and Impact.* New York: Scribners, 1968.

Guerin, P. J. (Ed.). *Family Therapy: Theory and Practice.* New York: Gardner Press, 1978.

Haley, J. *Strategies of Psychotherapy.* New York: Grune and Stratton, 1963.

Haley, J. *The Power Tactics of Jesus Christ.* New York: Groseman, 1969.

Haley, J. *Changing Families.* New York: Grune and Stratton, 1971.

Haley, J. *Uncommon Therapy: The Psychiatric Techniques of Milton J. Erickson, M.D.* New York: W. W. Norton, 1973.

Haley, J. *Problem-Solving Therapy*. New York: Harper & Row, 1976.

Haley, J., and Madanes, J. *Leaving Home: The Therapy of Disturbed Young People*. New York: McGraw-Hill, 1980.

Hoffman, L. *Foundations of Family Therapy*. New York: Basic Books, 1981.

Inshelder, B., and Piaget, J. *The Growth of Logical Thinking from Childhood to Adolescence*. New York: Basic Books, 1958.

Jackson, Don (Ed.). *Therapy Communication and Change*. Vols. 1 and 2. Palo Alto: Science and Behavior Books, 1968.

Johnson, Don. *The Protean Body*. New York: Harper & Row, 1977.

Jones, E. *The Life and Work of Sigmund Freud*. New York: Basic Books, 1953.

Jung, C. G. *Man and His Symbols*. Garden City, NY: Doubleday, 1964.

Keeney, B. P., and Sprenkle, B. H. Ecosystemic epistemology: Critical implications for the aesthetics and pragmatics of family therapy. *Family Process*, 21, 1–19, 1982.

Keith, D., and Whitaker, C. The divorce labyrinth. In P. Papp (Ed.), *Family Therapy: Full Length Case Studies*. New York: Gardner Press, 1977.

Kempler, Walter. *Experiential Psychotherapy in Families*. New York: Brunner-Mazel, 1981.

Kephart, N. *The Slow Learner in the Classroom*. Columbus, OH: Charles E. Merrill Books, 1971.

Kernberg, O. The treatment of borderline patients. In P. L. Giovachini (Ed.), *Tactics and Techniques of Psychoanalytic Therapy*. New York: Science House, 1972.

Ketty, Joseph. *Rites of Passage: Adolescence in America, 1970 to the Present*. New York: Basic Books, 1979.

Knapp, Mark L. *Nonverbal Communication in Human Interaction*. New York: Holt, Rinehart and Winston, 1972.

Koehne-Kaplan, Nancy. The use of self as a family therapist. *Perspectives in Psychiatric Care*, 14:1, 29–33, 1976.

Kramer, Charles H. *Becoming a Family Therapist: Devising an Integrated Approach to Working with Families*. New York: Human Sciences Press, 1980.

Kübler-Ross, E. *On Death and Dying*. New York: Macmillan, 1970.

Laing, R. D., and Esterson, A. *Sanity, Madness, and the Family*. New York: Basic Books, 1964.

Langs, Robert J. *Resistances and Interventions: The Nature of Therapeutic Work*. New York: Jason Aronson, 1981.

Langsley, Donald G., and Kaplan, David M. *The Treatment of Families in Crisis*. New York: Grune and Stratton, 1968.

Lazare, A. The Customer Approach to Patienthood. *Archives of General Psychiatry*, 32, 553–558, 1975.

Levenkron, S. *Treating and Overcoming Anorexia Nervosa*. New York: Scribners, 1981.

Leveton, Alan. The art of shamesmanship. *British Journal of Medical Psychology*, 35, 101–111, 1962.

Leveton, Alan. Time, death and the ego chill. *Journal of Existentialism, 6:*21, 69–80, 1965.

Leveton, Alan. Elizabeth is frightened. *Voices, 8,* 4–13, Spring 1972.

Leveton, Alan. Family therapy as play: The contribution of Milton H. Erickson, M.D.. In Jeffrey K. Zeig (Ed.), *Ericksonian Approaches to Hypnosis and Psychotherapy.* New York: Brunner-Mazel, 1982.

Leveton, Alan, and Leveton, Eva. Children in trouble, family in crisis. A series of 5 training films demonstrating a family counseling alternative. University of California at Davis, Administration of Criminal Justice, 1975.

Leveton, Eva. *Psychodrama for the Timid Clinician.* New York: Springer, 1977.

Luthman, S., and Kirschenbaum, M. *The Dynamic Family.* Palo Alto: Science and Behavior Books, 1974.

McGoldrick, M., Pearce, J., and Giordano, J. (Eds.). *Ethnicity and Family Therapy.* New York: Guilford Press, 1982.

McGrath, Patrick J., and Firestone, Philip (Eds.). *Pediatrics and Adolescent Behavioral Medicine: Treatment Issues.* New York: Springer, 1982.

Messinger, Lillian (Ed.). *Clinical Approaches to Family Violence.* New York: Aspen Institute for Humanistic Studies, 1982.

Minuchin, Salvador. *Families and Family Therapy.* Cambridge, MA: Harvard University Press, 1974.

Montalvo, B. Aspects of live supervision. *Family Process, 12,* 343–359, 1973.

Moreno, J. L., and Zirca, Z. *Psychodrama.* Vols. 1 and 3. Boston: Beacon, 1969.

Nagy, I., and Spark, S. *Invisible Loyalties.* New York: Harper & Row, 1973.

Napier, August, with Whitaker, Carl. *The Family Crucible.* New York: Harper & Row, 1978.

Neill, John R., and Kniskern, David P. *From Psyche to System: The Evolving Therapy of Carl Whitaker.* New York: Guilford Press, 1982.

Palazzoli, Maria Selvini. *Self-Starvation.* New York: Jason Aronson, 1978.

Palazzoli, Maria Selvini, Cecchin, G., Prata, G., and Boscola, L. *Paradox and Counter-Paradox.* New York: Jason Aronson, 1978.

Papp, Peggy. *Family Therapy: Full Length Case Studies.* Third ed. New York: Gardner Press, 1978.

Papp, P., and Aponte, H. J. The anatomy of a therapist: Paradoxical strategies and counter-transference. *American Journal of Family Therapy, 7,* 11–12, 1979.

Pearce, John K., and Friedman, Leonard J. (Eds.). *Combining Psychodynamic and Family Systems Approaches.* New York: Grune and Stratton, 1980.

Perls, Fritz. *The Gestalt Approach: An Eyewitness to Therapy.* Palo Alto: Science and Behavior Books, 1965.

Perls, Fritz. *Ego, Hunger, and Aggression.* San Francisco: Orbit Graphic Arts, 1966.

Rabichow, Helen G., and Sklansky, Morris A. *Effective Counseling of Adolescents.* Chicago: Follett, 1980.

Rabkin, R. *Strategic Psychotherapy.* New York: Basic Books, 1977.

Redl, F. *The Aggressive Child.* New York: The Free Press, 1957.

Redl, F., and Wineman, D. *Children Who Hate.* New York: Collier Books, 1952.

Rhyne, J. The gestalt approach to expression, art, and art therapy. *American Journal of Art Therapy, 12,* 237–348, 1973.

Robson, Elizabeth. *Getting Help: A Woman's Guide to Therapy.* New York: E. P. Dutton, 1980.

Rosen, S. (Ed.). *My Voice Will Go With You: The Teaching Tales of Milton H. Erickson.* New York: W. W. Norton, 1982.

Rosenheim, E. Humor in psychotherapy: An interactive experience. *American Journal of Psychotherapy, 10,* 584–591, 1974.

Satir, Virginia. *Conjoint Family Therapy.* Palo Alto: Science and Behavior Books, 1964.

Satir, Virginia. *Peoplemaking.* New York: Basic Books, 1972.

Schutz, William. *Joy: Expanding Human Awareness.* New York: Grove Press, 1967.

Searles, Harold F. *Counter-Transference and Related Subjects: Selected Papers.* New York: International Universities Press, 1979.

Searles, Harold F. *Collected Papers on Schizophrenia and Related Subjects.* New York: International Universities Press, 1965.

Siggins, L. D. Mourning: A critical survey of the literature. *International Journal of Psychoanalysis, 47,* 14–25, 1966.

Skinner, B. F. *About Behaviorism.* New York: Vintage Books, a division of Random House, 1976.

Snell, J., Rosenwald, R., and Rolley, A. The wife-beater's wife: A study of family interaction. *Archives of General Psychiatry, 2,* 107–113, 1964.

Spock, B. *Baby and Child Care.* New York: E. P. Dutton, 1976.

Taichert, Louise. Specific learning disorders. *California Medicine, 4,* 109, October 1960.

Tatelbaum, J. *The Courage to Grieve.* New York: Lippincott and Crowell, 1980.

Thorman, George. *Family Violence.* Springfield, IL: Charles C Thomas, 1980.

Tomkins, Calvin. The last skill acquired. *New Yorker,* September 1963.

Umana, RoseAnn, *Crisis in the Family: Three Approaches.* New York: Gardner Press, 1970.

Wallerstein, J., and Kelly, J. *Surviving the Breakup.* New York: Basic Books, 1980.

Whiffen, Rosemary, and Byng-Hall, John. *Family Therapy Supervision: Recent Developments in Practice.* New York: Grune & Stratton, 1982.

Whitaker, C., and Keith, D. Symbolic-experiential family therapy. In A. Gurnan and D. Kniskern (Eds.), *Handbook of Family Therapy.* New York: Brunner-Mazel, 1981.

Willi, J. *Couples in Collusion.* New York: Jason Aronson, 1982.

Williams, G. G., and Wood, M. M. *Developmental Art Therapy.* Washington, D.C.: Universities Park Press, 1975.

Wilmer, H. A. Television: Technical and artistic aspects of videotape in psychiatric teaching. In M. Berger (Ed.), *Video-tape Techniques in Psychiatric Training and Treatment.* New York: Brunner-Mazel, 1978.

Winnicott, D. W. *Therapeutic Consultations in Child Psychiatry.* New York: Basic Books, 1971.

Index

Da

CLINIC A